Praise for *Rural Rebellion*

"At a time when social and political differences tend to be portrayed in stark binary terms, Ross Benes adds depth to our understanding of rural Americans' attitudes about abortion, immigration, big government, and other issues of contention. And while Nebraska shares plenty of cultural and geographic characteristics with its neighbors, Benes suggests that each state in this often-stereotyped region has its own story to tell. Folks who don't have relatives and friends in Nebraska can thank Benes for lending us his."

C.J. Janovy, author of *No Place Like Home: Lessons in Activism from LGBT Kansas*

"Ross writes interesting sentences and takes stories down paths the reader wouldn't or couldn't travel without him. He knows this Nebraska because he's lived it and processed it as a kid, a wannabe rock star, a college student, a football fan, a social scientist, and more. Now he translates it, and he does it all with an intellect that forces us to rethink our suppositions about each other. A great read no matter where you are on the rural-urban or red-blue divides."

Scott Winter, associate professor of journalism, Bethel University, and author of *Nebrasketball: Coach Tim Miles and a Big Ten Team on the Rise*

"Raised as I was in Kansas, I've entertained theories of how my neighboring state—where Willa Cather once lived and Warren Buffett still lives—became such a bastion of Trump support. This engaging book by a writer who knows Nebraska firsthand explains why, and in so doing enriches our understanding of rural America."

Robert Wuthnow, Gerhard R. Andlinger '52 Professor of Sociology, Princeton University

"In *Rural Rebellion* Ross Benes provides a deeply personal look at how the Nebraska we both know and love has taken a hard right turn over the past quarter century, turning the state and its neighbors in flyover country into a no-fly zone for Democrats. How Nebraska went from being a notoriously independent and bipartisan state into a place governed by the most conservative elements of a conservative party is a complete mystery to most liberals—and one that Benes decodes adroitly. Must reading for anyone who wants to know how we got where we are and how to chart a roadmap out of the great divide in American politics."

Jack Todd, author of *Sun Going Down: A Novel*

"Written with deep insight, and with a keen appreciation for how politics unfolds through specific stories, this book is indispensable for anyone trying to understand how American politics got to be so profoundly divided along overlapping lines of partisanship and geography. At the same time, Benes's Nebraska roots lend the narrative an empathy that distinguishes this book from so many others. At root, this book reminds us that our problems aren't fundamentally about other Americans—they are about a politics that pushes us into incompatible camps."

Daniel Hopkins, professor of political science, University of Pennsylvania

"This is a story of a young man trying to make sense of both his past and present—how the place he came from shaped him and why that place ceased to exist. This is more than a coming-of-age story, more than a nostalgic look back to a simpler time when we know that no time was ever simple. With *Rural Rebellion* Ross Benes does the impossible: he combines an honest personal narrative with extensive reporting and research, making it an invaluable resource to all of us who look at the country and ask, 'Why?' This book does more than explain Benes, more than explain Nebraska. It helps us understand modern America."

    Sridhar Pappu, author of *The Year of the Pitcher: Bob Gibson, Denny McLain, and the End of Baseball's Golden Age*

Rural Rebellion

RURAL
REBELLION

HOW NEBRASKA BECAME A
REPUBLICAN STRONGHOLD

Ross Benes

University Press of Kansas

Published by the University Press of Kansas (Lawrence, Kansas 66045), which was organized by the Kansas Board of Regents and is operated and funded by Emporia State University, Fort Hays State University, Kansas State University, Pittsburg State University, the University of Kansas, and Wichita State University.

Library of Congress Cataloging-in-Publication Data

Names: Benes, Ross, author.
Title: Rural rebellion : how Nebraska became a Republican stronghold / Ross Benes.
Description: Lawrence : University Press of Kansas, [2020]
Identifiers: LCCN 2020022324
ISBN 9780700630455 (cloth)
ISBN 9780700630462 (ebook)
Subjects: LCSH: Nebraska—Politics and government—21st century. | Conservatism—Nebraska.
Classification: LCC JK6616 .B46 2020 | DDC 320.5209782—dc23
LC record available at https://lccn.loc.gov/2020022324.

British Library Cataloguing-in-Publication Data is available.

Printed in the United States of America

10 9 8 7 6 5 4 3 2 1

The paper used in this publication is recycled and contains 30 percent postconsumer waste. It is acid free and meets the minimum requirements of the American National Standard for Permanence of Paper for Printed Library Materials Z39.48-1992.

For the good people
of Brainard

Contents

Acknowledgments

Before I lay out some earnest thank-yous, I want to share a note with readers to give them some context of what they're getting into. This book blends several genres including memoir, journalism, political science, history, and sociology, but some subjects were much more personal than others. To tell the story of why my own views have evolved and why Nebraska politics have changed, I felt it necessary to include both personal essays and institutional critiques. In the first half of this book I talk more about my own experiences because the topics of religion, health care, and immigration are very personal matters. In the second half of the book I talk more about institutions—like the state's legislature, public university system, and political parties—so those chapters are less memoir driven. While various genres are imitated throughout the entire book, readers may find that the first part of the book is more memoir whereas the second part is more historical and journalistic. In citing where I obtained material, I tried to be thorough without overwhelming readers with endnotes, which led me to combine citations at the end of paragraphs. As part of my effort to limit endnotes, I excluded the numerous interviews I conducted from the endnotes section. Instead, I mentioned those interviews in the text and embedded them into my reporting. Quotes that have no endnote citation usually came from interviews I conducted.

Now on to the acknowledgments. I must begin by thanking friends and colleagues who fed my vanity by repeatedly telling me that my perspective was worth sharing. I'm amazed that you convinced me to write a political memoir. I appreciate the work you did building my ego.

My family deserves a shout-out. I've always been outspoken and not one to shy away from an argument. I appreciate that you guys keep putting up with me considering how often I disagree with you. And it's great that some of you were open to sharing your thoughts with me for this book. I'm glad that we get along well despite our differences. I know many others who moved away from their hometowns who don't have it so good. Similarly, I want to thank the people of Butler County, and to those throughout Nebraska, who make life easy there. Your friendliness is a cultural feature worth clinging to.

Thanks to my agent, Lane Heymont of the Tobias Agency, for believing in this project and assuaging my concerns. Thanks to my editor, David Congdon, and everyone else at the University Press of Kansas, for believing in the book and making it happen. Coming into this project, I was ignorant of how university presses work. Thanks, Jason Berry, Jon Lauck, and Scott Winter, for helping me understand this niche. Thanks, CJ Janovy, for your early feedback. Thanks, Matt Fraher, for your help creating charts. Thanks, Morgan Baskin, Zach Fulciniti, and Riki Markowitz, for your fact checking. Thanks to the peer reviewers for your constructive criticism.

Like most authors, my books haven't generated a substantial amount of money, so I take on other work. I'm grateful to *eMarketer* for employing me the past few years. It's been a good job that's allowed me to live more freely. I also want to thank editors I've worked with while freelancing. Sections of articles I wrote for the *Nation*, *American Prospect*, Deadspin, and *Esquire* found their way into this book in new formats.

Throughout the reporting process of this book, I spoke with many sources. I appreciate everyone who shared their time with me, including those who would rather remain unnamed. Sources who I want to personally thank include Greg Adams, Roy Baker, Doug Bereuter, Tom Brewer, Jon Bruning, John Cavanaugh, Vic Covalt, Sue Crawford, Frank Daley, Al Davis, Kara Eastman, Laura Ebke, Renee Fry, Amanda Gailey, Jack Gould, Ben Gray, Chuck Hagel, Gerard Harbison, John Harms, Burke Harr, Dave Heineman, Robert Hilkemann, Bill Hoppner, Megan Hunt, Jim Jansen, Ron Jensen, Jerry Johnson, Bob Kerrey, Jane Kleeb, Connie Knoche, Jon Knutson, Ari Kohen, Rick Kolowski, David Kotok, Bob Krist, Doug Kristensen, Paul Landow, Chris Langemeir, Rich Lombardi, Preston Love, John McCollister, Janece Mollhof, Randy Moody, W. Don Nelson, Ben Nelson, Patrick O'Donnell, Tom Osborne, Dave Pantos, Mary Pipher, Vince Powers, Barbara Raya, Walt Radcliffe, David Reneicke, L. Lynn Rex, Crystal Rhoades, Kim Robak, Chris Rodgers, Michael Rose-Ivey, Barry Rubin, Drey Samuelson, Judith Schweikart, Lee Terry, Tony Vargas, Don Walton, Sändra Washington, Gerald Wright, and Jeff Yost.

My research led me to ask librarians and state officials to help me find particular documents and statistics. I'm grateful for the patience of Brooklyn librarians at my neighborhood branch who helped me file many interlibrary loan requests. University of Nebraska librarian Signe Boudreau went beyond her required duties to find an old, rare report that helped inform my reporting. Workers at the Nebraska Accountability and Disclosure Commission were also helpful.

It has been rather strange finishing this book while stationed in the US epicenter of a global pandemic. As I write this, I've been shut in my apartment for three months, unable to go anywhere besides my neighborhood's grocery store, pharmacy, and park while New York City tries to control the spreading coronavirus. Having nowhere else to go helped me finish this project quicker, and producing this book gave me something to look forward to during these long days. By the time you read this book, I hope like hell that we've overcome the virus and our daily routines have resumed.

Last, I want to thank my fiancée, Rachel. Ever since she's met me, Rachel has heard a lot more about Husker athletics and small-town nonsense than she would prefer. Once I started working on this book, she then had to hear about Nebraska politics, which she doesn't care about at all. Yet, she's been patient and a helpful editor. Whether we're quarantined in our home together or traveling abroad, I'm always lucky to have her, and our hounds Cooper and Snoopy, who've done their part to calm my nerves, make me smile, and appreciate how good I've got it.

Rural Rebellion

Introduction

Man, Chi-Chi looked gorgeous strutting down the ramp. Bright lipstick made red lips pop, a pink bandanna accentuated dark, thick curls, and a blue dress with a hemline high enough above the knees to make your imagination run wild. Butler County, Nebraska, would never witness another drag queen so magnificent.

Chi-Chi was a character played by actor John Leguizamo in the 1995 movie *To Wong Foo, Thanks for Everything! Julie Newmar*. The movie was filmed about a six-minute drive from my parents' house. As the area's heating and air conditioning repair man, my dad got called when Leguizamo's trailer had a malfunctioning unit. While Dad fixed the AC, he saw the movie's stars Wesley Snipes, Patrick Swayze, and Leguizamo walk out the trailer and down a ramp wearing high heels and short skirts. The image burned in his mind.

"Leguizamo looked like a woman," Dad said. "He was decent-looking actually. Snipes was the ugliest. God, he made an ugly woman."

In case you haven't seen it, *To Wong Foo* is about New York City drag queens on a road trip to Hollywood for a pageant. On their way to California, the drag queens get stranded in a fictional midwestern small town called Snydersville. They deal with locals' ignorance of drag, take the townswomen shopping for new clothes, and engage in other novelty plot twists you'd expect from this sort of campy film. "Snydersville" is actually Loma, Nebraska, an unincorporated area where *maybe* thirty people live that sits just outside my hometown, Brainard. In Loma, there's a bar, a church, an old schoolhouse, a handful of houses, a cemetery, and . . . that's really it.

Loma is so rural, it makes Brainard and its elitist paved roads feel like Los Angeles in *Blade Runner*. Driving through the town's dirt strip (there's just the one) gives a feeling of *Walker, Texas Ranger* meets the Great Depression. The Loma bar is a national treasure, and I genuinely enjoyed drinking Boone's Farm in its empty pastures as pickup headlights and torched coaches guided us through the dark. When my fiancée visited Nebraska for the first time, I drove her up a hill outside Loma, turned off the engine, rolled down the windows, and watched fireflies dance in a ditch full of tall grass while we gazed at an orange moon and a sky full of stars that we normally can't see in the city. As much as I appreciate Loma, the place hasn't changed since Tom Joad headed Californee way. People there still talk about the time Leguizamo, Snipes, and Swayze stopped in town for their drag gig, *more than twenty-five years ago.*

It's not just in people's memory that the movie remains alive. Several buildings, including the Catholic church, received paint jobs, new wiring, and fixed-up storefronts from the movie production—and most haven't been touched up since. A building made for the movie that says "Welcome to Snydersville" still stands and is used by a family as a storage shed. In my closet back home, as in many other people's closets from Butler County, a "Loma Goes Hollywood" T-shirt hangs as a relic of a bygone era.

Over the years, I've talked to many people who were extras for the movie or owned land that was used in the filming. They are always eager to share their brief film experiences. My dad is no different, which is amusing given his heteronormative views.

My dad is essentially Hank Hill, which makes me an awkward and bewildering Bobby. He grew up a farm boy who's now in his seventies. He's a plain, straight, ordinary, blue-collar, old-fashioned man who never misses mass. His distaste for change is reflected in his loyalty to Bud Light. Whenever we go to a baseball game or bar where his favorite beverage isn't offered, Dad buys an alternative lager the server recommends. Without fail, he remarks, "This ain't Bud Light" after taking the first sip.

When Leguizamo, Swayze, and Snipes came to town dressed as women, people in Brainard like my dad didn't obsess over their differences with their Hollywood visitors. Sure, the idea of two men marrying each other at that time was perceived as an abomination by most folks in town. But the movie's deviation from heterosexual norms was viewed as harmless campy fun. Opportunists didn't use the movie to weaponize the anxiety that rural people have about gay rights. Fox News didn't exist yet, and no news publications were stoking people's fears by turning "Loma Goes Hollywood" into "Hollywood Assaults Small-Town Values." Evangelical groups weren't out picketing the movie set for its lax attitudes about sex. Talk radio hosts weren't propping it up as an example of liberals tainting the values of "real Americans." There were no fringe online forums spreading conspiracies about the town or the actors. The movie wasn't leveraged as an excuse to target gay people who lived in Nebraska. Everyone in Brainard was just thrilled that famous people acknowledged their existence briefly.

It'd be a stretch to say the philosophies of *To Wong Foo*'s filmmakers were embraced throughout Butler County. There's a reason gay kids from our area wait until college or later to come out. My hometown isn't always welcoming to those who are "different." However, in this specific case the outsiders presenting a different view on life were at least welcomed and politely tolerated. Because the movie wasn't instantly tethered to political or identity issues, my dad and many other Nebraskans who are apt to vote against gay marriage fondly remember the drag queens who delivered Loma its fifteen minutes of fame. Rather than upset people, *To Wong Foo* is a source of nostalgia for Brainard. The only thing I can do when faced with this dissonance is smile that there exists a condition in small-town Nebraska where cross-dressing has brought joy, not to mention a little renovation.

If a movie like this were filmed in Loma nowadays, the experience would likely be different. Pundits and political groups would turn to the internet and cable TV to nationalize and weaponize the situation. Operatives from Washington and New York would pour their attention onto Brainard to turn the filming into a controversy so that they could rally support by aggravating people's most basic emotions. With everyday life interactions increasingly turning into culture-war proxy battles, someone from Brainard would go "viral" and those who caused the sensation would be gone and have moved their attention elsewhere by the time the aftermath set in. Luckily for the good folks of Brainard, they didn't have to deal with this nonsense.

What I find intriguing about the making of *To Wong Foo* is that people from distinct parts of the country guided by dissimilar beliefs were able to respect each other's personal differences while being exposed to new experiences. We the people—and that equally applies to those who live on farmsteads and those who dwell in cities, and everyone in between—should strive for this type of openness and understanding when it comes to our politics. We have a long way to go in fulfilling this ideal. Like so many other states, Nebraska politics have become more extreme since Chi-Chi came to town.

———

The story of Nebraska is about how a once independent state full of gracious people became baptized into placing their hopes in fortunate sons and narcissistic TV stars. My story is about loving those whom I've left behind.

To understand my viewpoint, you should know that John Mellencamp's small town is a metropolis compared to where I come from. In Brainard, Nebraska, there are no stoplights, movie theaters, grocery stores, parking meters, concert halls, rec centers, car dealerships, public gyms, convenience stores, or chain restaurants. The tallest structures are the Catholic church's steeple and the grain elevator showing that God and farm reign supreme here. The town's bar, aptly titled Husker Bar in honor of the beloved University of Nebraska Cornhuskers, functions as a coffee shop, restaurant, saloon, community center, and psychiatrist's office. Whenever a family moves out of town it reduces our population by a few percentage points.

According to the 2010 Census, Brainard was 99.7 percent white. In 2000 it was 99.4 percent white. Our racial diversity was cut in half when my Hispanic high school Spanish teacher left to teach at another school. If you never left Brainard, you'd be under the impression that Lutherans and Methodists are ethnic minorities since nearly everyone attends the same Catholic church.

The population density is so low that you don't just know everyone's name in town. You also know who they are related to, who they've dated, where they work, and what type of beer they like. My graduating high school class was the biggest in East Butler history, yet it had fewer than four dozen students. Because my mom specializes in gossip, I knew more information about our neighbors than J. Edgar Hoover ever had on suspected communists.

Psychologically and geographically, Brainard is far removed from big city life. Sure, Omaha is just over an hour's drive away, but the closest city with more than a million residents is five hundred miles away in Chicago. Isolated areas of working-class religious white folk usually vote conservatively, and that has been the case with Brainard for a long time. What's been overlooked by many analysts is how much areas like Brainard have changed politically. Small towns throughout the Midwest have shed their interest in moderate candidates and embraced the hardened right.

Lots of people were puzzled by the level of support that the Midwest gave Donald Trump during the 2016 and 2020 presidential elections. In the greater Butler County area that Brainard is a part of, about 80 percent of voters picked Trump in 2016. In trying to explain the shock of Trump's victory, CNN sent cameras to my home county, which was unprecedented. What resulted was a three-minute segment of local farmers talking about their love for Trump set against the backdrop of tractors rollin' through alfalfa fields. "Nobody took that guy serious," a local Vietnam veteran donning an army helmet and fatigues told CNN. "Well, they forgot about us deplorables here in the Midwest. They totally forgot about us."[1]

When the clip was shared on Facebook and Twitter, commenters yucked it up over how backwards rural Nebraska appeared and how they never want to visit there. I think the same people calling Nebraska Trump supporters "disgusting" and "inbred drug dealers" would be blown away by how nicely rural Nebraskans would treat them if they ever got the guts to go there and talk to people who challenge their worldview. The disparaging comments directed at Nebraskans in reaction to the video showed why the "deplorables" line resonated so strongly with folks who were fed up with being looked down on.

While Trump's rise was unparalleled, much of middle America has been moving to the right for a while. Having spent the vast majority of my life in Nebraska, I've seen a gradual shift in the types of candidates we elect to our state legislature and the US Congress. The accumulative changes over the past few decades have made it extremely difficult for Democrats to be competitive outside of certain parts of our two biggest cities, Omaha and Lincoln, and even there, it is often an uphill battle for liberals. Nebraska is not alone in this regard, as the aversion toward Democrats has grown in several states in the middle of the country. Following the 1980s farm crisis, states with large rural voting blocs saw many seats flip from red to blue. By appealing to economic issues, such as federal support for agriculture, Democrats in Nebraska as well as in North Dakota, South Dakota, Iowa, Missouri, Oklahoma, and other states were able to defeat Republicans tethered to conservative doctrine. Republicans wrestled back that power. These states that once helped Democrats become the majority in the Senate are now an albatross for the party.[2]

It took a bizarre outcome to get news outlets like CNN to look at places like Brainard. But the dynamics that push small-town people away from liberal and moderate candidates have been in the making for many years. Now that I've spent over half a decade living in New York City, I have experienced how painfully unaware both rural and urban Americans are of how the other half lives. I realize that the people I grew up with around Brainard are some of the sweetest folks on Earth, even though I often disagree with them.

———

Nebraskans like to think of themselves as independent minded. It's in our blood. The state's settlers were explorers who took a gamble coming west to make a life for themselves on America's frontier. When presented with the chance to become a state in 1860, these prairie people voted against it. Statehood came seven years later, and not long after that Arbor Day was founded in Nebraska. The holiday was started by conservative Democrat Julius Sterling Morton, who took a liking to environmentalism and briefly served as Nebraska's governor and US secretary of agriculture. During that era, Morton's biographer wrote, Nebraska belonged to "a section of the country that seemed for a time to produce only radicals."[3]

For years, the state eschewed the Republican-Democrat dichotomy. Many Nebraskans supported the People's Party, an agrarian movement that arose back when the word "populism" actually meant something and wasn't just a watered-down buzzword that pundits use in varied ways to try to make themselves sound smart. These rebel farmers fed the rise of William Jennings Bryan, a political liberal and fundamentalist Christian who railed against big business when he represented Nebraska in Congress. He became the Democratic Party nominee in three presidential races, all of which he lost. Bryan's contempt for big business interests was best exemplified in his famous 1896 "Cross of Gold" speech wherein he stated that banks had become too dominant in society and that maintaining the gold standard would crucify the working class.

Nebraska asserted its political independence once again in 1937 by doing something truly radical and removing party labels from its state legislature. It remains the only state to have a nonpartisan as well as a single-house lawmaking body. Almost every newspaper in the state opposed this move, but it was adopted largely because the effort was spearheaded by George Norris, a man popular enough in the state to get elected five times apiece to both the US Senate and House of Representatives.

"Every mile of the road, it seemed to me, I had been in conflict with the Republican leadership; and I knew it considered me as a thorn in its side," Norris wrote in his autobiography, *Fighting Liberal*. Norris served the majority of his career as a Republican before becoming the only registered independent in the 1940 Congress. He was religiously agnostic, a supporter of liberalism, and wildly popular in Nebraska.[4]

Nebraska had become more conservative by the time I was born. In 1989

I welcomed the world in Butler County's only hospital in David City, notable for being the birthplace of Hallmark's founder. In that era we still elected people who were willing to take unpopular stances if they believed that what they were doing was right. Senator Bob Kerrey defended gay marriage before most politicians in blue states did. Congressman Doug Bereuter chastised his party for leveraging Christianity for political gain. Senator Chuck Hagel sponsored bipartisan immigration reform and was one of the first major critics of the Iraq War even though it put him at odds with fellow Republicans. Nowadays, the most rebellious action Nebraskans can hope for from their representatives is Senator Ben Sasse sending some terse words Donald Trump's way before voting in lockstep with the president's agenda.[5]

The difference between the Nebraska politicians who were in power when I grew up and today's elected officials can be seen in how differently they responded to Robert Mueller's investigation. Several of the most prominent politicians who presided over Nebraska during my upbringing added their names to a bipartisan group that urged the US Senate to protect American democracy as Mueller's investigation faced resistance heading into 2019. Meanwhile, Nebraska's current state lawmakers condemned the Mueller investigation before it got off the ground as a "perversion of equal justice." It's unlikely that the Nebraska GOP is swayed by the indictments and guilty pleas Mueller secured or believes its resolution would have an actual effect on his approach. The group just wanted to express party loyalty and hail to the chief.

In the year I was born, both of Nebraska's US senators were Democrats, as was one of its three House reps. The following year, Nebraskans elected Democrats for governor, auditor, and state treasurer. By 2020 all those seats were firmly held by Republicans. We haven't had a Democrat governor for more than two decades, and the Republicans we elect continue to get more conservative.[6]

Other states have had this experience too. Five of the six individuals South Dakota and North Dakota sent to Congress in 1989 were Democrats, but the two states have zero Democrats combined as of this writing. Kansas used to have two Democrats in Congress, but now it has one. Eight of the eleven people Tennessee sent to Washington were Democrat, and now only two are. Oklahoma, Arkansas, and Kentucky went from a combined fifteen Democrats to one. Missouri sent five Democrats to Congress in 1989; now it sends two. Indiana's congressional Democrats went from seven to two. During the New

Deal and Great Society, the moderates and liberals these states used to send to Congress were instrumental in getting progressive laws passed that supported unions and public-power projects. Throughout the 1980s and 1990s, representatives from these states backed public education initiatives, legislation that supported the well-being of the working class, and equal rights laws. Those days are gone. These states no longer give Democrats the incremental votes they need to pass legislation. And the Republicans they elect now are much more conservative than Republicans politicians were thirty years ago, which adds further difficulty in getting progressive legislation passed.[7]

I didn't realize it at the time, but bipartisanship peaked in Nebraska when I was a young boy chasing salamanders in my neighbor's cellar. Coming out of the womb in 1989, I entered a world where Nebraska straddled the middle of the political spectrum. Just a few years before I was born, Nebraska—not New York or California—became the first state to have a governor's race where both parties nominated a female candidate. We didn't start leaning hard right until the late 1990s, and from there the move rightward only gathered steam. Now we're so far from the center it feels blasphemous to suggest that things haven't always been this way. Figure 1 uses data from the congressional vote tallying website Voteview to show just how far Nebraska's political representatives have strayed.[8]

What's happened in Nebraska is that the uniformity and polarization of national political parties made it harder for Democrats to get elected there, and loyal Republicans filled this vacuum. This is a new development that sprung up in my lifetime. "Historically, party identity and loyalty has often played a secondary role in determining the support Nebraskans have given political candidates," wrote Nebraska historians James Olson and Ronald Naugle. "Correspondingly, the Republican or Democratic labels have not necessarily connoted the degree of conservativism and liberalism which at any point might describe the same parties on a national level."[9]

Democrats unintentionally helped enable Republican domination in my home state by pulling back their campaigning in Nebraska, struggling to build an infrastructure in the heartland to support local candidates, bickering among each other, and only reaching out to Nebraskans when there was a high-profile race they thought they could win. The perception among the people I grew up with is that Democrats pushed their party so far to the left that they've made elections insurmountable for Democrats who used to win in the

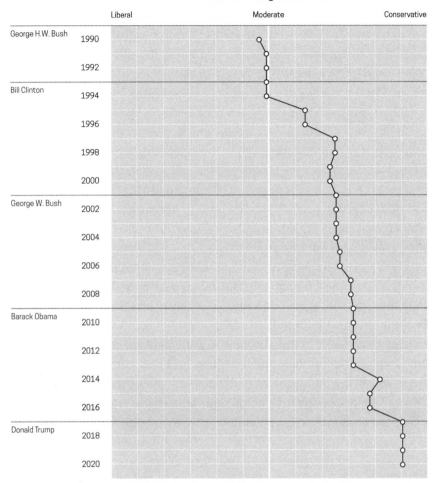

Nebraska's Rightward Shift

Liberal   Moderate   Conservative

George H.W. Bush — 1990, 1992

Bill Clinton — 1994, 1996, 1998, 2000

George W. Bush — 2002, 2004, 2006, 2008

Barack Obama — 2010, 2012, 2014, 2016

Donald Trump — 2018, 2020

This chart shows the average ideology scores of Nebraska's five congressional members for each year between 1990 and 2020. Scores range from –1 for the most liberal (Massachusetts Democrat Elizabeth Warren is –0.77) to 1 for the most conservative (Texas Republican Ted Cruz is 0.82). The horizontal axis ranges from –1 to 1. Between 1990 and 2020, Nebraska's average congressional ideology score went from –0.04 to 0.50. Put in today's terms, in 1990 the average Nebraskan congressperson's ideology was similar to Alabama Democrat Doug Jones, whereas today it resembles Texas Republican John Cornyn. *Source:* Voteview.com.

heartland. This has led Nebraskans to disassociate themselves from the party. When I was born, 42 percent of Nebraska voters registered Democrat; today just 29 percent do. The dwindling share of Democrats makes it all but certain that for most races the winner is decided in the Republican primary. Democrats win so few races that Nebraska public service commissioner Crystal Rhoades let out a subdued laugh during a conversation in 2018 when she told me she was the "highest-ranking Democrat elected in the state of Nebraska."[10]

Meanwhile, Republicans trump opponents with their ad spending, unite behind their candidates, and get their messages continually amplified by Fox News, local Rush Limbaugh imitators, churches, and coffee shop gossipers who keep regurgitating the same messages back and forth to the point that nobody knows who generated the arguments to begin with. This feedback loop enables conservatives to ride to glory on the wings of cultural wedge issues like guns, abortion, and immigration.

There's no single bullet that stripped Nebraska of its political moderation. In this book we will examine various trends that drove Nebraska far right. Over the past few decades, obsession over abortion politics has made many elections unwinnable for Nebraska Democrats, who can't seem to figure out a winning strategy. The state has gone in so hard on illegal immigration that the legendary football coach and congressman Tom Osborne ended his political career with a loss to a hard-line immigration opponent. As their influence slipped, Democrats kept infighting—and their bench of candidates who were willing to run shrank to the point that Republicans regularly run unopposed in several of the state's top races. In 2018, state Democrats turned to a former Republican to run for governor and nominated an attorney general candidate who dropped out of the race after strangling his eighty-two-year-old father. Even Democrat Bob Kerrey, a war hero and popular former governor and US senator, got crushed when he tried to recapture a Senate seat. Nebraska's last Democratic US senator, Ben Nelson, exited office after his Obamacare vote contributed to a controversy dubbed "the Cornhusker kickback."[11]

The state that used to make life hell for monied interests now nails itself to the Cross of Gold. Aside from placing faith in a bombastic reality-TV star, it elected a governor from a family worth billions who uses his connections and wealth to target fellow Republicans he finds too moderate. Due to deregulation of campaign finance laws, many donors remain hidden as they spread their Washington-led partisanship into our state. Brain drain, the glut of elderly voters, the growing rural-urban divide, and people increasingly choosing to live among like-minded folks play their part too in creating polarization across the heartland.

We've become so conditioned to follow arbitrary political alliances that it seems preposterous that until very recently, our state's two statues in the National Statuary Hall at the US Capitol were of a conservative environmentalist (Morton) and a liberal Christian (Bryan). Glancing at Republicans' dominance of Nebraska's elections gives the impression that the Cornhusker State is more right wing than any other place in the United States. However, Nebraska is not a monolith. Nebraska's unique legislature, grassroots activism, refugee resettlement programs, and ballot measures show that there's still some progressivism in the state, which markets itself with the slogan "Honestly, it's not for everyone." These initiatives indicate that areas like Nebraska—where Democrats routinely lose—aren't lost causes for progressives who are willing to work outside of traditional partisan politics when advancing their cause.

As much as I'm irritated by my home state's unquestioning loyalty to the Republican Party, I'm also frustrated by how ignorant many liberals I've met on the East Coast are about places like Nebraska. Some liberals I've met view the plains as a hopeless cause, populated by racist and backwards people, even though they haven't stepped foot in the Midwest outside of northern Chicago. These same liberals will insist that those who don't share their views are by default bigots, and they talk down to anyone who so dares to disagree with them, which is an ineffective form of persuasion. They see small-town conservatives as deranged, not as rational people who are reinforced by their environment to come to much different conclusions than those who dwell in cities. They don't like to encounter opinions or beliefs that don't align with their own, but they sure as hell enjoy feeling like they're right all the time.

Alongside the numerous insufferable liberals that one inevitably meets living in New York City, I've also met many folks on the left who are good people and who are genuinely curious about rural America. Many don't have a single friend who voted for Donald Trump, and while they can't imagine voting for Trump themselves, they truly want to understand what life is like in places where people overwhelmingly vote for Trump. These people are more interested in understanding those who differ from them than in shutting down people they disagree with. Many of the hardcore Christians I know could learn from their altruistic outlook on life. These caring and well-intentioned liberals (who I believe outnumber but are less vocal than their pompous counter-parts) have nothing in common with Fox News caricatures. I wish people in Brainard were more familiar with how caring and rational most liberals are. Brainard is an amazing place, but if I never left it, I wouldn't have been exposed to these views. I also wouldn't have realized how conditioned my own conservative outlook was.

I spent the first nineteen years of my life in an eastern Nebraska village of three hundred people before spending five years in the state's capital, Lincoln, where I attended Nebraska's flagship university. After college, I had a brief stint in Detroit before I chased an internship in New York City. At my first New York job, I became the worst-dressed man to ever work for *Esquire* magazine, which prompted a *Devil Wears Prada* makeover wherein the owner of a high-end salon insulted me for looking like a "Nebraska farm boy." At another job, my bosses joked that I—white, straight, Christian, male—was their real "diversity hire" even though the company employed people from around the world. No one else on staff nurtured pet squirrels, went coon hunting, witnessed an ultralight plane crash during a high school football game, or discovered the Insane Clown Posse in fifth grade while sitting in a garage watching pro wrestling videotapes next to a friend's thirty-year-old cousin who tripped on meth. I didn't fit in that great in the New York media world, but I kept working there, putting out books and articles for whoever would pay me. We'll trace how my own political views evolved as I've shifted from being a right-wing small-town Nebraskan to a card-carrying member of the East Coast "fake news" media.[12]

Following the 2016 presidential election, a strange thing happened: people suddenly started caring about where I came from. I never thought it was a big deal to be from Nebraska. But now when I tell people I'm meeting for the first that I'm from a tiny Nebraska town, it regularly turns into a half hour of giddy questioning. During these conversations, I've been told enough times to write a book about my experience that I decided to just do it so people would quit bugging me. I also wanted to shed some light on an area that is usually misunderstood by the national press corps. On the seldom occasion that Nebraska receives attention, its residents are often depicted as caricatures.

Nebraska is easy to mock for people who've never been there, but I loved growing up there. To me, Nebraska is the Good Life. And I wish more people would experience places like it. Hopefully this book will help people who have never been in the heartland understand what life is like there. Ideally, it will lead people to consider how their own environment shapes their opinions before they judge others solely by political differences.

I'm acquaintances with admirable and loathsome people across the entire political spectrum, but it turns out many Biden and Clinton voters don't really know Trump voters, and vice versa. Living in small-town Nebraska and New York City has given me a balance of Republican and Democrat friends that I wouldn't have if I spent my whole life in one area. Scrolling through my Facebook feed is maddening because I constantly see my friends on both sides of the divide being presented as something they're not. This book is about the dissonance of moving from one of the most rural and conservative regions of America to one of its most liberal and urban centers as the two grow further apart at a critical moment in our country's history.

CHAPTER ONE

Pro-Life License Plates

The Catholic Church's strict rules about contraception are the reason I'm even alive. I come from a line of big Catholic families where surplus children became farmhands at a young age. My dad's parents had six boys and two girls. My mom's parents had six girls and two boys. Both were the second-oldest kids in their families. Through several generations, my family's reluctance to use birth control spread out numerous children over many years and allowed me to be born. If my parents weren't observant Catholics, my entire existence would have been nothing more than a brief shot in the dark.

My sister is seventeen years older than me—old enough to be my mom. If my parents were nonreligious, or had lived in cities where it is economically prohibitive to have children, they may have decided to prevent themselves from having another child in their forties. Instead, they pumped me out just a few years before becoming grandparents.

People usually think it is strange as hell when I tell them I became an uncle at age four. Truth is, I didn't find it too unusual after my nephew was born. Hell, my mom is older than one of her aunts. As the youngest child in my family, I'm happy I have nephews and nieces near my age because it makes me feel like I have younger brothers and sisters.

Nebraska's teenage birth rate is on par with the national average. But those stats don't reflect how I experienced living in a Nebraska village for two decades. According to the Centers for Disease Control and Prevention, the teen birth rate in small towns is 63 percent higher than it is in cities. This aligns with my experience of knowing many people who had kids when they were still in high school. One of those people is my brother Kellen.[1]

In high school, Kellen was a beer-guzzling, deer-hunting, twelve-sport letter winner who raised all sorts of hell in Butler County with his lipstick-red

14

Pontiac Firebird. He also knocked up his sweetheart on his way to becoming class valedictorian. Her parents and my parents met to decide how to proceed. Abortion, adoption, and raising the kid on your own all flash through a teen's mind when they see their life changing. My parents even offered to raise the child. Eventually, everyone agreed that Kellen and his girlfriend would raise their child themselves.

My dad was angry as hell his son got his girlfriend pregnant at such a young age, and he gave Kellen a reaming. Then he made my brother visit our grandparents to tell them about the situation, which was undoubtedly awkward. But after my niece Brook was born, my dad stopped yelling. He became a goofy grandpa who would glow whenever he picked her up, contorting his face in funny poses to get her to smile. Brook and her cousins brought out a silly, tender side of my parents that I didn't know was inside of them.

After Brook was born, she lived with her parents. Then they split up. Her mom was working and attending college while her dad was preparing for grad school. They made sure they didn't live too many miles apart so that they could both raise Brook and be a part of her life. They continued this arrangement even after they both changed jobs and started families with new partners.

I'm just six years older than Brook, so we grew up together. When she was only four years old, she'd fill out crossword puzzles with my grandpa and spot four-syllable nouns in word searches. In high school she was a star athlete. She then competed for an NCAA Division I athletic program, running track at the University of South Dakota, a feat that no one else in my family came close to accomplishing. She got an MBA and started a successful career in healthcare administration. Through it all, she's taken no flak from anyone. During a long car ride to a high school football game in northeastern Nebraska several years ago, one of my relatives ranted about the accomplishments of the men in my family. Brook, then a freshman in high school, chimed in: "Why didn't you mention the things that your wife and I have done? Is it because we're women?" The corresponding silence was superb.

The high teen pregnancy rate in small towns would lead many to feel that these areas are where abortion services are needed most. But in small towns, the odds of opposing abortion are about three times higher than they are in metro areas. In less populated areas, you see a lot of these kids grow up and contribute to their community. When I see Brook, I realize her parents went through a really difficult situation, but I'm glad they did because she's enriched the lives of her family and friends. As he spiraled deeper in debt helping to provide for a child, Kellen spent a lot of time in his twenties going to Brook's dance recitals and soccer practices. Now he is joyous whenever he talks about his daughter's track meets or home-brews a six-pack of "Brook's Brew" that she can take to her apartment. I wish some of my progressive friends who have never been to Nebraska could observe these moments before they denounce pro-lifers as deranged.[2]

Most people in Brainard have deep connections with their family and can rely on them as a safety net should they have an unexpected crisis. If Kellen and his girlfriend couldn't raise their daughter, my parents would have been glad to raise her. Because the standard of living and the cost of land are so cheap in rural Nebraska, it is a lot easier to be poor in Brainard than it is in a big city, which is something many young parents grapple with. If you've lived in Brainard your whole life, you won't witness how defunding family planning clinics places more women at risk of falling into poverty. These dynamics aren't clear to people who have to drive through several counties just to reach a Planned Parenthood location.

In Brainard, what you see is people rejoicing whenever someone in town has a kid or grandkid. You're in a town where you need every physical body you can get to fight depopulation, and everyone in town will by default have a relationship with the new baby. Most people in Brainard haven't spent much time in economically distressed urban areas, so they don't comprehend the poverty, homelessness, lack of child services, and unavailable affordable housing that single mothers in cities may deal with. The way life is experienced in Brainard leads most people there to view abortion in strictly moral terms while ignoring economic considerations. The feedback loop from the church parking lot, the bar, talk radio, and Fox News just further instills the mindset that finds legal abortion untenable. For most of my life, I too found the subject unquestionable.

In third grade I won an art contest for creating a pro-life sign. To this day, I can't cut a straight line and my handwriting looks like a Rorschach inkblot, but I edged out my classmates by writing a concise anti-abortion slogan that my mom helped me decorate. This would be the first and last time my artwork received praise.

A handful of kids from my parish's CCD (the Catholic version of Sunday school) program had their signs chosen to be presented at the Knights of Columbus hall in David City. The reward was a free dinner and the chance to speak about your poster in front of an attentive audience. My parents already fed me for free every night and I didn't want to talk about abortion in front of adults, so I thought this reward was garbage. I just wanted to stay home and play video games and watch TV. Unluckily for me, the Knights liked my poster and sent me to a banquet in Lincoln to talk about it in front of a bigger crowd. This seriously cut into my precious *Ninja Turtles* time.

Throughout the 1990s, the only thing more reliable on the weekends than the Huskers winning football games was hearing a sermon about abortion. I was confirmed into the Catholic faith by Bishop Fabian Bruskewitz, one of the most conservative bishops in the United States. Bruskewitz was the only Roman Catholic bishop in the country to ban female altar servers in his diocese. He said good Christians shouldn't do yoga. He excommunicated Catholics for joining groups that advocated for church reform. He made sure that Lincoln was the only diocese in America to not cooperate with audits designed for protecting young Catholics from sex abuse. And he was the only bishop in the country to refuse to cooperate in the John Jay College of Criminal Justice's investigation of sex abuse in the Catholic Church. Even before I'd been confirmed by Bruskewitz, I'd already been bombarded by enough pro-life lectures to feel that abortion was a bigger issue in our country than wars, disease, poverty, unemployment, crime, and education combined. Nothing less than the entire moral fabric of our nation was at stake. Any day now our culture would become overrun by abortionists resembling the emotionally detached denizens of *Brave New World*.[3]

The Catholic Church became more politically driven by abortion during my childhood. Across denominations, abortion became *the* political issue for many Christians. It also became *the* issue for the Republican Party, said Nebraska state senator Robert Hilkemann, a Republican doctor in Omaha. Republicans put so much emphasis on abortion that they started sending pro-life politicians to Washington who "couldn't have found their way out of a culvert with a bright light at both ends," said Hilkemann.

When your community feels so passionate about abortion, it becomes your duty to make a pro-life sign. Anything you can do to protest the "baby killers" is welcomed by the community with open arms. My mom wasn't intentionally making a political statement by helping her son with a class project. Like most folks in Brainard, the last thing Mom wants to talk about is politics. She was just being a good parent making sure that I did what was required of me. Yet, assisting her son with this project would be viewed as political indoctrination by many of the people who shape our nation's news coverage.

If you're progressive, you may think that Nebraskans hate abortion just because they want to put women "in their place." I get why outsiders could perceive Nebraska that way given how many people I grew up with prefer stereotypical gender roles. My home state also overwhelmingly votes for candidates who fail to improve family leave that would make it easier for new parents to raise their children.

When a bill in favor of paid family leave made its way through the Nebraska Legislature in spring 2019, the conservative state senator Mike Groene complained that it would increase taxes. He said, "This is progressive socialism at its worst." Machaela Cavanaugh, a registered Democrat who was the first Nebraska state senator to nurse a baby on the legislative floor, countered, "We claim to be a pro-life state, we claim to value life . . . but our policies do not reflect that."[4]

Just as there are undoubtedly racists in Nebraska, there are undoubtedly misogynists, too. But, unlike some others in the press, I am not convinced the bigots are in the majority. I know so many pro-lifers who are genuine and want to help out the single mothers in their lives. Hell, at least half of the pro-lifers I know are women. The *New York Times* editorial board and some feminist academics may view pro-life women like my grandma, my mom, my sister, and dozens of my female friends as gender traitors, but doing so negates their humanity. The pro-life women I grew up with are not vandalizing abortion clinics, harassing doctors who provide abortions, or shaming the pregnant women in their lives. They're trying to comfort their pregnant friends and volunteering time and resources to organizations like Catholic Social Services that provide diapers, milk formula, and other goods free of charge to mothers in need.[5]

People in places like Brainard get made fun of for clinging to their religion. I wish the enlightened atheists who mock us could see *why* people in Brainard cling to their church. The same institution that repeatedly tells my family and friends to fight abortion also provides personal, social, and psychological fulfillment to people in areas where there is little else to do, see, or believe in.

What many people on the outside fail to really appreciate is how in Brainard, and across many small towns, church is the pillar that brings the community together. Aside from Sunday service, churches bring townspeople together by providing religious education for youth, hosting volunteer events like blood drives and soup kitchens, and opening up their halls for weddings, anniversaries, and graduations. After mass ends in Brainard, congregants spend twenty minutes in the parking lot chatting with their fellow parishioners before driving home. I can recall a lively discussion I had with my dad's friends right outside our church the day after Arizona State shutout the Huskers in 1996. Once a year, parish members put on carnival games and prepare a chicken dinner. Extended family members and people from surrounding towns pour in to support Brainard's Catholic church. The church will sell 1,500 meals even though there are only 300 people who live in Brainard.

Above all, the church is where Brainard socializes when it's not at the bar. It's where you come together with other people and feel part of something bigger than yourself. In politics, religion is something else altogether. Vocal Democrats are more apt to see religion as a punching bag whereas Republican officeholders wield it as a cudgel. Liberals couldn't help but laugh when Donald Trump, a pro-choicer most of his life, flipped his stance just before he ran for president. Cognitive dissonance is at work when Trump—a man who has been on the cover of *Playboy*, boasted about cheating on each of his three wives, had an affair with a porn star he allegedly (and very likely if we're being honest) tried to pay off, and been accused of sexual harassment by at least twenty-five women—wins over conservatives with family values positions supporting abstinence-only education and vowing to crack down on internet porn. I cannot stop my eyes from rolling when priests who blamed moral relativism for everything ranging from declining church attendance to unemployment do all they can to evangelize a political party that believes in "alternative facts." This has happened at a time when white evangelicals went from being the least likely group to the most likely group to say they will support politicians who commit immoral acts. "There's hardly any group in American politics that is as easily won over or seduced by power as Christians," said Peter Wehner, a Christian political operative who worked for Ronald Reagan and in both Bush administrations. "The fact that the Trump people are paying attention to them makes them feel very, very good, and especially because they didn't expect to be paid attention to very much. So they're just over the moon."[6]

Trump's election has seemingly outed many Christians as hypocrites, but don't let this sway you to believe that religion is a bad thing in and of itself. Americans who regularly attend religious services give more of their money to charity and spend more of their time engaging in civic activities. "By many different measures religiously observant Americans are better neighbors and better citizens than secular Americans—they are more generous with their time and money, especially in helping the needy, and they are more active in community life," wrote political scientists Robert Putnam and David Campbell. These researchers found that participating in religious activities matters more than belief itself when it comes to how much people give back to their community. "It's the friendships and group activities, carried out within a moral matrix that emphasizes selflessness," according to psychologist Jonathan Haidt. "That's what brings out the best in people." This is certainly how it felt in Brainard.[7]

The church is my hometown's foundation, and I have no doubt that it does more good than harm. However, when I was living a comfortable life in the Brainard bubble, I found it difficult to critically examine the institution that gave my life purpose and meaning. It didn't dawn on me how churches could enable extremist political ideologies.

Just as the people of Brainard get their socializing, spiritual fulfillment, and sense of community from church, they get their politics from the pulpit, too. Throughout my life, sermons functioned as a perpetual infomercial for the Republican Party.

The Catholic Church doesn't officially endorse candidates, but that's just semantics. It tells people who to vote for by encouraging single-issue voting. When I sat in the pew, I knew our priest wanted my parents to vote for the Republican George W. Bush. Why else would he keep publicly disparaging Democrat John Kerry for being too soft on abortion? The week Barack Obama was elected president, our chaplain was distraught and gave a homily about the dark times ahead of us as a result of the election.

As I sat in the back of our church, I heard priests say all sorts of things related to pro-choice: You shouldn't vote for anyone who is pro-choice because it is basically a mortal sin to do so; you could go to hell if you vote for someone who is pro-choice. You're not being true to your faith if you dare to vote for someone pro-choice. Our culture is being tested by God this election and you're disobeying Him if you vote for a pro-choice candidate, aka a Democrat. In addition to the shade thrown at Democrats, I heard many digs at liberals in general. It was a mortal sin to see heretical movies like *The Da Vinci Code*. Godless progressives in Hollywood were destroying our culture. Our universities are full of freethinkers who lack a moral compass, so be careful where you send your children to college. If you support the liberal agenda, you'll go to hell.[8]

In Brainard, morality is rooted in respecting traditions and institutions. Most people I knew believed that being a good person meant obeying the law and going to church. Patriotism is seen as a virtue, and the military remains very popular. In town, everyone knows someone in the service given that America's armed forces are disproportionately made up of people from rural areas.[9]

Brainard's institutions are cherished in a very personal way. That's why people volunteer at church events, regularly show up to high school games even after their kids are no longer enrolled, worship the traditional nuclear family that they're familiar with, and revere the Husker football program that they root for with their neighbors. Republicans have done an effective job appealing to these sentiments while Democrats have not. Nowhere is this clearer than with abortion politics.

"You had some wedge issues that I think the Republicans very masterfully made use of," Frank Daley, executive director of the Nebraska Accountability and Disclosure Commission, told me. "Abortion is probably the classic one.... I think the Democratic Party was asleep at the switch on this. In fact, [Democrats] did some things that actually had the effect of driving people out."

"Being pro-life never used to mean being Republican," wrote the Catholic News Agency's Mary Rezac, a friend of mine who was valedictorian of my high school class. It wasn't terribly long ago that Democrats like Joe Biden, Ted Kennedy, and Al Gore took pro-life stances before they flipped to conform to their national party's platform. And people forget that the Republican Party has ties to the biggest supporters of legal abortion.[10]

Eugenics supporter and Planned Parenthood founder Margaret Sanger worked with the wife of Republican presidential nominee Barry Goldwater to set up Phoenix, Arizona's, first birth control clinic, and Sanger died as a registered Republican. Planned Parenthood later named an award after Goldwater. Michigan Republican governor William Milliken, and the Michigan state GOP, once supported abortion rights. Republican governors Ronald Reagan and Nelson Rockefeller legalized abortion in New York and California before the Supreme Court made it legal nationwide. Republican feminists helped lead the fight for abortion rights in the Midwest during the 1970s. The author of the *Roe v. Wade* decision, Justice Harry Blackmun, was appointed by Republican president Richard Nixon. When Nebraska passed a "partial birth" abortion ban, the Reagan-appointed Republican Supreme Court justice Sandra Day O'Connor was the deciding vote that overturned Nebraska's pro-life law. And Nebraska native son Charles Munger, a Republican billionaire executive at Berkshire Hathaway, made significant investments in pro-choice organizations and helped back legal cases against abortion restrictions.[11]

When Nebraska politicians battled for a US Senate seat in 1984, both nominees took positions that seem crazy for their parties today. Democrat Jim Exon, the incumbent, backed an amendment to restrict abortion rights and opposed using federal funds for abortions. (Exon is the most successful Nebraska Democrat in the past century. He built up the party as a national committeeman, controlled state politics as governor, and became a national figure as a senator. He would be loathed by today's Democrats given his stances against abortion, immigration, and gay rights.) Exon's Republican opponent, Nancy Hoch, opposed abortion restrictions and said that the government should stay out of regulating women's decisions. Hoch gave Exon the closest race of his career but lost by a few percentage points. When interviewed years later about the race, she stated: "It was my pro-choice position that hurt. I didn't leave the Republican Party; they left me."[12]

Over time, Republicans attracted more Christian voters and nominated more anti-abortion candidates. As conservatives left the Democratic Party, it became less ideologically diverse and more liberal. Subsequently, the number of pro-life Democrat politicians shrank. According to the advocacy group Democrats for Life, in 1978 there were 125 pro-life Democrats in Congress. By 2012 there were just seventeen. In 2018 there were only three Democratic senators whose Planned Parenthood scorecards weren't 100 percent. There wasn't a single pro-life Democrat running competitively in 2018 in the ninety-one districts the party was trying to flip from red to blue. This led liberal-leaning publications to ask: "Where have all the pro-life Democrats gone?"[13]

When I was a kid, pro-life Democrats weren't an endangered species, which helped moderates like Democrat Ben Nelson get elected. Because there was diversity on this issue within parties, being a Democrat didn't automatically brand a candidate as unelectable to us rural churchgoers. Progressives may find this characterization unfair, but it's the reality in states like Nebraska.

"No issue brought churches as directly into the political sphere during the late 1980s and 1990s as abortion," wrote Robert Wuthnow, a Princeton sociologist from rural Kansas who studies rural politics and religion. "Clergy and parishioners organized pro-life groups, hired lobbyists, participated in demonstrations, and were arrested. They set up watchdog committees, published newsletters, and launched Web sites. Leaders hosted public officials whose views they endorsed and banned others from appearing in their churches."[14]

Exon told a local reporter that the national Democratic Party knee-capped Nebraska Democrats by taking a hard-line position on abortion, which pushed Nebraskans away from the party. Sue Crawford, a Nebraska state senator who is a registered Democrat, told me her party's monolithic abortion platform "has been a terrible albatross for Democrats in places like Nebraska." Mary Pipher, an author and liberal environmental activist living in Lincoln, said that "abortion will always be the big anchor on the ass of the Democratic party in this state."[15]

With Democrats becoming more liberal and uniform on abortion, the most devout people I knew found the party untenable. The business buzzword "synergy" comes to mind when I think about how Republicans rely on Christianity for their marketing.

In Brainard's Catholic church, I didn't hear many sermons about seeking justice for the poor, sick, and incarcerated. I mostly heard about protecting the unborn, and later, about the evils of same-sex marriage. We were taught to despise abortion. Over time, many people began to believe that abortion and Democrats were synonyms, so they began despising Democrats too. Their hatred for Democrats led them to support Republican positions like reducing health-care access for poor people and enforcing the death penalty, both which go against Catholic social teachings. Basic tenets of Catholic social teaching include that people should "put the needs of the poor and vulnerable first," that workers are entitled to "decent and fair wages," and that faith requires Christians to "care for the earth." On these tenets, the Republican Party strays far from the church.[16]

Republican Doug Bereuter was Brainard's US House representative for most of my life. At the 1998 Nebraska Republican Convention, he warned his colleagues about the dangers of this dynamic in a speech that's more relevant now than it was then: "I question no individual man or woman's religious sincerity, but . . . a lot of people got religion lately when it seemed to be especially good politics with certain voting blocs. . . . That is called exploitation and it leads to further cynicism and distrust of all who cite their religious views or act upon them."

Bereuter, a congressman whose political claim to fame lies in his foreign policy work, then addressed the issue of abortion, asking the attending delegates: "Have we permitted this issue to tear us apart?"[17]

The Roman Catholic Diocese of Lincoln is more fervent than most. According to Georgetown University's Center for Applied Research in the Apostolate, Lincoln has a diocesan priest for every 762 Catholics in its region. This means that, per capita, Lincoln has more priests in its parishes than anywhere else in the United States. The high number of priests is bolstered by a seminary that receives many out-of-state applicants who are attracted to Lincoln's exceptional conservatism. Most of our priests are homegrown though. I've probably met a dozen seminarians from Lincoln's Catholic high school alone. My best friend from high school, who was our quarterback, spent six years in the seminary before dropping out. The guy who quarterbacked our rival is a priest now. In a conservative and orthodox diocese, vocations to religious life are adulated. I personally visited our diocese's seminary several times and considered, for a brief moment, joining.[18]

I met the most beautiful people through our church and befriended many clergy members. I went on a service trip to Arizona where we worked with nuns from Mother Teresa's order who dedicated their lives to serving addicts and homeless people. When my grandfather was dying, a priest took great time out of his schedule to visit each week and comfort my family, even though he was new to the parish and hardly knew us. I went on spiritual retreats and camping trips, and to Lincoln to do simple things like play

Putt-Putt golf with priests who cared more about their parishioners than they did about themselves.

I am still very selfish at times, but I'd be a worse person had I not spent so much time in the church. I wanted what our best priests had. I saw how they became joyous from living selflessly. I've tried to incorporate that outlook in my own life, with varying success.

In popular culture, clergy are usually presented as caricatures. They're sexually deviant, obsessed with secrecy, careerist, or presented as comic relief. I've occasionally seen priests display these characteristics, but the majority of the ones I met were complex, caring, thoughtful, witty, and personal. They dedicated their lives to something bigger than themselves. Their sacrifices are beautiful. In New York, most of the people I hang out with think America is too religious, and they envy more secular European countries. In Brainard, we believe that America would be better if there were *more* priests and nuns who pledged their lives to serving others. Many people have issues with their religion because they were wronged by their congregation's leader. I have issues with my church despite how much I love most of the clerics I met.

When you hear a lot of politics from the pulpit that repeatedly tell you to vote Republican, you start to feel like Republicans are your team. It becomes very tribal. You want Republicans to whoop Democrats on election day just like you want the Huskers to beat the Hawkeyes the day after Thanksgiving. Once you fully identify with the party, it almost doesn't matter if that party pushes policies against your personal economic interest. You just want them to win. Besides, you are too busy working on your feet to constantly analyze the impact of Washington's rules anyway.

The coalitions that make up a political party often have arbitrary connections to one another, but Brainard doesn't care about that if it means keeping those pro-choice Democrats out of office. This is part of the reason why many people back home oppose criminal justice reform, immigrants living in their neighborhood, universal health care, taxes of any form regardless of how the funds are used, and anything remotely resembling a gun limitation. People in Brainard will look the other way as long as the person they vote for professes to be pro-life. Because so many people across the state are mired in abortion battles, politicians trying to capture votes have incentive to inflame animosity. No wonder no one in power bothers with olive branches.

There used to be more pro-life Democrats and pro-choice Republicans. The divide wasn't so stark like it is today. The goalposts have moved farther apart on this issue, which has increased the volume on the megaphone for those who push single-issue voting. Democrats continue to move leftward on abortion, which may appease their urban voting blocs, but expanding abortion rights contributes to bigger losses in places like Nebraska. And due to the way that local politics are nationalized by news sources, social media, pressure groups, and the political parties themselves, abortion laws debated in states halfway across the country now are political fodder in Nebraska. "Just as an Egg McMuffin is the same in every McDonald's," wrote political scientist Daniel Hopkins, "America's two major political parties are increasingly perceived to offer the same choices throughout the country."[19]

The abortion wars ain't going away anytime in the foreseeable future. In recent years, states like Alabama, Mississippi, and Georgia pressed for more abortion restrictions. Meanwhile, New York's legislature reduced restrictions for late-term abortions. Virginia's Democratic governor Ralph Northam faced backlash after making controversial comments about a Virginia abortion bill that some people perceived to be in support of infanticide. Nebraska's Republican US senator Ben Sasse went on Fox News to say that Northam should "get the hell out of office." Instead of trying to bring folks together or promoting legislation aimed at improving life in his own state, Sasse, like so many other politicians of our era, used the abortion controversy across the country to drive a wedge between people. Sasse's office did not reply to interview requests.[20]

"This is not abortion, this is infanticide," Sasse stated emphatically during the broadcast. "And every Democrat should have to answer for whether they stand with little baby girls who are born alive surviving an abortion, or whether they stand with Governor Northam's repugnant comments. I think the 2020 Democratic presidential candidates should have to answer for this."

By coming out strong against abortion and nationalizing an issue that solely affected Virginia, Sasse scored brownie points with Nebraska churchgoers regardless of whether they've ever stepped foot in Virginia. It's hard to blame Sasse for using this strategy when emotionalizing proves to be an effective political tactic that gives politicians in his position cover for what little they've done to help Nebraskans. Sasse likely realizes that most Nebraska voters recoil at New York's and Virginia's attempts at expanding abortion coverage (especially as the laws are described by Fox News). Coming out against those states gives the impression that he's working for the good folks back home. As Harvard law scholar Noah Feldman has noted, politicians benefit from forcing people to pick sides.

"What a wedge issue that's effective does is it forces you to stand up and say 'I am for this or I am for that,'" Feldman said. "And this kind of a position that you are required to take can be a tremendously powerful political tool. But it is almost profoundly divisive because that's the whole point of it. The whole reason you have a wedge issue is to drive a wedge between people and make them stand up and take a stand on one particular issue. And this elevates that issue in importance above everything else, no matter how important the other issues really are."[21]

Feldman was talking about how hysteria over alcohol prohibition tore the United States apart during the Great Depression. He might as well have been describing the abortion playbook that Sasse and other Nebraska politicians rely on to eke out votes.

In Brainard, we will support anything Republicans do as long Republicans say that abortion is evil. I know sweet little old church ladies who insist that we found thousands of weapons of mass destruction in Iraq, thus validating the US conquest that was pushed by a pro-life Republican president. I know others who believe the former GOP vice president nominee Sarah Palin is an outstanding public speaker even though the *Saturday Night Live* spoofs of her awkward speeches are indistinguishable from her own. Attendees at Nebraska bishops' pro-life banquets treat Governor Pete Ricketts like a celebrity despite his fetish to make the death penalty great again, which goes against everything the pope preaches. Nebraska's bishops say they're against the death penalty, but they'll look the other way as long as the politician they embrace claims to be anti-abortion and culturally conservative.

The most common phrase I heard in sermons wasn't "hallelujah" or "amen." It was "culture of death." It's a phrase intended to make people angry that abortion is legal. The priests who wield this phrase throughout the Lincoln diocese are mostly good men, but man, did they drive up my paranoia. Going to church every week gave me the impression that we were in a major crime spree, everyone around us is dying from doing too many illegal drugs, we all harbor seventeen sexually transmitted diseases, no one cares about each other outside these walls, Christians are a persecuted minority group in America, and we live in a materialistic country not because of the greed that capitalism incentivizes but because the legality of abortion has made Americans reckless.

If you're told the world is going to hell in a handbasket enough times, you'll probably start believing it. I thought we lived in a society that became more decadent by the day. I had no idea that kids were actually having less sex than their parents' generation and we were in the midst of a dramatic decline in violent crime. Once you believe the outside world is corrupt, like I did, "law and order" and "family values" candidates become appealing under the guise that they'll restore stability to a collapsing society.[22]

In an ideal world, one would expect local political candidates to focus on practical matters like improving schools and keeping zoning laws reasonable. Once the abortion battle lines were drawn, many Republican candidates focused on their pro-life credentials as if state senators and city mayors served on the US Supreme Court and could reverse *Roe v. Wade*. Because nearly all Democrats run as pro-choice, this strategy works in Nebraska.

Bill Hoppner ran Nebraska's last competitive Democratic gubernatorial campaign in 1998. I was nine years old at the time and campaigned for Hoppner's opponent—Republican Mike Johanns, who was then Lincoln's mayor. Because Johanns was pro-life, an ardent Republican, and knew one of our relatives, my parents supported him, which meant I did too. While campaigning for Johanns I found myself at the Saunders County Fair parade in Wahoo, Nebraska, which served as "the home office of David Letterman" for two decades because the talk show host liked saying the word "Wahoo" on TV. I wore an oversized navy blue Nike bucket hat, fake Oakley sunglasses with yellow tint peeling off of them, and a "Johanns for Governor" white T-shirt as I ran around in my baggy counterfeit Tommy Hilfiger jean shorts handing out campaign stickers.[23]

Hopper earned 46 percent of the vote in a loss to Johanns. In the five gubernatorial races since, Democrats on average won 31 percent of the vote. A supporter of legal abortion, Hoppner told me, "The number-one thing I ran up against with an audience who should have been supportive of my pro-government message was the abortion thing took them off the table." One state senator told me, "If you're talking about abortion, you're losing."

———

Abortion affects much more than presidential and congressional votes. The 2017 Omaha mayoral race is an example of how Democrats shoot themselves in the foot in red states by getting entangled in abortion controversies. Omaha's mayoral race is officially nonpartisan, though it felt like anything but.

In the race, former state senator and registered Democrat Heath Mello tried to unseat the incumbent mayor and registered Republican Jean Stothert. Some observers saw the race as a bellwether for the resistance movement against President Trump. To bring some energy to Mello's campaign, Bernie Sanders came to Omaha.

"My first gut instinct was Bernie Sanders [coming to Omaha] is going to be bad because we are getting into a litmus test," said Chris Rodgers, a Democrat county commissioner in Omaha. Sanders himself should be given some credit for venturing into Nebraska. Many other Democrats are reluctant to step foot in our state. Nebraska was the last state Bill Clinton visited as president, and by the time he came here he had visited California fifty-six times. But given the zealousness Sanders provokes among liberals, bringing him to campaign for a moderate candidate is not an effective strategy in Nebraska.[24]

David Kotok, a former exec at the *Omaha World-Herald* who once oversaw the paper's news coverage, said that Sanders coming to Omaha did two things. "It partisanized the race and brought Republicans out [to vote], and the Democrats said, 'How can you support a pro-life Democrat?'" According to Mello's campaign strategist, his plan was to win the election by turning out voters who tend to stay at home in city elections. That didn't happen. Mello lost by 7 percentage points, and voter turnout was low in the more liberal areas of Omaha that Mello was expected to carry. "You have Democrats attacking other Democrats in ways that suppress turnout and make it more difficult to win elections," said Ari Kohen, a political scientist at the University of Nebraska. "Some percentage of the Democratic Party decided that Heath Mello was not progressive enough on an issue that was important to them, and so they didn't turn out for him." Vince Powers, a Democrat who chaired the state party a year prior to Mello's run, said that bringing Sanders to Omaha was "the worst political decision in my lifetime."[25]

After Sanders visited, Washington-based abortion-rights activists slammed the Democratic National Committee (DNC) for supporting Mello. Though Mello's voting record in his legislative session had a favorable rating with Planned Parenthood's Nebraska chapter, he publicly opposed defunding

Planned Parenthood, he advocated for more comprehensive sex education and easier access to contraception, and he stated that he "would never do anything to restrict access to reproductive health care," all this wasn't enough for activists in our nation's capital who suddenly cared about Omaha, Nebraska.

As a state senator, Mello cosponsored a bill that required abortion providers to tell their patients that they can receive an ultrasound before getting an abortion. To make matters worse for liberal purists, Mello, like many Nebraskans, is a Catholic whose religious convictions led him to identify as pro-life.[26]

Mello's votes were public information and old news. The pandemonium came after the Rupert Murdoch–owned *Wall Street Journal* ran a story about divisions in the Democratic Party, citing Mello's mixed backing of reproductive rights. This prompted Washington's biggest abortion activists to scream that "it is politically stupid" for the DNC to support Mello. National media including HuffPost, *Newsweek, Rolling Stone*, Politico, the *Atlantic*, NPR, and CNN amplified their voices by writing about the activists' press releases and tweets, and suddenly Heath Mello's abortion views became its own national news story for a minute before everyone reporting the story went back to pretending that Nebraska didn't exist. The liberal mouthpiece Daily Kos withdrew its endorsement of Mello once he became part of the news. The *New York Times* ran the headline "Of Course Abortion Should Be a Litmus Test for Democrats" while simultaneously publishing countless articles about the media's blind spots in "Trump country."[27]

Very few of the national commentators slowed down to examine Mello's voting record. The controversial bill Mello backed was originally designed to force women to get an ultrasound before having an abortion. It was Mello's negotiation with pro-life legislators that made the bill more favorable to the pro-choice lobby. Mello's bargaining helped change the bill so that it would merely provide women information about where to receive an ultrasound instead of forcing them to do so. Abortion rights activist and University of Nebraska–Omaha health professor Sofia Jawed-Wessel said: "It was the most frustrating situation I've ever been involved in. Mello got thrown under the bus." Throwing Mello under the bus was more about giving political candidates a lesson in loyalty than it was about widening reproductive rights in Nebraska. Mello did not reply to multiple interview requests.[28]

Mello received blowback from liberals for engaging in the art of compromise. DNC chairman Tom Perez denounced Mello by name and said that every Democrat should be pro-choice. "That is not negotiable and should not change city by city or state by state," Perez said. The DNC didn't consult with the Nebraska Democratic Party before denouncing Mello. "Neither Heath nor I got a phone call from the DNC to discuss this at all," said Nebraska Democratic Party chair Jane Kleeb. "I learned about it in the parking lot at Walgreens, when a reporter called me. All of this was extremely frustrating because on the ground Heath was supported by numerous board members of Planned Parenthood."[29]

Ben Nelson, the last Democrat in Nebraska to serve as governor and in the US Senate, told me that Perez's denouncement of Mello was boneheaded. Nelson said: "I got calluses on my fist from hitting the table about that and not picking up the phone to chew [Perez] out. . . . It was enough, enough to make you really angry. Gratuitous! He shouldn't have done it in a partisan race, let alone a nonpartisan race."

Before Mello got dragged into this mess, one of the biggest planks in his platform was fixing Omaha's potholes. The outage over Mello's voting record is emblematic of how liberal activists want one-size-fits-all candidates, who stand little chance of winning in deep red states. Bringing Bernie Sanders to town got national power players to pay some attention to Omaha, which culminated in Washington activists and New York journalists turning a nonpartisan mayoral race in a medium-sized city in the middle of the country into a test about the future of the Democratic Party. The spark that ignited the tinderbox came from a publication that had the same owner as Fox News. And Fox News got in on the action by bringing a Democratic strategist on air so that the hosts could literally laugh at him during a live broadcast for belonging to "the Planned Parenthood party." Seeing that the Democratic Attorneys General Association requires candidates it endorses to be pro-choice, it's easy for Fox to brand the party this way. All the pawns played their parts perfectly, and their manufactured news left Nebraskans feeling more resentful toward outsiders who impose their views and policies onto the heartland.[30]

The national commentators who wanted to see Heath Mello go down in flames got more than they bargained for. They helped conservative Jean Stothert win reelection. "It was about that time that [Sanders visited Omaha] we had a good feeling," said Stothert's campaign consultant.[31]

In a Nebraska Right to Life survey of political candidates, Stothert said she would "support efforts to divert tax funds for government programs away

from Planned Parenthood and any such organizations which perform, promote, counsel or refer for abortion." There is momentum for her to accomplish this. The Nebraska Legislature passed a bill to defund Planned Parenthood, and the governor signed it. With state politicians looking to further
restrict abortion access, don't expect the mayor in Nebraska's biggest city to
mount any opposition. By targeting Mello, progressive activists also helped
eliminate a candidate who backed social programs that liberals typically support. Multiple unions endorsed Mello, and his platform included support
for immigrants, public schools, LGBT workplace protections, and Medicaid
expansion. After Mello lost, a writer at the left-leaning magazine the *Nation*
wondered "whether a party that sets the bar so high that it excludes Heath
Mello can ever hope to become a majority." The answer in states like Nebraska
is hell no.[32]

Before abortion dominated American politics, Catholics voted for Democrats
more often. In the five presidential elections that took place during the 1950s
and 1960s, Catholics, on average, voted Democrat 64 percent of the time. Democratic support among Catholics began slipping in the 1970s after abortion
became legal nationwide. Catholic votes didn't immediately vanish though.
In the late 1980s, Nebraska communities settled by Catholic immigrants still
leaned Democratic. That base dried up as unions disappeared and FDR-
sympathetic churchgoers began to perceive that Democrats cared more about
liberal cultural values than working-class protections. In 2016 most Catholics
voted for Trump, and when you break the stats out by ethnicity, 60 percent of
white Catholics went for the Donald. I suspect that among the devout, these
figures are higher. They are in Nebraska, anyways.[33]

Catholics—and Christians of some other denominations—oppose legal
abortion with such intensity that they become embroiled in culture wars that
lead them to support anyone who agrees with their abortion views. Folks who
are otherwise quite kind get a mean streak in their eye when they talk about
people who want legal abortion. Like the absolutist Sith lords in *Star Wars*,
they think that anyone who disagrees with them is their enemy. They perceive
that those who support legal abortions are in a conspiracy to unravel society.
That's why I heard about the "culture of death" so frequently.

When you get this deep in the culture war, it doesn't matter if people on "the other side" do good things. They are the enemy. I didn't hear much about social justice and helping poor immigrants because those are things Democrats support, and Democrats are by and large pro-choice, so we must ignore them whenever we're not chastising them. The pope endorsed labor unions in the late 1800s in response to dramatically changing worker rights created by the Industrial Revolution, but again that's a Democrat thing in America, so labor is not a battle to dredge up even as income inequality widens and blue-collar towns wither away. When Barack Obama mentions that most of our nation's income gains end up in the hands of America's wealthiest citizens, it's a lot more convenient to tag him as an anti-American socialist because he runs on a pro-choice platform than to notice that his comments have a lot in common with Pope Benedict's advocacy for wealth redistribution. Pope Francis can declare that the death penalty is never permissible, but you should still vote for a Republican governor who taps into this family's billions of dollars to legalize the death penalty because all blemishes are forgiven for self-described pro-life politicians.[34]

Pro-life mania in Nebraska has reached such a fever pitch that it has its own merch. It isn't enough for die-hard political types to partisanize our congregations and nonpartisan public servant positions. As in thirty-one other states, the license plates that Nebraska issues must contain some political opinions too.

Just in case you want the Chevy Malibu behind you at the traffic light to know how you feel about fetuses, you can now show off your political tribe with your license plate. The state legislature commissioned the creation of "Choose Life" license plates that show a woman and child walking through a meadow hand-in-hand. In response, Planned Parenthood unveiled Nebraska license plates that say "My Body My Choice" on them. The Nebraska Catholic Conference stated that pro-life plates give Nebraskans "an opportunity to put our deeply held pro-life values into action." An abortion-rights group near Omaha declared that "anti-choice license plates threaten women." Similar to academia, license-plate politics are so intense because the stakes are so small.[35]

"The special interests on both sides don't help it," Jane Kleeb told me. "It has now become a fundraising tool for different groups at the national level, rather than groups on all sides of the issue coming together with elected officials to reduce the amount of abortions."

Even though Kleeb is pro-choice and upfront about having had an abortion herself, she insists there is room in the Nebraska Democratic Party for diverse viewpoints, including pro-life positions. She acknowledged that abortion has been a big hurdle for her party.[36]

"I think as Democrats, we have done a really bad job at telling stories of why we are pro-choice and why we stand up for women's right to choose," she said. Kleeb went on to say that Democrats in Nebraska need to better explain that this "one issue that has divided individuals and kept our state in one-party rule and that is very dangerous and reckless for all of the other issues that we care deeply about, including things like public education, clean energy, and property rights. But I think Democrats have done a really bad job of that in rural communities."

The party that Kleeb chairs isn't really helping to change the perception that Democrats use abortion as a litmus test. In 2018 the Nebraska Democratic Party adopted a platform to "continue to oppose any state and federal laws that would impede a woman's constitutional right to a safe and legal abortion." This is the first time the state party officially included abortion rights in its platform. The adoption of this language reflects how state parties have become less distinctive and more aligned with their national counterparts. In Kleeb's book about attracting rural voters, she admonishes Republicans for using abortion to divide people. Then she states: "The laws Republicans are passing will not reduce abortions. The laws Republicans are passing will kill women. And quite frankly, they should be forced to sign the death certificates of all the women their reckless laws will kill." I don't see that kind of talk winning over rural Nebraskans who tend to identity as pro-life.[37]

Kleeb has a point that rallying around abortion has provided Republicans cover on other issues where they diverge from voters' preferences. Nebraska governor Pete Ricketts is currently in a battle to slash education budgets. The cuts to education budgets prompted backlash because, compared to many other states, Nebraska has a pretty robust public education system. According to the National Center for Education Statistics, Nebraska has one of the highest high school graduation rates in the United States. Some large local Republican donors, like University of Nebraska regent Howard Hawks, publicly chastised Ricketts for his attack on public education. Ricketts has also opposed increasing the minimum wage and expanding Medicaid, which puts him at odds with most Nebraskans because those initiatives passed ballot measures. There is also a need in rural Nebraska for better economic development, health-care access, and broadband service (which I notice when I stay at my sister's farmhouse and have to use my mobile data to browse the web). These are the types of pragmatic issues the Republicans in power are failing everyday people on. Democrats could gain votes with these issues. But that's difficult to accomplish when a powerful conservative movement and some influential progressive activists do what they can to ensure that divisive social issues like abortion dominate our politics, just like in every other state.[38]

My own view on abortion began to shift once I realized that within the Catholic Church there is plenty of advocating for charlatans who claim they're pro-life.

I was sitting in a confessional when I first heard Dinesh D'Souza's name. I was a college junior struggling with my faith and dealing with a health scare. Aside from uncertainty over what was going on with my body, I tussled with intellectual faith topics: whether Christ was really God, why I'd been under the impression that "the church never changes" even though several important doctrines have drastically changed, why an allegedly forgiving and welcoming institution could be so hostile to outsiders, and why the Catholic Church resorts to dismal rhetoric without ever concerning itself with social science.

I laid out these concerns during confession with a priest I trusted. He was wildly popular on campus, and remains one of the most sincere, selfless, honest, kind-hearted, and humble people I've ever met. He listened patiently to my concerns and told me to check out D'Souza's book *What's So Great about Christianity?* The book would help me find answers, he said.

In case you are unfamiliar with D'Souza, you should know that he has been indicted for campaign fraud, forced to resign as president of King's College because he was engaged to his girlfriend while still married to his wife, called President Obama "Grown-Up Trayvon" after Trayvon Martin was murdered in Florida, and mocked school shooting victims. D'Souza built his career off outlandish conspiracy theories like the idea that a Kenyan anticolonial worldview is driving Obama to savage the world. He likes to lionize Trump as the next Abraham Lincoln while comparing Democrats to Nazis. He's a quack who is embraced by ultraconservatives to the point that he's become required reading in the confessional.[39]

His book about the greatness of Christianity is just a diatribe. It implies: all atheists are immoral, Christianity is the only religion based on reason,

Muslims are violent but Christians no longer are, people who aren't hardcore
Christians are joyless, all bad things that occur in our society are due to declin-
ing religious participation, Christians are a persecuted minority group in the
United States, and without Christianity civilization will collapse. The book's
wild overgeneralizations and contempt for non-Christians made me feel like
Christians believe they're inherently pitted against everyone else.

After reading the book, it felt a little odd that the priest recommended it to
me since he really made the effort to empathize and meet people where they're
at. As I thought about it more, it began to make sense. Many Catholics in Nebraska have become so conservative that they favor the Republican Party over
the church itself. It's only in an environment like this where Dinesh D'Souza
gets praised.

To stand strong against abortion, it's not uncommon to hear sermons
sprinkled with apocalyptic overtones that strongly imply it's your duty to vote
Republican. You're told to solely obsess over reproductive issues as needless
wars leave thousands dead, income inequality grows, basic health care costs
consume the poor, our environment degrades, and the foreign laborers (many
of whom are Catholic) our economy depends on receive few rights. Sublim-
inal safeguards shut down, and the mania of right-wing propagandists goes
undetected. They even occasionally get confessional endorsements.

And what is most unfortunate is that shortly after college, another priest
who I was close to got expelled from the priesthood. This was a man who
helped instill in me an intellectual distaste for anything modern, secular, or
liberal. I never knew why this priest, who used to crank Rush Limbaugh's radio show and praise George Weigel on our interstate road trips, got purged
until he blew the whistle on our diocese. In an essay for the magazine American Conservative, he detailed how his relationships with adult women got
him booted from the priesthood. He also wrote about how our great diocese,
with its record numbers of priests, hid sexual abuses committed by its former
seminary director and parish priests. Following his essay, scandals erupted
around the state and multiple priests were removed from their duties for having inappropriate relationships with the people who they were supposed to be
watching over. I'm pretty sure we both still pray for each other even though we
haven't spoken in years and no longer believe in the same God.[40]

Dinesh D'Souza himself did not damage my faith. Like Limbaugh, D'Souza
is just another shrewd attention getter, interchangeable with the rest of the

far-right news circuit. What shook me is how the sincerest church leaders I knew will support con men in an intimate setting as long as whatever they're recommending is antagonistic to the pro-choice movement. The well-meaning priest probably didn't intend any of this, and unfortunately he might not even see anything inflammatory within D'Souza's writing, given the pro-Republican, politicized environment of our congregations. Reading D'Souza's book wasn't the first or the only thing that made me question my Catholic upbringing. But it made me question why I keep seeking, if this is what I find.

The women I've dated shaped my outlook on reproduction issues. When I was living in a Nebraska town spending lots of my spare time at church events, I dated women whose convictions against abortion were stronger than mine were. One girl who I went out with for a few months believed doctors were corrupt if they ever prescribed birth control pills to women who were sexually inactive but wanted to have more predictable menstrual cycles. To her, selling pharmaceuticals that could prevent conception was an evil injustice even if the person taking the pills just wanted a more regular period. Others who I went out with saw no distinction between condoms and third-trimester abortions. The only contraception they used was dry humping.

To be clear, the conflict between faith-based and evidence-based contraceptive practices cropped up outside my dating life, too. Like when I had heart-to-heart talks with my best friend, Tom. I first lived with Tom in Lincoln when we both went to UNL, and many years later we lived together in New York and accompanied one another on vacations. We still share a sweet hound that we adopted from a shelter. Like me, Tom grew up in a deeply Catholic household in a tiny Nebraska town and received Pell Grants to attend college. Tom briefly considered the seminary before enrolling in medical school and becoming a doctor. He planned on being a doctor who refused to prescribe contraception because doing so conflicted with Catholic teaching. Now that he's serving patients in the poorest areas of the Bronx, he changed course and recommends IUDs when patients seek contraception. He's still pro-life. But after gaining hands-on medical experience, he realized that giving patients reliable contraception would be the best way to prevent them from getting abortions.

"I'm not going to be able to stop anyone from having sex," Tom demurred one night over a sweltering Hudson Valley sunset as we walked our dog along a meadowy riverbank.

While moments like these that I've shared with platonic friends have affected my views on reproduction, I've been more influenced by romantic partners. In New York City, my dating experiences have been much different than in Nebraska.

For over five years, I've dated a woman named Rachel. (Yes, that's her real name. No, I don't like the show *Friends* but I recognize that my life has become a sitcom cliché.) Like me, Rachel struggles with her Catholic upbringing. Her disregard for some church precepts has not prevented her from being an entirely selfless person who spends her energy raising money for children's nonprofits, volunteering at soup kitchens, and helping her family whenever possible. Rachel is pro-choice but does more than most pro-lifers when it comes to caring for children once they're out of the womb. She teases me whenever I wear my bright red "Nebraskans for Life" scarf to brunch with our friends. Her experience led me to change my views about pro-choice organizations like Planned Parenthood.

Rachel's parents are Filipino immigrants who arrived in New York in their early twenties. Shortly after arriving, Rachel's mom became pregnant with Rachel, who is the oldest of her siblings. Poor and confused about how to navigate the convoluted US health-care system, Rachel's parents sought the help of a Planned Parenthood clinic. They felt ambivalent because they were pro-life Catholics who were discouraged to support such organizations. Nonetheless, they received free ultrasounds and clinic visits from Planned Parenthood. It was with the help of Planned Parenthood that the pregnancy went smoothly. The biggest pro-choice organization in America helped ensure that the love of my life was born healthy.

When I lived in Nebraska, I went to pro-life rallies where we marched around the state capitol chanting anti-abortion slogans, demanding the government to defund Planned Parenthood. Once, I even rode a bus to Washington, DC, to attend such an event. (Although I didn't go out of pure altruism. My secondary aim in participating in pro-life rallies was to meet Catholic women.)

These days I hang out with a female friend who dons a button on her backpack that says "abortion providers are heroes." Since moving to New York, other people have recalled to me how they or their pregnant friends got help from Planned Parenthood. Their stories always involve someone who became unexpectedly pregnant and couldn't afford health insurance. This kind of advocacy for family planning clinics is something no one I knew back home would discuss publicly. And it's something that I still feel a little apprehensive about given how conditioned I've become to oppose abortion. Rachel's experience made me reconsider how my own birth may have been handled differently were the circumstances different. Given that my parents lived in a trailer after they got hitched and I certainly wasn't a planned pregnancy, I can't help but wonder if my own family would have to seek help from a group like Planned Parenthood if my mom were young and unexpectedly pregnant today during our current era of rising insurance premiums.

What Rachel taught me is that it's an outright travesty how the United States set up its laws and institutions in a way that predisposes young mothers to a life of poverty. Because of the lack of affordable health care and childcare combined with workplace discrimination and draconian maternity policies, I cannot ever fault a woman for getting an abortion to improve her circumstances, especially when the man who got her pregnant refuses to help out. I was told time and time again growing up that people only want legal abortion because they want to "live sinful lifestyles." I think what's more realistic is that pro-choicers feel that legal abortion helps keep many women out of destitution and helps prevent some children from being brought into unstable circumstances. It's worth pointing out that the laws that create this dynamic, including the *Roe v. Wade* decision that legalized abortion nationally, were written by men.

My own experience living in Brainard and New York City is that there are rational people on the opposite ends of this issue who have good intentions but will probably never see eye to eye. Whenever I see my niece and brother together, I can't help but believe there's beauty in pro-life philosophies because Brook could have easily been aborted but instead was allowed to live. She continues to bring joy to all of our lives. And I'm only alive because my mom is pro-life and didn't want to use contraception even though she was entering middle age and wanted to be done having kids. So, in some sense, it is in my self-interest to be pro-life. I still describe myself as such.

But when I see my fiancée, I think about how family planning clinics play a crucial role in the American health care system, giving poor women the medical help they need but can't afford otherwise. When I hang out with pro-choice friends, they remind me of the destitution many young pregnant women face if they don't get an abortion because several of our domestic policies are designed against them. In the culture wars, each side demonizes those they disagree with. Having been embedded among pro-life and pro-choice crowds, I've grown to see a lot of gray areas where I used to see a clear good-evil dichotomy.

Pro-lifers call pro-choicers "baby killers," and pro-choice candidates are repeatedly run into the ground for their stance on this single issue. When Nebraska politician Ben Nelson supported Obamacare, pro-life groups hammered him for backing an "abortion funding" bill—as if the health-care reform act was solely about abortion. A once popular governor and US senator, the moderate Nelson never entirely recovered from this kerfuffle and exited public office. When pro-life feminists wanted to join the Women's March, they were shunned even though they shared the same desire as the event's organizers to protest President Trump. Groups like Planned Parenthood and NARAL help poor women receive health care, but they have worked against their own interest in our state by creating controversies in political contests that hurt Democrats' chances of winning. These groups' abortion-rights orthodoxy goes beyond what most Americans find sensible, and even by European standards they're extreme in the restrictions they oppose. Everything is absolutist, and there is little compromise bringing both parties together to actually reduce the number of abortions in society.[41]

The intense conflict over abortion that influences politics in Nebraska, and nationwide, doesn't really align with how people in Brainard proceed through their daily lives. In Brainard, there are no abortion clinics to vandalize. No one from NARAL is staging a protest outside the church. Really, abortion is a conversation that doesn't come up much unless someone is talking about it on TV, talk radio, or from the pulpit. Yet, this topic has more sway over our local politics than any other issue.

Across Nebraska, billboards featuring Jesus and babies decorate cornfields that grow so tall that you can't see past the country road intersection. Little kids gaze out the car window searching for ideas for their own pro-life posters, which they'll create alongside their parents just like my mom and I did. They probably won't realize that they're advertising someone else's politics. When you're isolated in a depopulated area that consists almost entirely of people who look like you and share your beliefs, you don't really question these things. Abortion was just one of many areas where I took influence from my surroundings. Immigration was another.

CHAPTER TWO

A Soccer Town

Sweating bullets while installing air conditioners with my dad in an unfinished country house on a scorching July day, I eagerly left work early to play American Legion Baseball with my best friends. I got through half of Bob Seger's greatest hits album before arriving at our opponent's ballpark in Schuyler. Although Schuyler (which we pronounced Sky-ler) with its six thousand residents was quite a bit larger than the villages that the kids on my team came from, we expected to crush them because Schuyler was "a soccer town." What we meant by that is Schuyler kids didn't share our heritage. They were different from us.

Like many other towns throughout the country, in recent decades Schuyler witnessed tremendous demographic change. Between 1980 and 2000, the number of Latinos living in rural areas in the United States more than doubled. This happened as meatpacking plants moved from cities to smaller towns in a movement influenced by access to free land, cheap labor, and tax breaks. Meatpacking plants influenced some US citizens to relocate and attracted laborers from Mexico, Guatemala, and other Latin American countries. Plant workers came to small towns seeking employment and their own American dream. After crushing unions and lowering wages, the agribusinesses running the show recruited cheap and undocumented laborers willing to work jobs that the local white folks wouldn't touch. The people who I hung around weren't always welcoming.[1]

Schuyler wasn't exactly in my backyard, but it belonged to the same legislative district as Brainard. The town was close enough that people around Brainard frequently complained about it. "That town is really goin' to hell," I heard at many family and community events. When we played Schuyler, my teammates and I joked that we were playing kids "who know how to kick a ball but don't know how to hit one."

What I saw in Schuyler at the time was a violation of the law. And the law was something that my family ritually observed.

My dad never broke the law. He's never had a speeding or parking ticket. He's so by the book that he cautiously follows informal rules and norms. Whenever he'd leave his car in an Applebee's parking lot, he'd ask the manager three times just to make sure the business was okay with a vehicle sitting in one of its many empty spots for twenty minutes while we went across the street to check out a nearby store. His stomach churned when the grass hadn't been cut in over a week. When customers offered him keys to buildings they own so that he could fix appliances whenever it best suited his schedule, he often declined because he felt uneasy having access to other people's homes. Why the hell should *his* hard-earned tax dollars pay for the education, welfare, and social security of people breaking the law to enter our great country, I genuinely wondered after hearing everyone around me espouse this point.

From relatives and townsfolk, I heard story after story of illegal immigrants creating chaos. There were stories of illegal immigrants buying cars with cash and getting in crashes, but instead of staying at the scene, they'd flee and leave the car there because being identified by authorities would lead to deportation. There were stories of illegal immigrants taking advantage of social services like welfare, public housing, and food stamps without paying any taxes into the system. There were stories of gangs and violence, where illegal immigrants victimized some innocent white lady. It usually wasn't clear where these stories came from, or if there was any truth to them. They could be anecdotes plucked from the news or pulled from some internet forum. They could have happened to a guy who knew a guy who knew the guy my uncle split shifts with at the Kwik Shop. These things certainly didn't go down in Brainard, where there were no immigrants and everybody was whiter than Barry Manilow. Over time, the stories added up and my surrounding environment pulled my perception to be in line with those around me.

Like so many others in Brainard, I wanted fewer illegal immigrants in my country. I wanted them deported. I wanted stricter border patrol. Our safety depended on it. We law-abiding citizens didn't deserve to be exposed to those who don't respect the law. It was right there in the name: *illegal* immigration.

In small towns like Schuyler, politics aren't intense like they are at the state level or in big cities. When I arrived at the short concrete square slab that is Schuyler's municipal building, I was the only guest sitting in the lobby, which also functioned as the city council meeting room. The biggest commotion on the block that morning was two guys moving a six-foot-tall display honoring the 150th anniversary of the Union Pacific railroad's arrival in Schuyler. No one was around as they discussed the easiest way to move the display to the town museum a block and a half down the street. The railroad they honored was arguably the most powerful force that drove the settlement and development of Nebraska. Using assembly-line tactics that predated factories, the railroad expanded rapidly and helped quadruple the state's population between 1860 and 1870. During that decade, Schuyler grew from one hundred to six hundred residents and became "the first of Nebraska's cow towns," as about fifty thousand head of cattle were sold in Schuyler one summer. De-skilled labor and the cattle industry still make Schuyler run, but the new power brokers are agribusinesses. Trains roar down the old tracks every fifteen minutes or so, but they no longer carry passengers, just commodities.[2]

Mayor Jon Knutson arrived a half-hour late for our meeting, dressed in Schuyler Central High School's green and black colors. He wore a gray-and-green long-sleeved T-shirt, black-and-green athletic shorts, and gray mesh Adidas running shoes that were stained from freshly cut grass. Knutson profusely apologized the rest of the day for forgetting our meeting time because he was absorbed with mowing on a bright summer morning. We got in his gray Mercury Milan and drove three minutes to his home while Knutson dabbed sweat off his forehead.

After teaching and coaching sports at Schuyler's high school for a quarter century, Knutson retired and became mayor, which entitled him to a $5,000 salary, no benefits, and a hell of a lot of meetings. Knutson sees the mayor job as another gig to keep him busy. During tax season, he works part-time for H&R Block. Since retiring, he also worked as a corn inspector and substitute teacher.

Whereas Brainard hasn't changed much during my lifetime, Schuyler rapidly evolved since Knutson moved there from South Dakota in 1990. When he came to town, the high school had a handful of Latino students. That changed after Cargill expanded its beef plant on the edge of town and used migrant laborers to fill low-paying jobs. Now Schuyler has the demographics befitting an international municipality. Pamphlets at the library tout Schuyler's "Strength Through Diversity," which isn't messaging you ordinarily see in small Nebraska towns. "You don't have to speak English to live in Schuyler," Knutson told me as he cooled down with a glass of cold water at his kitchen table.

As an elected official, Knutson is eager to point out that most people, of all races, get along pretty well in Schuyler. He sees the various ethnic communities in town coexisting. I saw this at Hunters Bar, where I ordered a smooth margarita for $4 and the Latina bartender had all the bar's patrons, who were mostly white, laughing and in good spirits. Another day I had lunch at the Burrito House that sits a block north of city hall. Its menu had Mexican and Central American staples like burritos, tostadas, and tacos, as well as burgers, hot dogs, and chicken strips that white Nebraskans are accustomed too. The clientele, which included a group of local police officers sporting gun holsters on their hips, was racially mixed too. Most of the white people ate nachos and tacos. I noticed that few whites and Latinos sat together at the same table, though. And many of the town's churches tend to cater to a single ethnicity.

Another thing that stood out in Schuyler is how people drive. This rhythm of daily life has become political since state lawmakers turned the ability of undocumented workers to obtain driver's licenses into a campaign issue. Whenever I visited Schuyler, I noticed that Latino drivers sometimes waved me through the intersection when they had the right of way. No one is driving over thirty miles per hour on Schuyler's brick streets downtown, and there are few cars on the road in the middle of the day. But when I met people at four-way intersections that relied on stop signs instead of traffic lights, white drivers would blow on by when they had the right of way while Latinos were more apt to let me go through first. The reason behind this is that there are immigrants in Schuyler who don't have driver's licenses, and in some cases, they aren't even allowed to. This means they can't get car insurance. If they get into a car crash, a financial and legal mess is awaiting everyone involved. To avoid this they take extra caution on the roads, even when there are only a few cars around.

Outside city hall in downtown Schuyler, I spoke to a middle-aged man who had lived in the area his whole life. The man bemoaned the loss of the town's former bars and hardware stores, which he felt were not supported by Schuyler's newcomers. He complained that the golf club was the only place in town that served a decent meal anymore and it served steak just twice a month. Schuyler went through an upheaval because an international ag corporation decided to expand its beef operations, but now there is nowhere in town to regularly get a good steak because of it.

Mayor Knutson insists racial relations are improving but acknowledges there have been growing pains. My baseball team certainly wasn't the only one to refer to Schuyler as "a soccer town" or "Little Mexico." During a soccer game against Lincoln's Catholic high school fifteen years ago, the referees tried to ban Schuyler's kids from speaking Spanish, Knutson said. The refs said it was an unfair advantage and that Schuyler's kids could be talking about the refs without them knowing about it. Knutson and school administrators got involved and called out the officials for discrimination. Parents heckled the refs. A few fans got tossed. Lincoln won the game in a blowout. Later, administrators from the Catholic school apologized for the fiasco although they weren't the ones who instigated it. The severity of that incident was unusual, but unfortunately, Schuyler kids are familiar with being targeted. Schuyler's high school athletic director said that Schuyler fans regularly hear things like "Yeah, we are playing a bunch of Mexicans, it should be an easy game," "Those kids can't even speak English," and "Wait until Trump sends them all home." He noted that in recent years, the heated political climate has given some people "a free pass to say some things that they wouldn't normally say."[3]

Before he became mayor, Knutson spent twenty years on Schuyler's city council. He got calls for all sorts of petty infractions, many of them aimed at Latinos. People let their grass grow too tall. A house had too many cars parked in front of it. There were too many people living in a single-family dwelling. When he first started on the council, the group listened and acted on complaints by bringing people to court whenever they violated single-family dwelling ordinances. Knutson said the reason for pursuing these infractions was safety related and that a house fire erupted in a home that wasn't properly circuited for the twelve space heaters that were running in it. The courts rejected the claims, so the council took a different approach.

"We said instead of trying to alienate them, let's try to educate them," Knutson said. "Our economic development came up with [pamphlets] with English on one side, Spanish on the other, of things you should and shouldn't do. It had pictures. Don't put a stove in the basement with a DC outlet. We thought that made a difference. A lot of the people that moved here, it just wasn't a big deal if their grass grew too tall. That bugged the neighbors. But I'm not gonna pick on where people came from. So they just had to learn."

Like most towns, Schuyler has its issues. But its set of issues looks different than those facing Brainard.

Schuyler experienced white flight after the packing plant expanded and more immigrants moved in. People who live on the border of multiple school districts in the area became less likely to choose Schuyler. Those who were on the bubble between districts usually came to Schuyler because it had more programs and activities to offer than smaller schools. Families whose oldest kids had attended schools in Schuyler send their younger children to schools in Columbus, North Bend, and Howells, Knutson said.

Compared to most Nebraska high schools, Schuyler's Central High School has a higher number of families moving in and out of town each year, which means it has more student turnover. It also has more kids who are unfamiliar with the US education system. Some of its students haven't been in a formal classroom for years. Due to its low scores on standardized tests, the high school was labeled a "priority school" by the state. This led the state to intervene in fixing Schuyler's high school with a $4,000 per-day consultant. It's unclear how much help the state will be. One critic of the move is Schuyler city councilmember Barbara Raya, who said the labeling is akin to a scarlet letter. Born in Mexico, Raya and her family moved to Schuyler in 1998 and have been there since. Raya is the first Latina on the city council and is a teacher at a Schuyler preschool. According to Raya, whose daughter attends Schuyler's high school, after the state-paid consultant began coming in it fueled a negative perception of the school and made students "feel like you know what, we're already bad anyway and this is just proving it."[4]

Schuyler also has a housing shortage that came about after the town's population expanded faster than the supply of homes. Fixing the housing shortage isn't as simple as increasing construction. Undocumented workers seeking housing will often have no recorded work experience, no savings, no rental history, and they come in unfamiliar about how to set up utilities and rent payments, said Chris Langemeier, a realtor in Schuyler who served as our representative in the state legislature when I was in high school. Property owners will require a deposit and background check before renting, but without much information to go off, it can be hard for newcomers to find a sympathetic landlord. "So what you see is motels doing long stays because they can easily rent a room by the day, week, or month," Langemeier told me. "They don't ask all those questions."

Like many small communities, Schuyler has several vacant lots downtown. In the summer of 2019, trusses supporting a dilapidated building took up half a block. Most of the apartments above storefronts haven't had tenants in years. But I wonder how many more vacancies the town might have if immigrants didn't enlarge the town. The African Store, Chichihualco Supermarket, Novedades La Sorpresa clothing store, and Paleteria Oasis ice-cream stand are just some of the businesses run by immigrants that help keep the town alive. I've been to a lot of withering towns in Nebraska that would kill to have as many operating businesses as Schuyler has.

"A lot of smaller communities are going to have trouble keeping their population," former Schuyler mayor Dave Reinecke told me. "I was glad people wanted to come to Schuyler. I didn't care who they were, as long as they were good people."

Reinecke served as mayor from 1998 to 2018. He runs his family's Ford dealership, which has been in business since 1926, making it the oldest Ford dealer in the state. The dealership is next door to the Schuyler municipal building, making it convenient for him to work both jobs. Even though Nebraska is a good thousand miles from any ocean and you can't get any more landlocked, immigration became a critical issue in our state's politics when Reinecke was mayor.

Republicans used to address immigration with a more compassionate conservatism. Speaking at Metropolitan Community College in south Omaha on a sweltering June afternoon a week before the 2006 College World Series, President George W. Bush pushed an immigration reform package. Bush's speech took influence from Chuck Hagel's bill that made it easier for illegal immigrants who had been in the United States for several years to obtain legal status. "I like to remind people, when we think about this immigration debate, the first thing people have got to remember is we are a nation of immigrants, that we've had this debate before in American history," President Bush told 400 Nebraskans in attendance.

> This isn't the first time the United States of America has had to take a look at our nature and our soul and our history. . . . This is a tough debate for America, it really is. It's a tough debate because it's one in which the language can sometimes send the wrong signals about what we're about. People are very emotional about this issue. And my admonition to people who are concerned

about the immigration debate is to remember that language can send signals about who we are as a nation. That harsh, ugly rhetoric on the debate tends to divide our country. It tends to forget the values that have made us great.[5]

As Bush gave his speech, the Republican Party that made his family a political dynasty splintered over the immigration issue. To many congressional Republicans, the only appealing reform was increased border patrol, and their allies flooded the airwaves with ads denouncing amnesty. Hagel's reform bill passed the Senate, but it never became law even though it was approved by Christian leaders, had bipartisan support, and was backed by the president. Republican House Speaker Dennis Hastert refused to negotiate with the Senate because the majority of the GOP House delegation didn't support the bill. (Hastert went on to become the highest-ranking US politician to serve prison time after he was convicted of using hush money to silence teenage boys he sexually abused.)[6]

The GOP had already moved rightward on immigration by the time Donald Trump descended his golden escalator and called Mexicans rapists during his presidential announcement. Trump proceeded to campaign for a border wall, deride migrants as animals, advocate travel bans, and insinuate that he'd ban immigration altogether temporarily. When Trump accepted his party's nomination at the 2016 Republican National Convention in Cleveland, he drew on a tragedy that happened in Omaha when a drunk-driving illegal immigrant killed twenty-one-year-old Sarah Root just hours after she graduated from college. Failures by the courts and law enforcement agencies made the situation worse when mistakes and bureaucratic failures led them to release the suspect, who then vanished and remains at-large. Trump blamed Democrats for the incident and described Root's death as "one more child to sacrifice on the altar of open borders." Years prior to Root's unfortunate death, the politicization of immigration had already come to a head in Nebraska when Governor Pete Ricketts and the legislature battled over whether undocumented immigrants who came to the United States as children (known as Dreamers or DACA youth) should be allowed to have driver's and occupational licenses. Given that a Nebraska Republican was one of the original supporters of the Dreamers and President Bush used his Omaha visit to push immigration reform, Trump's and Ricketts's strict stances against illegal immigration showed how much the party changed.[7]

"I don't know what the Republican Party stands for," said Hagel, emphasizing that Republicans' priorities on immigration, fiscal restraint, and international trade have flipped. "I think the reality is it's the Trump Party, there is no Republican Party. . . . The Republicans have no courage and the Republicans just support [Trump]. They are scared to death to challenge him."

Because immigration has become a more heated topic, towns like Schuyler have become political focal points even if their local politics are low-key. A few years ago, Reinecke had lunch with Governor Ricketts at the Burrito House when the governor was in town for Schuyler's annual Labor Day parade. The Schuyler mayor position is nonpartisan, but like Ricketts, Reinecke is a registered Republican. The two didn't see eye to eye.

"I think he was just feeling out how I felt about immigration," Reinecke told me as we sat in his cramped dealership office with his orange cat Leo prowling around the front desk. "And I could tell at that time I don't think he agreed with me. I told him, 'You need to support the Dreamers.' He said, 'I support the laws of the country.' And I said, 'OK governor, when you walk down the streets of this parade, I want you to look at all of these people. Look at them good. Because every one of them is gonna be directly or indirectly affected by this. So take a good look at these people. We need these people here. The whole state needs them. The whole Midwest needs them. We don't have enough white people who want to work. Who in the heck wants to work in the packing house? It's hard, hard work.' He didn't really say anything after that."

The necessity of immigrant labor in Nebraska was evident during the COVID-19 pandemic. Feedlot and packing plant workers kept the food supply chain moving under poor working conditions that left them exposed to the virus. As more people became infected, a few meat processing plants temporarily shut down. Protestors advocated for indefinitely shutting down the plants until the public health situation improved. Grocery stores started limiting customers' meat purchases. When the ag economy became threatened, Nebraska's most powerful figures worked behind the scenes to ensure that the plants stayed open and migrants kept working.[8]

"It has been immigrants all the time who have been essential workers," said Sergio Sosa, executive director of the Heartland Workers Center, a nonprofit in Omaha that advocates for immigrant workers. "These essential workers became invisible. Because of COVID-19, they've become visible again."[9]

When the state isn't faced with a recession or health crisis, our most powerful elected officers regularly target immigrants. Nebraska's recent governors have opposed bringing Syrian refugees to the state, giving in-state tuition to Dreamers who graduated from Nebraska high schools, granting professional licenses and driver's licenses to DACA youth, and offering any state services for illegal immigrants. Additionally, the state sued the federal government to end DACA. Voters incentivized politicians to take these positions. Lately, Nebraska politicians who come out as strict against immigration are likely to be rewarded with getting elected. Of course, outside money influences these campaigns, and many Nebraskans remain critical of this strategy.[10]

When viewing how Nebraskans align with Republicans who abhor immigration, consider that there are Nebraskans who are fed up with the Democratic Party and that moderate candidates have become rarer. A conservative state, Nebraska is more likely to go far right than far left when those are the perceived choices. Republicans presented on the general election ballots are being picked by zealous primary voters. There are also many people in the state fearful of change. My family is like that too. Most of us don't like to leave the area we came from, and many of my relatives refuse to drink any beer that isn't Bud Light. Being unwilling to try different types of booze is inconsequential and kind of endearing, but the general aversion to change becomes serious when it negatively influences other people's lives.

Take for instance the struggle that blacks in Omaha faced in passing an open-housing ordinance that would allow them to live anywhere in the city. In the 1940s, racist redlining policies kept the city segregated and confined Omaha's black residents to housing that Republican county board chairman Roman Hruska described as "abominable." After Hruska's remark, it took another two decades for the legislature to pass a housing ordinance that prohibited racial discrimination in selling and renting property. To this day, the city remains effectively segregated in multiple ways. "Most Caucasians," said Hruska, a David City native who went on to serve in both houses of Congress, "are not bigots or malicious but only bewildered and misinformed bystanders . . . overwhelmingly possessed with inertia and . . . likely to be governed by tradition rather than by conviction."[11]

It is concerning when people vote for reactionaries because they're afraid of what will happen when they hear that Nebraska's Hispanic population could grow from one-twentieth of the state's total population to one-fourth over a fifty-year span. Liberal critics don't do themselves any favors when they reflexively denounce the concerns that people in small towns have when they see their town's demographics change. I can't help but think that Mayor Knutson's approach of educating instead of alienating would be more helpful than calling everyone on Twitter racist.[12]

The righteous anger I once had over illegal border crossings whenever I played baseball in Schuyler has been effectively weaponized for political purposes. Meanwhile, Democrats, who have a small yet dwindling base in Nebraska, have become more lenient on immigration. These dynamics bolster the perception that the divide between people who identify as Democrats and Republicans is widening. Yet, it wasn't long ago that President Bush expressed sympathy toward foreigners and President Obama deported record numbers of immigrants. Donald Trump made masterful use of isolated people's anxiety, but the immigration fervor had already been building for some time in states like Nebraska. Things really took off when I was in high school in 2006. The most popular person alive in Nebraska couldn't overcome a hard-line immigration opponent and wound up leaving politics after a surprising defeat. To get a sense of how much elected officials have changed on the issue, it's worth looking back at how Nebraska politicians used to tackle immigration.[13]

When I was a young boy playing pickup football in open lots next to Brainard's condemned houses, Nebraska's top elected officials took a more moderate approach to immigration. In the late 1990s the Immigration and Naturalization Service (INS) launched an operation where investigators subpoenaed employee records at Nebraska, South Dakota, and Iowa meatpacking plants and compared them to federal databases of authorized workers. About a fifth of the investigated employees had discrepancies in their records. Nearly three-fourths of those with erroneous documents fled before the INS could interview them. At one Nebraska plant, the investigation prompted 350 workers to leave.[14]

Agribusinesses didn't want to lose cheap labor. They got former Nebraska governor Ben Nelson, a conservative Democrat, to lobby for their cause. The pressure the INS raids put on farm commodity prices led Nebraska's then governor, Republican Mike Johanns, to organize a task force to oppose the investigations. US senator Chuck Hagel, another Republican from Nebraska who would later serve as secretary of defense in the Obama administration, pressured the Justice Department to end its immigration crusade. Hagel also cosponsored legislation intended to provide a pathway for illegal immigrants who grew up in the United States to obtain legal permanent residency. Although their actions were aimed more at protecting business interests than promoting humanitarianism, during the 1990s and early 2000s there were situations where Nebraska's most powerful politicians worked across the aisle to protect illegal immigrants. This is a far cry from how the state's current politicians handle immigration.[15]

To outsiders, Nebraska may seem like a weird place to campaign against immigration since the state sits smack-dab in the center of the United States. Nebraska's unemployment rate consistently ranks among the lowest in the country, so there aren't many displaced workers to yell "They took 'er jobs!" at illegal aliens. Local newspapers routinely publish stories about business leaders worrying that the state has too few employees to fill their companies' open jobs. And historically, community developers and regional think tanks put more emphasis on fighting brain drain and keeping the state's population from shrinking than keeping immigrants at bay.[16]

Between 2000 and 2010, Nebraska's Hispanic population nearly doubled; Hispanics now account for 10 percent of the state's residents. Towns like Schuyler, Lexington, and South Sioux City absorbed a surge of migrant workers who came to take low-paying factory jobs. As the Hispanic population swelled, state politicians took stricter immigration stances. It didn't take long before immigration controversies found in other states swallowed Nebraska.[17]

Tom Osborne's popularity couldn't save him from a hard-line immigration opponent. Born in the same Nebraska town where Kool-Aid was invented, Osborne coached the Nebraska Cornhusker football team to three national titles and won more than 80 percent of his games throughout a twenty-five-year career. His successes turned Nebraska football into a cult. When full, the university's football stadium is nearly double the size of the third-largest city in the state. Yet, it has sold out every game since 1962, which is an NCAA record. Tom Osborne is our Jim Jones: many Nebraskans would do whatever he wanted, no questions asked.

When Osborne and the Huskers lost the 1983 national championship by going for the win with a two-point conversion rather than settling for an extra

point that would have given his higher-ranked team the title, he become symbolic among sports moralists as the humble midwesterner who "does things
the right way." After retiring from coaching, Osborne became a politician. Beginning in 2000, he won three consecutive elections in Nebraska's Third Congressional District, where he captured at least 82 percent of the vote each time.

In 2006 Osborne ran for governor. In the Republican primary, ran against
lieutenant governor Dave Heineman, who had recently assumed the governor's office when his predecessor took a cabinet position in the Bush administration. Although technically an incumbent, Heineman hadn't been elected
governor—and he was running against a cultural icon who looked untouch-
able. Heineman was definitely the underdog.

Both Osborne and Heineman are Republicans, so like in many Nebraska
races, the real race was the GOP primary. Because Osborne and Heineman
took the same positions on many issues, campaign strategists emphasized the
few areas where they slightly disagreed. What resulted was a profusion of immigration messaging.

As governor, Heineman vetoed a bill that allowed children of illegal immigrants who were born in the United States to pay in-state tuition rates at public
colleges in Nebraska as long as they had lived in Nebraska for at least three
years and graduated from a Nebraska high school. Nebraska's legislature overrode Heineman's veto, but he wisely clung to this issue and aired ads that portrayed illegal immigration as a taxpayer burden.[18]

Osborne believed that illegal immigrants who were brought to the United
States as children by their parents deserved a right to affordable higher education as long as they had a good record. "You don't punish somebody for
something they had no control over," Osborne said during a 2006 debate with
Heineman. Osborne asked: "Why would you take away that opportunity to
better themselves?" This wasn't a hot take. Osborne was agreeing with the law
the legislature passed.[19]

Osborne said that his stance on immigration was "being misrepresented
in campaign materials" and that voters had formed "inaccurate perceptions"
about his immigration views because of the messaging Heineman used against
him. After his clash with Heineman, Osborne ran a TV ad touting his stances
against illegal immigration. When he spoke to the press and voters on the

trail, the congressman emphasized how he supported legislation that clamped down on illegal immigration. Osborne and Heineman were battling for support from the state's most ardent conservatives. They were not trying to swing moderates their way. By this point, the governor's primary in some ways transitioned into a contest over who attacked illegal immigration hardest. Heineman won this contest by 6 percentage points. Even though Osborne won in the cities, Heineman defeated him by winning overwhelmingly in the rural communities located throughout Osborne's former congressional district. It's in rural communities west of Lincoln and Omaha where anti-immigration sentiment is strongest.[20]

When I interviewed Heineman he downplayed the role immigration played in his victory, but others saw it differently. Dave Nabity, a Republican who finished third in the 2006 primary, accused Heineman of "inappropriately politicizing immigration to gain votes." The way Nabity saw it, the immigration issue surfaced "solely for the governor to exploit it." Former state Republican Party chairman David Kramer believed the immigration issue helped put Heineman ahead of his opponents. Kramer said: "It was the defining issue of his campaign. It was the issue that made the difference between him winning and losing."[21]

A few years after Heineman became governor, he aimed to apply Arizona's strict immigration laws to Nebraska. (Arizona allowed local police to demand documents from people they suspected to be illegal immigrants. I asked Mayor Knutson if he ever flirted with the idea of adopting these policing tactics in Schuyler, and he responded with an exceptionally long sigh.) When the legislature passed a bill that restored Medicaid funding for prenatal care for illegal immigrants and their unborn children, Heineman vetoed it even though another pillar of his campaign was being pro-life. Activist groups like Nebraska Right for Life sparred with Heineman over this, but the governor said that he refused to provide undocumented migrants affordable prenatal care because it would make the state "a magnet for illegal aliens."[22]

It's probably tempting for progressives and immigration activists to label Heineman as a misguided leader imposing his views onto his constituents, but that's a mischaracterization. Heineman won nearly three-quarters of the vote in each general election and his approval rating hovered between 60 percent and 70 percent, making him one of the most popular governors in the United States. The former governor and his colleagues were simply better than their opponents at capitalizing on the emotions of their constituents. Heineman's tactics were a sign of things to come.[23]

After Heineman became governor, state senators including Kathy Campbell and Charlie Janssen tried to pass bills to eliminate public benefits like food stamps and Medicaid for many *legal* immigrants who have been in America fewer than five years. And some state senators wanted to give local law enforcement the authority to detain people they suspected to be in the country illegally.[24]

Following Heineman, Nebraska elected a new governor even further to the right—Pete Ricketts, who swept into office on a pledge to oppose taxes and illegal immigration. In some ways, Ricketts just did what his voting bloc wanted when he targeted immigrants. Ricketts first ran for office against Senator Ben Nelson in 2006, the same year that Heineman defeated Osborne for governor. Despite being a Democrat, Nelson went to the right of Ricketts on immigration. Nelson voted against giving "guest workers" a chance at permanent residence, and he ran against providing Dreamers a pathway to citizenship. Nelson implied that helping Dreamers become citizens was tantamount to amnesty. He said that the United States needed a "hard barrier" on the Mexican border. Ricketts was more pragmatic about helping those already here obtain citizenship. "Practically speaking, we can't round up 11 million people and send them all home," he reasoned. Nelson crushed Ricketts despite getting outspent.[25]

When Ricketts ran for governor in 2014, his opponent accused him of supporting amnesty. This time, the tag didn't stick. Once elected, Ricketts used his power to show Nebraskans that he was hard on illegal immigration. At the time, Nebraska was the only state that denied driver's licenses to DACA youth. When the legislature ended the driver's license ban, Ricketts targeted incumbent Republicans in an attempt to replace those who voted against his wishes with ultraconservative newcomers. Ricketts's office did not reply to numerous interview requests.[26]

During Ricketts's and Heineman's reign, Fremont, Nebraska, became an immigration battleground. My parents briefly lived in Fremont after they got married in the early 1970s, but back then the city wasn't a political hot potato at the center of immigration debates. Fremont is a city of 26,000 (yes, 26,000 people is a city in Nebraska) just northwest of Omaha. It's named after John C.

Frémont, who, according to some historians, is responsible for giving our state its name. Frémont was the first-ever Republican Party presidential candidate, and the town named after him remains a GOP bastion. It's where Heineman, Janssen, and US senator Ben Sasse cut their political teeth. It has become infamous among politicos for its city ordinance that restricts landlords from renting to illegal immigrants, and employers from hiring them. When a Costco chicken processing plant broke ground near Fremont in 2017, it became a touchstone issue in immigration debates due to conflict between Costco's reliance on migrant labor and the anti-immigrant policies of the town where the laborers lived. Nebraska author Ted Genoways wrote that before the ordinance passed, Fremont residents' bitterness toward immigrants had been building for years: "Many remember when a spot on the line at Hormel was the most coveted job around. But ever since the union-busting of the 1980s and the reduced-inspection agreements of the 1990s and 2000s, those jobs have been largely taken over by a workforce of undocumented immigrants willing to work twice as fast for lower pay—a fact that many old-timers blame for the swift decline of Fremont and surrounding communities."[27]

When I asked former Schuyler mayor Reinecke if he ever considered pushing a similar ordinance in Schuyler after the town started absorbing waves of immigrants, he immediately shut down the idea. "I'd never let it happen," he said. "No way. I think Fremont is bad news because of it. As far as I'm concerned, they've got themselves some issues with that because of this Costco plant coming up. I don't think they've thought that out very well." Councilmember Raya added: "Schuyler wouldn't be able to afford that. If they enforced something like that, to be honest, Schuyler would be dead."

Opposing illegal immigration continues to be a well that state Republicans draw from. Ricketts and other top GOP lawmakers backed President Trump's pledge to end the DACA program. In 2018 Nebraska was one of seven states to sue the federal government to end DACA. Yet, one of the early cosponsors of the DREAM Act of 2005, which provided a route for illegal immigrants who grew up in the United States to obtain permanent residency, was a Nebraska Republican—Chuck Hagel.[28]

"I get the deal about illegal immigrants, yes that's true, we have to protect our borders," Hagel told me. "But let's start with security. The biggest security threats in this country are not coming from our southern border, believe me. They are coming from cyber."

By the time Donald Trump became president and rallied his base by refer-
ring to Latino gang members as "animals," calling illegal aliens from Mexico
"rapists," and vowing to make Mexico pay to build a wall that stretches across
its shared border with the United States, several politicians had already conditioned Nebraskans to openly and furiously oppose immigration. Through
politicians, think tanks, and partisan media outlets, Nebraskans have been
told that oncoming waves of immigration are one of the main threats to their
way of life, even though Nebraska remains nearly 90 percent white, most immigrants are here legally, and the number of illegal aliens in the United States
has declined since the Great Recession.[29]

"Politicians have made immigration an issue," Hagel said. "Donald Trump
is the one politician who made immigration more of an issue than any politician in my memory. That was a huge part of his campaign. 'All of you good
people in Nebraska and all over the country, who are not doing as well economically, it is the fault of those damn immigrants. They have taken your
jobs.' . . . The facts don't back that up. Matter of a fact, immigrants take the
jobs Americans won't take. For seventy-five years, the only reason we have a
tremendous sugar beet harvest out in Scottsbluff is because immigrants come
in from Mexico for three months and work in the fields and harvest them."

Ben Sasse holds the Senate seat that Hagel used to control. In interviews with
the press, both guys come off as thoughtful, conservative Republicans. But
their differing approaches on immigration are a sign of the times.

Sasse repeatedly insists he is all about limited government. He criticized
Trump's emergency declaration over the border wall as an instance of the executive branch overstepping its bounds. "Over the past decades, the legislative
branch has given away too much power and the executive branch has taken
too much power," Sasse said. Despite his talk, Sasse fell in line with the president when it came time to vote. Which is what Sasse almost always does.[30]

Sasse fashions himself an "independent conservative" who thinks about
leaving the Republican Party every morning. "Neither party seemed to have a
plan for the future, so I ran against both of them," Sasse wrote. The reality is
this: Sasse votes in line with Trump's position 85 percent of the time and votes
with his party about nineteen out of every twenty times. Sasse may personally
disagree with Trump's style and criticize the president to the press, but he

is not above doing the president's bidding if it helps him stay in office. Self-preservation is a key tenet of maintaining political power, and Sasse probably realized that if he opposed Trump too stringently, he could suffer the same fate as former Republican congressmen Jeff Flake and Mark Sanford and find himself on the sidelines, exiled from his party.[31]

Sasse's voting record shows that he is a party loyalist, but the first person to challenge him in the primary for reelection was a Republican businessman whose primary campaign platform was criticizing Sasse for not supporting Trump enough. Sasse is the fifth most conservative person in the entire US Senate, but this is apparently not enough for some state Republicans who want to push the party further rightward. Curiously, when Sasse announced he was seeking reelection in 2020, his criticisms of Trump quieted. About a month after the reelection announcement, Trump tweeted an endorsement for Sasse, which effectively stymied the primary challenger.[32]

It's expected that politicians will do what's in their best interest to retain power. On that front, Sasse is being smart by bending to the party that controls his state. Being very conservative isn't something to criticize in and of itself, especially given that Sasse is representing a conservative state. What makes Sasse more prone to criticism than, say, that of other Nebraska Republicans in Congress, is that when he's out marketing his books or promoting a pet cause, Sasse makes a lot of hay out of being an independent, principled conservative who is above self-interested maneuvering, when his actions indicate otherwise.

During the hearings for US Supreme Court Justice Brett Kavanaugh, Sasse got a lot of attention for grandstanding on the floor and blaming Congress for not doing its job. About every conservative publisher picked up the speech, and Sasse appeared primed for the attention since it quickly turned into a byline for the *Wall Street Journal* op-ed page. Sasse said:

> The legislature is weak, and most people here in Congress want their jobs more than they want to do legislative work. So they punt most of the work to the next branch. . . . But the real reason this institution punts most of its power to executive-branch agencies is because it is a convenient way to avoid responsibility for controversial and unpopular decisions. If your biggest long-term priority is your own re-election, then giving away your power is a pretty good strategy.

Sasse loves to harp on how when Congress does nothing it gives more power to the executive branch. It's a stump speech he's recycled in various forms in the press, at Conservative Political Action Conferences, and on the Senate floor.[33]

Sasse disregarded his own well-worn critique of Congress after an immigration raid rocked the north-central Nebraska town of O'Neill. Instead of leading an effort to pass a needed but controversial bipartisan bill on the issue, like Hagel did, Sasse opted to punt away his power to the next branch. The statement Sasse's team put out about the raid read: "There's going to be a compromise, comprehensive immigration reform, at some point. The problem is you have a Congress that's really a broken institution right now. . . . It's really difficult to try to figure out what the pathway is to anything comprehensive. We're going to need some sort of executive branch leadership to resolve these problems."[34]

Online commenters who never visited Nebraska before, but insist that its propensity for Republicanism is solely rooted in racism and xenophobia, are missing a lot of the picture. When we rely on the internet for so much of our personal communication and media consumption, it is really easy to read a few tweets and articles and generalize that what you're reading reflects the beliefs of most of the people in that given area. It is especially tempting to succumb to this logic when you are angry at people in other states for voting differently than you wanted them to.

However, it is dishonest to totally deny the influence of the anti-immigrant fervor currently flowing through Nebraska. This is uncomfortable to confront. I have many acquaintances back home who want more brown-skinned immigrants purged from the state. They were excited by Trump's promises to build a wall and ban Muslim immigrants from entering America. "The politicians and the leaders have tapped into a reserve there of concern and insecurity and all the rest, and it just builds on itself," Hagel told me. "Then you get social media hammering it every day. Fox News hammers it every day. People will build on that, especially political leaders." Many people in Butler County say they only dislike *illegal* immigration, but that justification rings hollow when they also support politicians that further restrict who can come here legally. Some support these pledges silently, while others share memes on Facebook and post links to highly partisanized and pseudoscientific research that details the perils of what will happen when too many immigrants live here.

"Welcome to America, where people who are appalled with building a wall to protect our country from crime, illegal immigration, and drug trade," a devout Christian friend of mine ranted on her Facebook wall after the Democrats stymied Trump's efforts to build a border wall. "And yet those same people are okay with killing innocent lives who don't have a chance to have a voice. Makes total sense. #MakeAmericaGreatAgain#prolife."

An elderly woman I know who is otherwise sympathetic to people facing difficult circumstances repeatedly boasts that, unlike today's immigrants, her ancestors came here legally, didn't cost the government money, didn't require the country to adjust to them, and didn't burn the American flag. Her tirades start out with a face-valid gripe about immigrants being here undocumented, and they end with unfounded accusations that immigrants are driven by an agenda to desecrate the United States. On the anniversary of 9/11, a guy I went to high school with shared a picture of the Twin Towers on fire with the comment: "Now We Have Muslims In Congress That Hate Our President, Israel, And America. Wake Up And Smell The Curry." As someone who has worked as an advertising analyst the past few years, I can confidently say that social media rewards reactions and "engagement" over substance because the more time people spend on these apps, the more ads can be sold against their eyeballs. As such, these systems reward extreme ideas over logical ones. Posts that show opposition get more likes than those that show support while posts that take sides receive more likes and comments than neutral statements. Scrolling through feeds gives the discomfiting impression that stupidity is in vogue.[35]

The loudest people online don't represent what most people believe. But they've gained momentum from the press and some of our politicians, both at the state and national levels, who appeal to the lowest common denominator when discussing immigration. Trump holds rallies and press conferences where he's animated and entertaining while denying the humanity of Latinos. He imposes arbitrary travel bans with the intention of denigrating Muslims. When Trump retweets white nationalists, he makes the zealots I'm friends with on Facebook feel validated whenever they share blatant propaganda designed to attack immigrants. Meanwhile, Trump's ascension to power makes the low-paid workers that American agribusinesses rely on feel unwelcomed. "Once he became our president, it was devastating," said Raya, noting that it was difficult to see Schuyler's county vote overwhelmingly for Trump. "That fear, for a lot of people, turned to anxiety. We have a lot of kids and families in our community that are in that situation. They aren't here legally. They fear, 'When is the next raid going to be? Am I going to come back from work today? Are my kids going to be safe?'"[36]

In the Cornhusker State, city councils push ordinances aimed at making life unlivable for illegals despite their economic dependence on migrant labor. State legislators try to take away government funds for immigrants' prenatal care even though these lawmakers ostensibly oppose abortion. By voting for Trump and backing local elected officials who continually decry illegal immigration, white Nebraskans as a whole appear "backwards" and racist to outsiders, regardless of how most of these folks actually treat the people they interact with in real life. Heartland conservatives denounce these accusations of racism because they feel they should be judged by their interactions with others, not just by their votes. They say, if we are as racist as lefties say we are, then why do we donate time and money to charities and social services that serve many disadvantaged people? They'll point to the good relationships they have with friends and colleagues who are racial minorities, which of course just spawns more mockery from lefties who say that the mere act of pointing out that you have minority friends is racist itself. Coastal liberals insist that people who vote for a president who displays racism are automatically racist themselves regardless of how they treat others because pointing out good deeds is just another "dog whistle" meant to hide the oppression of marginalized groups. When people in Brainard hear these accusations, they don't sympathize with the people they're offending. Most folks in Brainard dismiss accusations that their votes enable racism. They feel that they're lectured by "elitists" whose liberal arts degrees brainwashed them into believing in made-up definitions of racism and justice. It's an ugly merry-go-round.

"We [have] got to be smarter how we handle these things, how we debate these things, how we address these things," Hagel told me, "rather than this approach that Trump and many of the real conservative Republicans are taking. It is not in America's interest, and it is not who we are."

Several Nebraska Republicans have relied on a strong anti-immigrant base to obtain power. But nuances exist that should be pointed out to people who have never been to the state and rely on national media platforms to inform them about what's going on there.

Democrats are actually changing their views on immigration more than Republicans are. The timing indicates their changing viewpoints are a reaction to Trump. In Gallup surveys, the number of Democrats who want to decrease immigration levels got cut in half in the past few years, from 50 percent in 2016 to 25 percent in 2018. Republican numbers have stayed steady, with about 80 percent saying they want less immigration. According to the Pew Research Center, Democrats are now twice as likely as Republicans to believe that immigrants benefit the country, but back in 2002 their responses were similar. About 80 percent of Democrats in a 2018 *Washington Post*/ABC News poll said immigrants "mainly strengthen American society," which is up 15 percentage points from 2016.[37]

Liberals may see Nebraska's political approach to immigration as flawed, but they should recognize that for years Nebraska settled more refugees per capita than any other state. Nebraska has a long history of welcoming foreigners, but the number of refugees living in the state took off in the 1990s when the US Office of Refugee Resettlement listed Lincoln, Nebraska, as a preferred community due to the area's low unemployment and cheap cost of living. Under President Trump, Nebraska, like many other states, experienced a significant decline in refugee resettlements, but the state is still accepting some foreign newcomers despite these restrictions. When I lived in Lincoln, I taught English classes to adult immigrants and refugees who gave me the impression that they loved living in Nebraska. Some of the greatest resettlement work was done by churches and synagogues. While religion is often used as a divisive political tool, I also witnessed religion inspire people of faith to be more welcoming toward their new neighbors. The entire state isn't hostile just because we have some politicians launching anti-immigration crusades.[38]

If you haven't visited Nebraska, you may think that Nebraskans have become more xenophobic over the past decade because several of the state's top politicians are taking stricter immigration stances. Outlandish politicians help to indirectly bolster this perception because when people in power show prejudice it drives angry people to the polls and makes bigots feel more comfortable to come out from under their rock. Meanwhile, social media allows the trolls to loudly and publicly spread their messages.

The rise of far right candidates in Nebraska has shone a light on immigration anxieties, but the loss of moderate representatives isn't necessarily primarily driven by changes in people's opinions. The state's fledgling Democratic Party, the polarization of both national parties, the influx of money into local races, loosening campaign finance regulations, and the fear of losing primaries have nudged Nebraskans to vote Republican while also stiffening many GOP politicians into following the orthodoxy of their party that continues to move further to the right. If all you do is look at the headlines and never talk to anyone who disagrees with you politically, you risk pigeonholing everyone from "the other side" into the stereotypical identity and demographic cohorts that politicians dice up.

"Trump tries to 'otherize' Muslims, refugees, unauthorized immigrants and other large groups," wrote Nicholas Kristof, an opinion columnist at the *New York Times* who grew up in rural Oregon. "It sometimes works when people don't actually know a Muslim or a refugee, and liberals likewise seem more willing to otherize Trump voters when they don't know any."[39]

Fetishizing over these labels leads people to ignore nuance and gloss over the uniqueness of individuals in any given cohort. Former Schuyler mayor Dave Reinecke voted for Trump even though Reinecke supports the Dreamers, advocates for the immigrants in his town, and stopped Schuyler from passing anti-immigrant housing laws. "I didn't like Hillary Clinton. There was no way I was going to vote for her," he said before smirking and adding, "I won't vote for him again unless Hillary runs."

It's easy to chalk up a vote for Trump to cognitive dissonance, but people are more complicated than the binary choice presented on ballots. On several issues, including immigration, GOP candidates are garnering support from moderate Nebraska voters like Reinecke. My brother Kellen falls in this boat, too. Like many people I know, my brother dislikes discussing politics and veers from the party's most outlandish ambitions, but he feels that lately Republicans usually better represent his interests.

Kellen lives in David City, the place where all of my siblings were born and the same small Nebraska town that CNN profiled after the 2016 election. He is a mythological creature as far as many of my New York colleagues are concerned. He once supported Barack Obama. He has a doctorate degree and is the most educated person in my family. He has a solid job with a managerial title. He treats the women in his life, including my mom and his wife and daughter, as well as anyone I know. He wants to make it easier for people who migrate to this country to become legal residents. And like most people in my family, he voted for Donald Trump.

Excited by Obama's pledge to pull troops out of Iraq and reform health care, Kellen voted for him. Since then, Kellen's health-care bills have skyrocketed and the United States still has troops in Iraq. Like nearly one-tenth of Obama voters, Kellen flipped to Trump after getting fed up with Democrats.[40]

"I can't fucking stand Trump," my brother told me one night in his garage as we sipped milkshake-flavored stouts he homebrewed and packed gunpowder into bullets he custom-crafted for his rifles. "I really can't. But I'm really tired of politicians and am ready for a businessperson to take command. I know Trump is a narcissist and self-interested. I'm just hoping his self-interests will align with our country's interests, but I honestly don't know if they will."

Kellen and others like him aren't on Twitter trying to make their mild observations go viral. Kellen isn't on social media at all, which benefits his sanity. If you haven't visited "Trump country" you probably won't encounter people with his viewpoint regardless of how much time you spend reading political blogs and following hashtags.

The never-ending amount of nonsense coming out of Trump's mouth irritates my brother and he's not a fan of Trump's immigration approach. But Kellen likes that Trump met with North Korea's leader Kim Jong-un, which he hopes will be the first step toward more peaceful relations between our nations. The US news media's critical approach toward this event has convinced Kellen that most American journalists are liberally biased and unable to see the historic significance of the event due to their hatred of Trump. Another thing he likes about the current administration is how the Republican-led tax cuts left more money in his wallet, something he's become more sensitive to since his health care costs went up.[41]

It is a bit peculiar to have so much in common with someone and yet feel worlds away from them due to an election. I admit I was mad when Kellen told me he voted for Trump since I think The Donald will go down as a stain on American history who made life undoubtedly worse for most Americans. For his part, Kellen didn't flip out that I voted for Hillary Clinton and Joe Biden, whom he saw as corrupt, compromised, and the embodiment of everything he hates about party politics. Whoever we voted for doesn't change the fact that the best concert I ever saw was when Kellen took me to an AC/DC show when I was nineteen; we wound up in a hotel lobby after midnight singing *Highway to Hell*. One of my favorite sports memories is when he was coaching my baseball team when I was thirteen and he got into an argument with an opposing coach—shouting "vicinity doesn't mean shit"—as they debated whether my teammate should be called out for running outside of the baseline. Kellen boosted my love for video games by bringing his Xbox home from college and playing Halo with me until 5 a.m. As the only person in our family who read for enjoyment, Kellen showed me books are awesome; you just have to find the ones you're interested in.

According to many pundits, Kellen and I should be at each other's throats for our political differences instead of treating these behaviors as a single aspect of our complex personas. Yet, even though I recognize Kellen is much more than his vote and I don't think he holds outstanding prejudices, I get an urge to critique him for helping put people in office who enact xenophobic policies. On the flip side, I'm sure Kellen and the rest of my family think that living in New York made me smugger, and they certainly don't want to hear me lecture anyone about politicians. They're already skeptical that I'm publishing a book about politics for a university press. Lecturing Kellen would only be unproductive. He is smart and can make up his own mind. In fact, one reason the Democratic Party, and the national press for that matter, have become such a toxic brand in rural America is because people in small towns are tired of being told by liberals in big cities that their views are outdated, their concerns invalid, and that they need to vote for Democrats if they know what is good for them.

Whenever Republican politicians attack immigrants, it is convenient for Democrats to believe that racism is the sole fuel pumping the GOP engine. There are many voters, including loud and influential trolls, who definitely vote for Republicans precisely because they want to kick immigrants out. Alongside that dynamic, there exist good people like Kellen voting for Trump and putting fringe right-wingers into Congress and state legislatures. Had I stayed in Butler County, I'd probably share my brother's views and vote for Trump. But once I left home, my experiences changed my outlook.

———

With my college days winding down, I had no idea what I'd do with my life. My girlfriend had just dumped me a few months before I planned to propose, and the unexpectedness of it all threw me into a tailspin that drove me to want to leave Nebraska. I did not have any concrete plans on how I'd utilize my degree to build a career. All I knew is that I wanted to get away from everything I found familiar. For much of my senior year, I planned to teach English in a foreign country like South Korea or Poland. I had no teaching experience, so I became an instructor at Lincoln Literacy, a nonprofit program in Lincoln that provides free English classes and tutoring . What began as a self-interested careerist act blossomed into a pleasant life experience.

Each Tuesday, I taught English to Vietnamese, Laotian, and Mexican adult immigrants and refugees. Refugees from around the globe brought diversity and culture to Nebraska cities. I've lived in New York for six years now, but the best pho I've ever had was in Lincoln.[42]

My lesson plans were unstructured and my own English skills were at times suspect, so my classes generally turned into casual group conversations. Most of my students earned measly wages working long hours at factories and packing plants, yet they were upbeat and very pleasant to be around. I don't know if my students learned much English from me, but I got a lot out of teaching them. On my last day, they sent me home with a card and baked goods. They were so sweet it was hard to stomach.

Those few hours I spent at Lincoln Literacy each week were a respite from what I was going through personally. When you're having a good time hanging out with someone in a classroom week after week, it is hard to be concerned about an individual's legal status. It's possible that many of my students didn't have proper documentation to work here legally, but I really didn't care. While I used to view illegal immigration as a blatant disrespect for the law, I now saw immigrants of all persuasions—both documented and un-documented—as decent people who are just trying to create a comfortable life for themselves like everyone else. As someone who has tried to learn Spanish as an adult but failed hard, I was wowed by the progress and persistence my adult students put into learning a foreign language. They could not be criticized for their effort.

After I graduated from college and was no longer teaching English in Lincoln, I moved to New York City, where my daily contact with immigrants significantly increased. In Brainard, it was memorable if you happened to have a conversation with someone from another country. In New York City there are so many foreigners that people are really surprised when they find out I'm from Nebraska but don't bat an eye when my friend says she grew up in New Delhi, India. This response makes sense considering there are a lot more Indians than Nebraskans in the city.

Living in a multicultural neighborhood like Kensington Brooklyn, you rub elbows with immigrants from various nations whenever you get your hair cut, buy groceries, hang out at the park, or wait for the bus. People who live in diverse cities will find it laughable that I'm even printing this, but having a familiarity with people from other cultures and seeing them carry out the same banal routines that you do facilitates a perception that immigrants and native-born citizens aren't really all that different. Now that I'm dating someone whose family was born in another country, the fiscal conservative in me sees them as resourceful instead of law-breaking when I hear about how they used to cram three families into a single house so that they could afford rent.

These dynamics aren't clear when the only place you've lived in is Brainard. In Brainard, I hardly came across people who were born outside Nebraska. Social cues incentivized me to think that immigrants were flouting our laws and hastening the demise of our quaint rural life. I didn't realize that during the nation's first 100 years, there were no federal restrictions on how many immigrants could come here each year (though the 1790 Naturalization Act stated that only a "free white person" could be naturalized). The waves of European immigrants who arrived in the United States back then didn't have to deal with the confusing and ever-changing immigration system of today. People who want to come here legally now have to wait a long time and navigate through confusing laws that vary depending on whether an immigrant is coming here via an employer, family, or visa lottery, or is a refugee seeking asylum. Supporting laws to punish illegal immigrants was to support a theoretical principle. In Brainard, we'd hardly ever deal with the people affected by the harsher immigration enforcement we desired. But dammit, people shouldn't flout the law at all, so we should make the punishments tougher.[43]

My experience taught me it isn't coincidence that immigration backlash is strongest in areas where there are few immigrants. It is in states like Nebraska, where immigrants don't even make up 10 percent of the population, that support for the border wall is high. In states like California and New York, where more than one in five people are immigrants, the term "illegal immigration" is considered a slur by some. (In an effort to stop discrimination, the New York City Commission on Human Rights proposed that employers and landlords using the terms "illegal alien" or "illegals" with the intention of demeaning someone could be fined as much as $250,000. The conservative Heritage Foundation called the proposal "an assault on the Constitution.") Many of the congressional districts lining the southern border have flipped blue. Aside from swaths of Texas, the rest of the Congress members whose districts touch the southern border oppose Trump's wall. This hasn't stopped state lawmakers in North Dakota, a rural state that touches Canada, from passing a resolution supporting the wall. "The irony of the wall is it works best the further you are from the border," said New Mexico's Democratic US senator Martin Heinrich.[44]

Another thing that nudged me to view immigrants more favorably was realizing that I used to be the type of person that nativists ostracized.

A hundred years ago, a Nebraska court case changed US law forever. It came as a reaction to the superpatriotism that erupted around World War I. At the time, state officials did everything they could to stop perceived foreign influence. German books were burned. People suspected of disloyalty were forced to kiss the American flag. A thirty-minute drive from where I grew up, the village of Germantown was renamed Garland, in honor of Raymond Garland, the first Nebraskan soldier to die during World War I. University professors were interrogated, and in a few cases forced to resign, over their loyalty to the country. "While fighting to make the world safe for democracy, Nebraskans nearly lost it at home," wrote historian Bruce Nicoll.[45]

Shortly after the United States entered World War I, Nebraska's legislature repealed a law that required schools to offer foreign-language classes if more than fifty students requested them. Eliminating the law was a victory for the governor, who denounced it as being "vicious, undemocratic, and un-American." A separate measure that required all children in the state to attend public schools failed by a single vote. The legislature succeeded, however, in passing an act that prevented foreign languages from being taught to students who hadn't passed the eighth grade. Those who violated the law and taught foreign languages to youngsters could receive up to thirty days in jail. "If these people are Americans, let them speak our language," one legislator said at the time.

"If they don't know it, let them learn it. If they don't like it, let them move." When an official in Campbell, a south-central Nebraska town a half-hour drive from the Kansas border, asked the state attorney general if an ordinance forbidding the speaking of foreign languages in the village streets would be legally valid, the state's top law enforcement officer replied that he believed such an ordinance would be invalid. But the attorney general assured the local official that "prudence and public policy will, no doubt, in the near future, prompt those of foreign birth to desist as far as possible in the use of their native language." In response to the crackdown on foreign-language instruction, the renowned Nebraska writer Willa Cather stated that "no Nebraska child now growing up will ever have a mastery of a foreign language, because your legislature has made it a crime to teach a foreign language to a child in its formative years, the only period when it can really lay a foundation for a thorough understanding of a foreign tongue."[46]

Meanwhile, Nebraska's Council of Defense requested that schools stop teaching foreign languages. It pressured churches to eliminate foreign languages from their worship services even though many parishioners were immigrants who could not speak English. One county in the northeast part of the state ordered a Catholic priest to stop using foreign languages in mass, with the exception of Latin. And a Lutheran minister was rebuked for giving a speech in German at a soldier's funeral. At the Zion Lutheran school near Hampton, Nebraska, vandals blew out the windows with a shotgun and destroyed the school's German books in protest of the German lessons being taught there.

"Much of the animus against the use of foreign languages in religious services arose out of the suspicion with which many Nebraskans regarded the Lutheran and Roman Catholic churches, whose elaborate liturgies, richly decorated sanctuaries, and highly intellectual doctrines often seemed alien to Anglo-American Protestants," wrote legal scholar William Ross in his account of early twentieth-century Nebraska law.[47]

This conflict came to a head when Zion instructor Robert Meyer was charged for violating the prohibition against teaching foreign languages. Meyer fought the charge in court. He faced many detractors, including the American Legion—the same organization that supported the baseball league where we played kids from "soccer town" Schuyler. In an amicus brief, the American Legion echoed today's Trump supporters when it stated, "We must eliminate every influence that tends to perpetuate foreign ideals and foreign influences."[48]

Meyer saw things differently.

"This is a question of principle," Meyer said. "If I go to jail for doing what I know to be right, I go to jail. I shall not compromise what I know is not right."[49]

Meyer was convicted in county court. He appealed his case, only to lose again in the Nebraska Supreme Court. Eventually, the case made its way to the US Supreme Court, where Meyer was represented by Arthur Mullen, a powerful Roman Catholic lawyer and William Jennings Bryan's Nebraska campaign manager. Mullen feared that anti-Catholic nativist groups would be encouraged if restrictions against foreign language instructions became permanent. In a seven-to-two decision, the Supreme Court ruled that Nebraska's law was unconstitutional because it infringed on an individual's right to acquire knowledge and worship freely. The decision in Meyer's victory helped create the legal right to privacy that was later cited in numerous court cases, such as the *Griswold v. Connecticut* case that removed prohibitions around contraception access and *Roe v. Wade*, which legalized abortion nationally. The Meyer case is referenced in legal decisions about parental rights, homosexual conduct, and school vouchers.[50]

"Although the scope of the liberties recognized by *Meyer* is likely to continue to cause controversy, its ruling that 'the individual has certain fundamental rights which must be respected' is likely to endure as long as the nation has citizens who are as willing to fight for rights as courageously as did a Nebraska schoolmaster nearly a century ago," William Ross wrote.[51]

Some people will say that the anti-immigrant paranoia of the nineteenth and early twentieth centuries is ancient history that does not reflect today's affairs because we no longer rename towns because they sound too European or ban schools from teaching other languages. I suspect that the distance between suspicion and paranoia is shorter than most people think. The Republican Party that controls nearly all of Nebraska's political power officially wants to establish English as the official language, and it aggravates the fear of a foreign menace strawman by opposing "the instruction of Sharia law in our education system." Despite the ruling in the Meyer case, Nebraska's state constitution still features a provision stating that English is the state's official language and must be used as the language of instruction in schools. Voters overwhelmingly rejected efforts to redact this unenforceable clause. "There have been multiple attempts to remove it from our constitution, but we are never able to get it done because it always gets caught up in the fervor in what's going on today," said Frank Daley, executive director of the Nebraska Accountability and Disclosure Commission.[52]

As of this writing, migrants are dying while in custody of our border patrol, our policies are designed to tear undocumented immigrants away from their families, and immigrant children apprehended by border patrol are being held in cages. The people supporting the politicians who push these policies generally are the least likely to be affected by border crossings. Ensuring border security is a legitimate concern, but if we are not vigilant in supporting basic decency regardless of which nation a human being happens to come from, we are prone to become controlled by opportunistic hucksters who thrive in a climate of division by spreading fear in the name of justice.[53]

Thankfully, some people in the Cornhusker State resist this temptation. After the shock of the raid in O'Neill, Nebraska, set in, the Rev. Bernie Starman directly addressed the immigration issue afflicting his parish. On the Nineteenth Sunday in Ordinary Time, he began his sermon by acknowledging that following the raid, the town became a community divided between those who rejoiced in ICE's actions and those who were horrified by what had transpired. He grieved that mothers and fathers he knew might not ever see their children again. He admonished parishioners for reacting inappropriately with hostile phone messages and social media posts. He then asked the laity in their pews to be compassionate and merciful. "Until we understand the how's and why's our current immigration programs are broken, we can't begin to try to find a solution," Starman said. "Every day we deal with the 'lives' of real human beings, not objects."[54]

Actions like Starman's are rare. Despite the pope's plea for nations to protect the rights of migrants, the call has largely gone unheeded within the US church, whose membership increasingly relies on Latin American migrants. "Afraid of alienating a party they still want to influence, and grateful to it for its official opposition to abortion, the U.S. Conference of Catholic Bishops has so far been unwilling to denounce Trump's border policies as emphatically as it denounced the Obama administration's contraception mandate," wrote the editors of the progressive Catholic magazine *Commonweal*. "The latter was treated as an existential threat to the Catholic faith in America, while the former has too often been lamented as if it were just a lapse of judgment, perhaps a little excessive. The circumstances require something much stronger."[55]

Beyond my grandparents, I don't know much about my ancestors other than that they were poor Catholic farmers from the Bohemia region of Czechoslovakia. When they settled in the Midwest, they called their new home in Nebraska's southeastern hills "the Bohemian Alps." Like Meyer, they practiced their native tongue, which nativists loathed. Because anti-Catholicism was rampant in the United States at the time they arrived, the Slavic people who I derive from were scoffed at by the more established Anglo Protestants the same way that my friends and I mocked Schuyler kids. "The early Czechs who settled near the vicinity of Brainard encountered a great deal of trouble from the non-Czech element that had settled there previously," wrote one Butler County historian. "Fights were common there when the various groups went to town to do their shopping." Had I been born several generations earlier, I'd be the one facing ridicule over my loyalty to the United States. Like today's Muslim immigrants who trudge through obtuse travel bans and the Mexican laborers fighting discriminatory housing ordinances, Eastern European Catholics during Meyer's time were targeted for their otherness. I never realized this until I had the privilege to devote my time to education and relocate to a city full of immigrants. Most bohunks in Brainard don't get those opportunities.[56]

Like abortion, immigration has become a reliable wedge issue in Nebraska for Republicans seeking power. If I stayed in Brainard, I'd still probably be on the other side of this issue, but the places I've lived in since my Butler County days changed my thinking. Life experiences sure have a way of changing your views. I found out the hard way when I became terribly sick.

CHAPTER THREE

The Cornhusker Kickback

At the end of my junior year of college, I started finding blood in my stool. Lots of it. I was getting ready to graduate and this was definitely not what I needed. I couldn't go to class because every half hour I felt like tiny crows were flying around my stomach and shredding it. I went to the university health center, but their remedies did nothing. I didn't feel relief until I saw a specialist weeks later who diagnosed me with ulcerative colitis. The doctor gave me some drugs that stopped my colon from attacking itself. While I was relieved to no longer be defecating blood, the cost of the medication made me feel like I was still getting screwed.

My struggle with colitis taught me more about health care than any of my other maladies. Before we get to where I now stand on the issue, let's look at how and why my views changed. This story is best told through my medical problems, which are numerous.

In kindergarten, I became bored during one of my brother's junior high football games. I wondered around with some other kids and found a well near the field with its cover torn off. We spotted some toads at the bottom of the well, so we started throwing sticks down the hole to see if we could make the amphibians hop. I got carried away, slipped, and fell headfirst down the well. I didn't panic initially, but once blood streamed into my eye, I freaked out. I screamed and bawled. Parents came rushing over. Eventually medics followed them. An ambulance hauled me to David City, where a doctor stuck three staples in my skull to close the gash. I'm lucky I didn't break my damn neck. The next day, I missed school for the first time.

Later that year, pneumonia hospitalized me for four days. In seventh grade I got pneumonia again, in the same spot of the same lung, and stayed in the hospital for nearly a week. It took me four months to gain back the twenty pounds I lost. Losing weight sucked because I was already skinny as hell and I wanted to bulk up for sports.

Like my brothers, I played football. By the time I played, the well near the field was cemented shut. Unlike them, I never became a star player. But I managed to become the worst player to ever be named Nebraska Prep Athlete of the Week by Lincoln's CBS affiliate. The honor came after we played our county rivals, David City's Catholic school. Publications across the state named it their game of the week because both teams were rated and featured all-state backs. On a fluke play with next to no time remaining, I imitated Husker receiver Matt Davison by catching a tipped pass for the winning touchdown. Immediately following the game, TV reporters crowded around me, asking me what was going through the mind when I made the play. "When I saw it go up in the air, I just went up and got it," I screamed while trying to catch my breath. "When I caught the ball, I almost prolapsed." The folks at Husker Bar laughed their asses off when the nightly news aired the interview without cutting my crude remark.

Five years prior to that glorious moment, I experienced another memorable incident on that field. Right after a game in seventh grade, I walked off the gridiron looking so jaundiced teammates said I resembled Bart Simpson. I wanted to go home, eat chicken strips, and watch ESPN, but my parents said that wasn't happening. I pleaded that I felt fine. We were worrying about nothing. "Well, you sure as hell don't look fine," Dad told me. From that moment on I have dealt with a serious illness—and will do so for the rest of my life.

Once again, I was rushed from East Butler's football field to the David City hospital. The family doctor in David City had no idea what was wrong. After all, how many kids in tiny Butler County come in looking like a ripening banana caused by some indecipherable ailment? I was tested for many diseases, none of which I had. The doctor refused to send me to a specialist, insisting the local hospital could fix me. After I'd struggled through months of liver deterioration, my parents finally hauled me to the Children's Hospital in Omaha, where a specialist immediately diagnosed me with autoimmune hepatitis. From there, I got sent to the University of Nebraska Medical Center, where I still see doctors today.

I had no idea what "autoimmune hepatitis" was. "Hepatitis" made me think of drug needles and sexually transmitted diseases. I was confused because the only drug I abused was caffeine from all the pop I drank, and as far as sex goes, my left hand was the only partner I had penetrated at that juncture.

Plus, I got shots to prevent hepatitis. Didn't those things work? If there was ever a time to convert to antivaccination, this was it.

The specialist explained, calmly, that "hepatitis" just means liver inflammation, and "autoimmune" means my own body caused the illness. Unlike the hepatitis types that have a letter attached to them, autoimmune hepatitis isn't caused by a virus and isn't contagious. I realized then that my body attacked my own liver and I had a very rare lifelong liver disease. I kept my faith in vaccines.

After consoling me, the specialist scolded my parents. "You have a very, very sick boy here," he said in a demanding tone. "I don't know why you waited this long." He called them irresponsible. He told us I'd have a liver transplant the next day. Mom cried. He then apologized for calling them irresponsible. It was Christmas Eve.

As I began my second weeklong hospital stay of the year, I was too out of it to appreciate how serious the situation was. Luckily, the drugs that were inserted into me through an IV worked immediately and the transplant got postponed. My liver enzyme counts kept improving, and by the end of the week, the medical team called off the transplant. I had to regularly visit the specialist and maintain a punishing drug regimen, but those things were very minor compared to what we were prepared for, placing my life at the whims of a donor list and surgeon. Our family felt relieved.

In the months before I was told that my liver would be extracted, I dealt with a lot. My body was clearly messed up. In just one year I had bronchitis, pneumonia, anemia, strep throat, rapid weight loss, rapid weight gain, hemorrhoids, and anal fissures. I thank God that I didn't have to handle our bills.

My family had to provide its own health insurance since Dad ran his own business and Mom worked odd jobs that offered low pay and no benefits. The insurance we bought was so crummy that the company kept going out of business and getting bought by larger firms. While we dealt with my illnesses, the name of our insurance company changed several times. We couldn't switch companies because of my new "preexisting condition," which meant that a new insurance company would not pay for treatments for my illness. It was highly profitable—and then very legal—for insurance companies to discriminate against people who became sick through no fault of their own.

Due to our bad insurance policies, my diseases became a noose around the neck of our family's finances. I didn't know it at the time. Mom, who did the bookkeeping for our family's business, told me to not worry about it and that the costs weren't that bad. I knew she was full of it, but she was just doing her part. I knew Mom cared too much to tell me the truth so there was no point arguing about it. I was also too tired to argue because all the immunosuppressants and steroids getting crammed down my throat made me a fatigued insomniac.

Mom still doesn't like talking about medical bills because she worries I feel guilty about creating financial strain. Once I started paying my own bills years later, I got her to open up about what they paid so that I could be prepared for what to expect. She reluctantly shared the policies for the coverage we had in 2003.

For out-of-pocket expenses, we had a $5,000 cap for in-network providers and $5,000 cap for out-of-network providers. This didn't include monthly premiums. Our insurance didn't have a stellar network like Blue Cross Blue Shield does. So some of my visits and procedures were covered in-network and others were out-of-network.

"Guess what? We paid $10,000 out of pocket," Mom said, before launching into her own line of questions about how my liver counts are doing and if my insurance still covers my medications. Her experience with medical bills makes her skeptical that I can cover my bills, even though I have for many years. "It's a racket," she says of health insurance companies.

Because the upper crust of Butler County doesn't flash its wealth around and rich farmers are among the humblest people I know, I thought I grew up middle class. We *are* middle class by Brainard standards, which means we are actually lower class according to the rest of the nation. Technically, I grew up poor, though I was in my twenties before I realized it. This changed in college, where I met people who talked about their parents' vacation homes as I got by on Pell Grants and scholarships that were awarded to me for being a first-generation college student from a lower-income household. When I moved to New York after college, I encountered another level of wealth when I learned that in addition to being a season, "summer" was also a verb. People who "summered" at Martha's Vineyard, were raised by nannies, and frequented country clubs had upbringings that were a universe removed from Brainard. By their standards, I'm like the savage hillbillies from *Deliverance*.

If I had claimed to be poor when I was in Brainard, my friends would have said I'm full of crap because I always had enough to eat at home and my parents had jobs. My mom would have told me to stop pitying myself with such pontificating. Before Mom and Dad settled in Brainard in the 1970s to start a family-run plumbing, heating, and air-conditioning business, the newlyweds shacked up in a trailer in David City. According to Mom, they lived in "a nice trailer park"; therefore, we weren't poor.

My point is that we didn't own a bunch of properties or lucrative possessions. We bought used cars. We went to public school. Since my parents never had anyone giving them retirement funds, they parked their savings there when possible. They don't have enough in those accounts to retire at a reasonable age. Dad's still banging away on ACs and furnaces in his seventies. No matter how Mom frames it, I know my bills were burdensome.

Keep in mind the $10,000 was just for the first year. My disease was chronic. Our medical costs declined as I got healthier, but I had regular appointments with specialists, multiple prescriptions to fill each month, routine blood work, colonoscopies, endoscopies, biopsies, ultrasounds, and whatever other procedures the doctor ordered. Sometimes I got hit with other medical problems—becoming prone to sleeplessness, strep, flu, acne, rashes, anemia, bone density loss, perpetual bowel irritability—because my body was worn down from the drugs that simultaneously fought my hepatitis and suppressed my immune system. This in turn caused me to schedule more doctor visits and consume more meds. My disease became an annual tab that subsided some but never stopped. When I asked Mom how she and Dad dealt with unanticipated bills, she conceded that they borrowed money.

Mom and Dad have taken out two significant loans since they moved to Brainard. The first was a mortgage for the house I grew up in. They paid it off years ago. The other is a revolving loan that's been ongoing for many years, used primarily for business expenses. For instance, in the summer of 2019 my parents took out $6,500 to repair Dad's workshop and trade in his old pickup for a newer model. Back in 2003 when my liver's expense account grew, they leaned on a loan.

"The bank has always been good to us," Mom said. "That's how small towns are, you know what I mean?"

Mom's point is that small-town banks, like Brainard's First Nebraska Bank, know their customers. They support local businesses. Nearly everyone who works there has had my Dad install an air conditioner or a toilet in their homes at some point.

We support them in return. My parents do all of their finances through the Brainard bank. The catering business that the bank manager's husband runs has supplied food to every graduation, wedding, anniversary, and surprise birthday party we've had for the past thirty years. If the event venue allows us to bring our own caterer, we know who we're calling.

When I got sick, I was lucky my parents had easy access to funds when they needed it. If you don't personally know your banker well, it can be difficult to quickly get a credit extension. Small banks are constantly closing as big banks get bigger. The friendly dynamic my parents have with our local bank is a dying way of life in America that's being replaced by soulless encounters with banking websites operated by international conglomerates. Another thing to consider is that many families don't have good credit so they can't borrow from a decent institution during dire times. I'm lucky as hell my parents didn't feel forced to turn to predatory payday loans.

"We were really fortunate," Mom said. " A lot of people aren't set up like us. We found out a lot about insurance. We never really had anything until you had that."

The close relationship my parents maintain with the local bank is possible because Brainard is a tight-knit community. My best friend growing up was our polio-stricken seventy-seven-year-old neighbor Eddie. Though he never started his own family, Eddie was very much part of ours. I went to his house every day after school. He made *Matlock* and bird watching fun for a six-year-old. We went to Eddie's for holidays, and he bought us fireworks. When I went to my grandparent's or sister's house for a few days, I'd miss Eddie before I'd miss my parents or friends that were my own age.

How does a child so easily befriend an elderly man who is a disabled bachelor? It's because in small towns like Brainard, where everybody knows your name, people trust each other in a way that isn't possible in larger municipalities. At Husker Bar, the farmers who come to drink coffee in the morning pay whatever they wish. The standard rate is about a quarter per cup, but no one

checks. While many people in Brainard distrust the outside world, they always welcome their neighbors. The relationship I had with Eddie or my school
wasn't strange by Brainard standards, but I have trouble explaining how nor-
mal it felt to people I've met in college and the workplace who have no point
of reference to small-town life.

"Growing up in Nebraska, I was able to see first-hand that from the car
dealer in Grand Island to the guy walking bean fields in northeast Nebraska,
those people stand for integrity and hard work and caring about your neighbor and putting the needs of other people ahead of yourself," Scott Frost told
ESPN after the University of Nebraska hired him as its head football coach
in 2018. Frost, who grew up in a small town in Nebraska before becoming a
football star at our largest university, described Nebraska exactly how people
in Brainard would describe it.[1]

The model of our family business gives further indication of how close
people are in Brainard. My dad does the plumbing, heating, air conditioning,
and electrical work in many of the houses in Butler County, and like other
local merchants, he hates raising prices to offset inflation. Because he worries about charging the people of his community too much, Dad continues to
charge a fraction of what plumbers in Omaha and Lincoln charge. Part of the
reason I qualified for Pell Grants despite my parents owning their own business was because Dad cared more about friends and customers than profits.
In the surrounding counties, there are very few people in my dad's trade, so
they could easily band together and create an oligopoly to jack up prices if they
wanted to. Corporations do it all the time. If someone suggested this tactic to
my dad, he'd instruct them to go straight to hell.

Both of my parents grew up on farms outside other nearby small towns.
Every once in a while, someone moves to Brainard who grew up in Lincoln,
but that's rare. Meeting someone who lived in cities like Los Angeles or Miami
is unheard of, so you don't really hear many different viewpoints. Because few
people move out and your neighbors stay constant through generations, you
get a clear sense of where other people in town stand on issues. I can still recall
Eddie's distaste for regulations that restricted what types of fireworks we could
purchase before Independence Day. We complained as we road-tripped past
the Missouri border for bottle rockets and larger artillery shells.

When I got sick, the closeness of our neighbors came out in full force. At
times it got very repetitive when everyone in town asked if I felt okay whenever

they saw me. They meant well. There was genuine concern about my well-being because we were part of the community. When someone gets sick in Brainard, the town will do its best to make them feel loved and welcomed. My schoolteachers realized that some nights I couldn't sleep at all and that I might inevitably and suddenly crash during a sixth-period study hall. Instead of lecturing me or sending me to detention, which would have been the typical course of action if I were healthy, they'd wake me up without repercussion. In some cases they even let me sleep until the bell rang. Punishment would have done nothing to help me sleep at night and prevent me conking out during class.

One school day I woke up so loopy I barely made it to the front door. I insisted that my parents let me go to school because I wanted to be eligible to play in a basketball game that night. I was so out of it that I stumbled into lockers and nearly fell down. When I got to my desk, my biology teacher immediately said, "Hey Ross, you don't look good. You should go home." I said, "You're probably right. I feel like ass." The school called my parents to let them know I was going home sick. Someone offered to help me get home or wait with me until Mom could arrive to pick me up. I insisted I was fine to walk the two and a half blocks back home. I stayed home sick the next four days and was in the hospital by the end of the week with pneumonia. The teacher, who taught my older siblings and knew my parents, had looked after me.

Meanwhile, I don't know the names of any of the people who live on my floor in my Brooklyn apartment. And that's how I want it. Because New York City is so exhausting, when I come home, I don't want to talk to anyone or put in the effort to be friendly. Some days when I step off that crowded subway and walk home, I pray that the only living being I speak to that night is my dog. I never felt that way in Brainard.

Tight relationships are among many rhythms of daily life in Brainard that influence political opinion. Part of the reason so many people in small towns like Brainard hate the government, and initiatives like government-mandated health care, is because it runs counter to how they live their own lives. From their perspective, rejection of national liberal policies seems sensible.

When you live on several acres of land, rarely encounter law enforcement officers or strangers, and are used to doing whatever you damn-well please on your own property, forcing people to participate in a massive health-care marketplace feels restrictive of personal liberty. Plus, the government has bungled programs in the past, so there is not a whole lot of trust there. Environmental initiatives like the Green New Deal appear overreaching to farmers who take great care of their own land but see polluted cities whenever they turn on their TV. Farmers feed the world and agriculture powers our small towns, so they see it as an attack when Democrat politicians list farting cows as climate change contributors. The $25 trillion national debt and deficit spending don't make sense to people who save up and purchase vehicles with cash. Inventing arduous regulations to keep people in check is baffling when you don't see anyone losing their homes and you conduct your business through handshake deals and word-of-mouth referrals with people you know and trust. They distrust the government, so they protest tax increases in knee-jerk fashion. They see the government's ineffective hand influencing their lives in all sorts of unproductive ways. Diversity promotion is just liberal politicians' way of shaming us for who we are. No prayer in public schools is the government's way of keeping us God-fearing people down. So much as issuing a peep about preventing civilians from owning rocket launchers will invite lectures about the country being founded by rebel gun owners who believed that everyday people should have as much access to as much firepower as they desire. Anyone wanting gun control is an anti-patriot obsessed with big government controlling our lives.

Our system of government intensifies the urban-rural divide. Because the structure of government bodies is determined by geography as well as population, rural voters have a disproportionate influence over our country's politics. This is part of the reason why progressives are statistically underrepresented in Congress and state legislatures. Rural voters helped put Trump in office, they prevented Democrats from controlling the Senate in 2018, and they will play a major role in upcoming elections. Their share of the population may be dwindling, but rural voters will hold a lot of power for years to come due to how our government is set up.[2]

Liberals roll their eyes at conservative viewpoints at their own peril, often not realizing how much they are influenced by their own environment. I remember my cousin Hannah telling me how irritated she was after she moved from a small Nebraska city to attend college in New England. She was at a dinner party in Vermont and got grilled over what type of farm her parents operated. The people at the party didn't want her there if her parents ran a "factory farm." They rambled about how cows are bad for the world because they produce methane that contributes to global warming. When she told me this,

I wondered how kids at fancy schools in the Northeast differentiated between factory farms and regular farms if they've never worked on a farm themselves.

"It's not fair for them to look down on the Midwest and rural agricultural ways of life when they have never tried to understand it," Hannah said. "I didn't vote for Trump, but all these blue-collar people voted him in and I'm like, that's why. It was that feeling of feeling looked down upon that Trump tapped into ingeniously."

Whenever I meet people in New York and reveal that I'm from Nebraska, some are intrigued by my exotic origin but no one is surprised that I chose to leave home. From their view, it's natural for ambitious people stuck in the middle of the country to venture to greener career pastures in a huge city. Some ask: "When did you realize you wanted to live in New York?" When I tell them that randomness brought me here, I've always been ambivalent about the place, and I think often about leaving it, they're usually surprised I could view other living options more favorably. It's just assumed that many kids from the Great Plains will leave for cities like New York when they grow up. But the idea of New Yorkers moving to Nebraska is considered so absurd that the concept warrants a situational comedy that prompts the kind of shenanigans that happen when a single straight man pretends to be gay so he can share an apartment with two women. The conservative writer Dennis Boyles made the case that Middle Americans are more open-minded about learning about the East Coast than East Coasters are in learning about Middle America. Over time, the disdain becomes mutually reinforcing.[3]

"Almost every day, marching bands or drama clubs or debate teams or high school graduating classes board buses in Kansas or Nebraska or Oklahoma and end up in Washington, D.C., or Boston or Pasadena," Boyles wrote. "What does Nebraska get in return? Provincialism, ignorance, and condescension from the New York Times. Since the invention of buses, none has ever carried a bunch of inquisitive New York City students to Alma, Nebraska—and it's too bad for them."[4]

Given how much people in most geographical regions follow the same voting patterns, I can't help but feel that many of my New York friends would be conservatives if they spent their whole lives in Nebraska towns. On the flip side, I think my conservative high school friends would become more liberal if they spent a few years in New York City.

I also believe that press members on the coasts—which is a flawed group

I belong to and value—don't give enough consideration to how the attitudes that many people in the middle of the country have are formed in reaction their coverage. Working-class rural Americans have been portrayed as irrationally cranky and resentful of anything that is in their best interest. As press members, we need to examine what we're doing and saying about rural conservatives. We should ponder if we're provoking a response that creates a self-fulfilling prophecy. Mock a group of people long enough and they will resent you, but that doesn't mean the people who dislike you are being unreasonable.

Commentators working for left-leaning national publications should consider that the values they find to be common sense and logical don't necessarily appear that way in places like Brainard. When you're in a place with more cows than people, and you personally know most of the few people around, the benefits of regulating fireworks, guns, pollution, and housing aren't that apparent. On the other hand, if you are constantly bumping into strangers in a crowded city, the need for more government agencies to enforce rules and guide interactions is much clearer. Just as my New York friends are perplexed by rural conservatives' love of guns and aversion to taxes, whenever I go home people confess to me that they're puzzled by what big city folk care about.

"You have people in California who say it's wrong to declaw cats and have a law against it, and they're probably the same people who think it's just fine to suck a baby's brains out," said a small-town Christian woman interviewed by Princeton sociologist Robert Wuthnow. "I just don't understand people like that!"[5]

Even though my political views evolved since I lived in Brainard, the obsession with striving for self-reliance is something I can't shake. A few years ago, I finally saw the popular play (and later, movie) *Rent*, about poor creative types struggling to make a life in New York City as they battle HIV. Instead of feeling sorry for the characters, I hated most of them for being selfish and lazy. The exception was the character Angel, who hustled and made some money through music and drag performances. Angel even generously shared some of that hard-earned money with friends. I respected Angel much more than the others, which made it sad when Angel died. The worst character was Roger, a musician who thought he was entitled to sit around strumming his guitar all day without ever contributing to society or paying his rent.

The villain in *Rent* is the artists' rich landlord friend, who had the audacity to charge them rent after he let them live in his building for a whole year without paying. But I think the real villains are the bohemians like Roger who refused to get a job and leached onto their friend's generosity. If your landlord doesn't make you pay rent for an entire year and then you get mad when, after repeated warnings, the locks are changed, you're not a helpless victim. You're a selfish person who needs to do your part and get a job. Stop acting like the world owes you favors just because you think you're creative and special. I feel this way because I've seen my parents work really hard doing jobs that they often did not enjoy to earn what they've got. Like so many others in states like Nebraska, I've been conditioned to loathe people seeking handouts. For many years, I directed this animus at the government.

The view in Brainard is that if the banks are making risky bets out of greed, let them fail. If you can't get health care for yourself, that's your own fault, so don't restructure the government to get it for you. If you want more wealth distribution, go make billions of dollars yourself to give to the poor, but keep your tax reforms out of my sight.

Conservative principles like personal responsibility, fiscal restraint, limited government, respect for authority, and individual liberty align with how people in Brainard live their lives. The Republican Party has done an incredible marketing job convincing people in rural areas that it values these ideals and that it's the only party doing so. In many small towns, the predilection for the do-it-yourself mentality hinders Democrats and boosts conservatives into office.

My friends in Brainard hate whenever people think they know what's best for them. Telling rural voters that they're "voting against their own interests" doesn't get them to reconsider their beliefs. No one in Brainard is going to suddenly start voting for Democrats because an NYU graduate at NBC News said that Democrats will better serve their economic interests. Telling people that they vote against their own interests only angers them. This is why the best pro wrestling villain in America is a guy doing small-circuit shows in the South under the name "The Progressive Liberal." Not unlike liberal media pundits, "The Progressive Liberal" reigns in the boos from conservative crowds by calling them backwards and mocking their love of religion and guns.[6]

It's true that several Democratic policies, especially those concerning health care, would financially benefit working-class people in Brainard who consistently vote against Democrats. However, interests are subjective, and economics is just one type of interest that people have. As a whole, most folks in places like Brainard prefer the GOP agenda. Many are too proud to seek out the type of assistance Democrats propose. In her study of rural Wisconsin voters, political scientist Katherine Cramer stated that the idea of "help" in the small towns she visited was "about letting people work hard enough so that they can make it on their own." Writing about her turbulent childhood on a Kansas farm, Sarah Smarsh wrote that working-class people in the middle of America can "concede personal failure and vote for the party more inclined to assist them, or vote for the other party, whose rhetoric conveys hope that the labor of their lives is what will compensate them."[7]

Folks in Brainard prefer the self-reliance talk of Republicans.

People get sick all the time; I'm not unique there. Thousands of Americans right now are much, much sicker than I ever was, and many of them struggle to pay their bills. My illnesses aren't some sob story. I'm alive and I'm not bankrupt. Considering the situation, I'm fortunate.

Those who've never been to Nebraska and want progressive legislation passed may insist that it is in Nebraskans' best interest to pass free and universal health care. They'll say that Obamacare helps people with lower incomes get coverage, so working-class people like my family should unanimously support it. To understand the distaste that people in towns like Brainard have for Obamacare, and large nonmilitary government initiatives in general, it's worth considering their ideology of doing your part by helping your neighbor.

See, public politeness is always on display in Brainard. When my dad and godfather share a round of Bud Lights at Husker Bar, they trade light barbs for ten minutes over who should pay the bill because each of them insist that they owe the other one a favor. If the girls' basketball team makes it to the state tournament and you tell one of the player's parents you're impressed by their daughter's athletic skills, the parent will all but blush before saying their daughter is just lucky to be on such a team and that she doesn't deserve the credit herself. If an elderly couple has trouble electronically transferring files to their son in another state, a familiar face at the farmer's co-op will scan and email copies at no cost. When storms blow down trees, a friendly handyman with a backhoe will help you replant while insisting it's no big deal.

Nebraskans take incredible pride whenever they're told they're the nicest fans in college football. When the Heisman-winning Texas running back Ricky Williams tore up the Huskers, Nebraska fans chanted "Heisman" instead of booing him.[8]

All the politeness, even the false niceties, derive from a social obligation of doing your part. When you take out a loan to cover medical bills for your sick kid but assure him that everything is alright and there's nothing to worry about, you do your part. When you pay for your friend's beer, you do your part. When you compliment a kid to their parents, you do your part. When you help pull your neighbor's car out of a snowdrift, you do your part. When you salute the troops and profess adulation for your country, you do your part. When I worked with my dad installing air conditioners during the summers of my childhood, he'd yell "stop jacking around, pick up the Hole Hawg and do your part" whenever I goofed off. By contrast, the characters of *Rent*, who refused to pay for their apartments, did not do their part.

Living in Brainard, it is easy to fetishize personal responsibility, communal loyalty, and stingy financial habits. All of these things embody doing your part, as I was taught. I was told to keep working hard no matter how crappy your job is. Never rely on government handouts or complain about your lot in life. My parents said we should be grateful to live in a place like Brainard where you know everybody's name. And for god sakes, don't ever brag about having money if ever you should fall into some. My siblings and I often violate these ideals; nonetheless, these stereotypical midwestern values were hammered into us.

Surrounded by miles of farm ground separating villages of a few hundred people, I felt totally disconnected from whatever went on with our national politics. Instead of eyeing poll numbers, most of the people I knew prayed for elections to end so they wouldn't have to see those damn political ads souring their football watching. When my parents were working on their feet all day doing their part, they didn't care to mock awkward statements made by elected officials or gawk at the haircuts of presidential advisors or get caught up in the latest inane Twitter controversy. Instead of looking outward to the nation at large, they focused their energy on the local institutions they're loyal to, like our church, school, and bar. I felt that you can trust the good people of Brainard, but you can't trust those money-wasting good-for-nothing government bureaucrats, so what's the point of getting involved in politics?

Relying on the government, even for something as important as health care, was the opposite of doing your part. I saw government programs as the opposite of how honest people did business. The bloated budgets, the insurmountable debt, the wasted resources, the bureaucracy, the people pulling strings behind the scenes—none of that made any logical sense. Conservatives who slashed government spending and professed to hate Washington offered a message that appealed to the way I believed the world should work. When Republicans and conservative Democrats pledged to reduce government spending, I said hell yeah, bring it on. Promises to balance the budget aligned with my sense of responsible money handling. Problems affecting big American cities and other countries seemed so alien. If a new law prompted more governmental oversight, no matter how slight, I'd hate it because I wanted to be left alone.

My distaste for big government came out in full force during high school, when Congress passed an energy bill intended to phase out incandescent light bulbs. To most people this wasn't a big deal. Those who supported the bill argued that fluorescent and LED lights are more efficient alternatives that will benefit the environment and lower electric bills. I did not see it this way.

Like policy analysts at conservative think tanks, I saw government intrusion. I blamed everyone from my state senator to President Bush to hippy environmentalists for creating a problem out of thin air and burdening honest Americans with needless legislation. I raised my hand in home economics class and stood up near the warm steel radiator in the back of the classroom to rant to my fellow classmates about how the government's regulation of light bulbs was a harbinger that would be followed by more oppressive rules. Eventually, the liberals in the government would force us to drive fuel-efficient Priuses and eat vegetarian. Light bulbs were just the beginning, I tell you what.

The economy of Brainard benefits from enormous agricultural subsidies the government doles out, but for many years I did not see things that way. To me, government wasn't something that artificially propped up an industry that many of the people I knew depended on. The government wasn't what educated me tuition free. The government wasn't what ensured that our food was safe.

To me, the government was an onerous set of rules that told you what type of light bulbs you could use. The government was a nanny that paid lazy people for being lazy. The government paid thirty guys to do a job that required two people. Whenever me and Dad would drive through a state-funded construction site on the highway, disgust overcame Dad. He'd get pissed off by how many people were standing around doing nothing. When I took my sweet time soldering copper water pipes, Dad would bark: "What the hell you doin' over there? You ain't workin' for the state!"

My parents, like so many other people I knew growing up, dislike government assistance and view it as a collection of people who aren't doing their part. Like *Hillbilly Elegy* author J. D. Vance, they feel that "our government encouraged social decay through the welfare state." Whether or not this label is fair or true, most Nebraskans I know associate fiscal responsibility with Republicans and big government with Democrats. Consequently, they link monetary incompetence to Democrats. What makes this stereotype more pervasive is that Republicans run ads broadcasting this message and talk radio hosts continually extend it.[9]

Lately, the federal budget deficit has grown under Republican administrations and shrunk during Democratic control. Even though Republicans cut welfare programs, they keep growing the government's budget by funneling more dollars to defense and border patrol. Though small-town conservatives are apt to oppose increasing the size of government, these developments don't necessarily hinder them. Studies across several states show that small towns receive more government funding on a per capita basis than metro areas. Services like roads, schools, and broadband networks become more costly on a per-person basis in areas with low populations, so metropolitan taxpayers help subsidize rural coverage. Although big government can benefit people in small towns, it never *felt* that way. I felt budget cuts were always responsible because the people of Brainard practiced financial modesty. When the financial industry bailouts and health-care overhauls came along during Obama's tenure, they didn't *feel* financially modest.[10]

I know farmers worth millions when you factor in the land and equipment they own, but they still drive rusted-up Chevy trucks and rock worn T-shirts they earned with Marlboro Miles twenty years ago. Taking out a loan is something you're only supposed to do when you absolutely need money for things like paying college tuition or buying an affordable home for your family. Rich farmers aside, most folks here don't have much but that's fine enough by us.

I still view this type of financial modesty as a good thing. The lack of having to keep up with the Joneses helped shield areas like Butler County from the Great Recession. In high school, the recession was all over the news but invisible in my personal experience. I hadn't met a single person who lost their home or job because of the mess. We had good reason to think Nebraska was The Good Life because we have some of America's lowest unemployment and foreclosure rates. Paradoxically, my experience of the recession makes me think of an Alabama song: "Somebody told us Wall Street fell, but we were so poor that we couldn't tell."

Although we weren't too directly affected by the national catastrophe, I remember hearing stories about people in Florida and California who bought extravagant homes that they'd never be able to afford with their wages. Nobody in Brainard talked about the culpability of the financial institutions who banked off these terrible loans. We sure as hell didn't discuss the financial deregulations that made complex securities like collateralized debt obligations possible in the first place. We got pissed at people in those populous coastal states for losing their sense of responsibility.

As the recession unfolded, we didn't care who got caught in the mess. If people lose their jobs, banks go under, and the auto industry collapses, so be it. Screw 'em. They deserve it anyway. Maybe punishment will teach them a lesson.

Unlike the areas who were hit hard by the recession, home ownership in Brainard isn't an exercise in speculation. Land around Brainard is cheap and so is the local carpenter who everyone knows. No one comes to town hoping to flip their house and quickly turn a profit. If anyone buys property around here, it's because they want to live here for the long haul or invest in farmland. Because home purchases transacted so differently in Brainard, deregulation wasn't of interest here. Meanwhile, liberal pundits like the popular economist Paul Krugman wailed that big banks became too powerful and their deregulation led to the financial meltdown. "Banks are special, because the risks they take are borne, in large part, by taxpayers and the economy as a whole," Krugman wrote. "And what JPMorgan has just demonstrated is that even supposedly smart bankers must be sharply limited in the kinds of risk they're allowed to take on. . . . It's clear, then, that we need to restore the sorts of safeguards that gave us a couple of generations without major banking panics."[11]

There is some truth to Krugman's point, but hardly anyone in Brainard wants more regulation, even if it is intended to protect the working class. An op-ed from a New York City newspaper ain't gonna change their minds. The people of Brainard don't engage in credit default swaps or take out risky mortgages with no money down, so they don't really need rules that limit the risky behavior of bankers. When I started college, I saw financial regulations as burdensome rules that'd increase the power of the government and create more paperwork for tiny operations like our First Nebraska Bank. I thought, why should places like Brainard be punished for the sins of greedy city slickers? I never thought about how government oversight could benefit places I never visited. Despite how poorly the country's economy was doing, our state mostly avoided the crisis, so I just wanted the government to leave us alone.

When Barack Obama bailed out the bankers and automakers, it annoyed the people of Brainard. It made people feel like the government stuck its nose where it didn't belong and chose winners and losers. "All Obama cares about are those big wigs in big cities," I'd hear from townies at Husker Bar and on Fox News, which would air in the bar, creating an endless echo chamber. The target of the frustration morphed back and forth from materialistic people in populous states to people in big cities to special interests to liberal elites to the Democratic Party so frequently that these very disparate terms became interchangeable whenever people vented their political frustrations.

Mind you, unlike New York City, the vast majority of conversations in Brainard don't directly touch politics. Fox News broadcasts prompt a few folks to publicly comment, but most people in the bar just talk over the program so they can keep discussing Husker football. Instead of perpetually voicing their political opinions like journalists on Twitter do, these feelings brew under the surface and pop up sporadically, like during drunken rants in friends' garages or when people visit the ballot box. Similar to many other states, after the bailouts we began replacing moderate Republican lawmakers with bigger conservatives.

The furor for antiestablishment candidates hit a tipping point with the 2016 presidential election, but it simmered for a long time before that and it's bound to have consequences on ensuing elections. Given the appreciation Nebraskans have for performance modesty, it is ironic, if not hypocritical, they backed Trump, the least modest person in US history. By this point, most of the Nebraskans I know would back the Republican nominee no matter who it was. Many people just wanted someone in office who would stick it to professional politicians, government busybodies, liberals, and anyone else who they thought looked down on them.

"I was happy that a conservative would be in the White House," my college roommate Drew told me as he sat in the living room of his family's old farmhouse in southwest Nebraska. "You heard a lot of media sources, especially those in cities bigger than Omaha, saying that there was no way Trump could get enough votes to pull it off. But he did it. It kind of had that underdog victory feeling. Part of me found satisfaction in that it felt like a victory for middle and rural America."

The local animus toward Democrats increased with the bailouts and further ballooned with Obamacare. Seeing that Nebraskans voted in 2018 to expand Medicaid, there's an opportunity for progressive candidates to win over voters through health care. But Medicaid passed through a nonpartisan ballot measure, and only eight of Nebraska's ninety-three counties supported it. If Democrats are going to lead in Nebraska, they have some serious branding issues to overcome. "If our ballot said 'expanding Obamacare,' I feel like people would have voted against it," said Tony Vargas, a Nebraska state senator and registered Democrat. "Instead, we said 'expanding Medicaid and addressing the gap.' . . . It's a lot harder to attack the issue. It's much easier to attack the person."[12]

Nebraska played a role in getting Obamacare passed, but doing so came at a political cost as our Democratic senator who cast the crucial vote was replaced by a very conservative politician who helped push the state's political power further rightward.

I can't think of a recent government initiative that is more despised in Brainard than the Affordable Care Act, which we always referred to as Obamacare. Even more so than the bailouts, Obamacare violated our sense of personal responsibility and fiscal restraint while ramping up our hatred of big government. It left my high school friends feeling that liberals are misguided and assume they know what is best for Nebraska.

"It felt like something got shoved down our throats and we didn't have a say in it one way or the other," one of my friends from Brainard said as we sipped Bud Lights during halftime of the Big Ten football championship game.

The Democrats, who passed the legislation without a single Republican vote, failed to fully appreciate how Obamacare's stipulations wreaked panic in the heartland. People who grew up like me were conditioned to hate the law from the get-go. Since I resented the characters in *Rent* for failing to pay their landlord, I sure didn't have sympathy for people who didn't pay for their own insurance. As a religious kid, I saw liberals as evil when a priest friend turned on Rush Limbaugh who screamed through the radio that nuns were suing the government because the sisters refused to become Obama's contraception pill pushers. I didn't really reconsider my beliefs until years later when I developed a second chronic disease and had to navigate my way through health insurance markets.

Obamacare's contraception mandate that required all hospitals, including those with religious affiliations, to provide patients access to contraception kicked off a firestorm. A group of Catholic nuns sued the government for forcing them to break their vows. The optics of this fight were horrible. When I went on a road trip with a local priest to St. Louis, this court battle was blathered all over the radio. I couldn't get a haircut without seeing Fox News pontificate on the matter.[13]

Not everyone was so reactionary about it, but Obamacare further worsened the perception of Democrats in Nebraska. The hostility that came out of Obamacare helped mobilize Tea Partiers and other fringe conservatives, which moved the Republican Party further to the right. Even though the influential conservative think tank the Heritage Foundation originated the individual mandate concept and Republican Mitt Romney championed government-run health care as Massachusetts governor, the GOP didn't let those facts get in the way of rebranding the Affordable Care Act as an enabler of "death panels." Nebraska state senator Sue Crawford told me that fallout from Obamacare "is a big part of the polarization that has happened in Nebraska and in other states."[14]

Once people became conditioned to hate Obamacare, they started blaming it for all of the health industry's woes, including rising insurance premiums. This made it more difficult for Democrats like Bob Kerrey to get elected. One particular snafu associated with Obamacare tainted the political career of US senator Ben Nelson, the last Democrat to win a major statewide election in Nebraska.

As recently as 2010, Nebraska gave Democrats a key vote. Ben Nelson was more conservative than most Democrats (he had to be to get elected in Nebraska, after all) and often deviated from his party, so it wasn't clear how he'd vote on Obamacare. His vote was critical because without it, the Republicans who opposed Obamacare didn't have enough support for a filibuster.

To entice Nelson to vote with the Democrats, senior majority leader Harry Reid cut a deal that gave Nebraska federal funding for Medicaid expansion in exchange for Nelson's vote. If you're not from Nebraska, this may seem like a good deal when your US senator gets affordable health care expanded to more people in need while getting the feds to pay for it. But many Nebraskans didn't look at it that way.

The deal angered a lot of people who wanted to defeat Obamacare and prevent the government from expanding into yet another area of their lives. In his description of how the health-care bill got put together, former president Obama wrote that Nelson "could go sideways on us at any minute" and that "Senators Mary Landrieu and Ben Nelson made their votes contingent on hundreds of millions of additional Medicaid dollars specifically for Louisiana and Nebraska." It backfired for Nelson, who claimed he never asked for the deal to begin with and later had Nebraska's Medicaid exemption removed from the final legislation. According to one poll, following this controversy, Nelson's approval rating dropped from 78 percent to 42 percent. Some politicos believe Nelson did not seek a third term in the Senate because his popularity declined after the "Cornhusker kickback" and he would have had trouble getting reelected. Former president Bill Clinton privately told House Democrats in 2010, "that Nebraska thing is really hurting us." President Trump addressed Nelson's conundrum: "Their best senator did one of the greatest deals in the history of politics. What happened to him?"[15]

The reality is that deals like the one Nelson made with Reid are just a realistic part of politics. To get legislation passed, politicians make concessions and compromises. Political deals aren't always transparent to the public. That's just the way it is. Nelson told reporters he made the Obamacare deal "to move it forward, to see if they could put something together. That's called legislating. Sometimes you want to move something forward even if you don't agree with everything within the underlying bill, particularly when you know that you've got the role that I had."[16]

This deal would have benefited Nelson's constituents at the expense of taxpayers across other states. Fox News framed Nelson's negotiations as a "shady backroom deal." Republicans said it was "vote-buying paid for by the taxpayers." Mike Johanns, the former GOP governor and US senator who I campaigned for as a kid, said: "The special deal for Nebraska was wrong. . . . We now know this bill passed only because of back-room deals for Democrats and special carve-outs agreed to in the dead of night with the cameras off." Former Republican governor Dave Heineman told me, "What happened was the Obamacare vote went down, people were really upset and it basically ended [Nelson's] political career. I don't think he could have ran again and won."[17]

It is easy to feel that way if you already want to reduce the size of the government and are inherently suspicious of vote trading. Courting people behind the scenes just doesn't feel honest when it's not how business is handled in Brainard.

The pro-life lobby fought hard to make the Cornhusker kickback Nelson's albatross. To rally the troops against health-care reform, conservative strategists mixed health care and religious politics to portray Obamacare as an abortion bonanza. Because Nelson voted for Obamacare, conservative media said he funded Big Abortion. Once again religion—which is a source of meaning, community, and comfort for the people of Brainard—was wielded as a political weapon.[18]

The famous Republican political consultant Karl Rove and former Republican National Committee members blasted ads in Nebraska that said, "Ben Nelson sold out to Obama when it counted most." The powerful pro-life group Nebraska Right to Life condemned Nelson. Former governor Johanns said Nelson created "a watered-down accounting gimmick that leads to Nebraska taxpayers subsidizing abortions in other states." The National Right to Life Committee accused Nelson of having a 0 percent pro-life voting record and said he helped pass the "most abortion-expansive piece of legislation ever to reach the floor of the U.S. House of Representatives." Being a popular governor and senator didn't stop Nelson from getting heckled out of an Omaha pizzeria, according to Politico. (When I asked Nelson about the alleged incident, he said Politico's story was "fake news" and that he never got booed out of a restaurant.)[19]

The truth is that when Democrats courted his Obamacare vote, Nelson fought to restrict insurance coverage for abortions. Pro-life lobbyists praised Nelson when he cosponsored the Unborn Victims of Violence Act that recognized a fetus as an additional legal victim when a pregnant woman was harmed in a federal crime. When he was Nebraska's governor, Nelson signed a law banning partial-birth abortions. As a senator, he crossed party lines to oppose the nomination of Supreme Court justice Elena Kagan, who is pro-choice. In Nebraska, where running campaigns on pro-life platforms is a way of life, tagging Obamacare as an abortionists' dream worked even though the country's abortion rate declined under Obama.[20]

"A lot of [pro-life groups'] support is just partisan based," Nelson told me. "They are looking for reasons to drop you. You don't have to give them anything. It is shallow support. . . . I appreciated the support when I had it. But I think I deserved it and I don't think I ever deserved not to have it."

When he came up for reelection in 2012, Nelson declined to run. When I spoke with Nelson at his corporate law office in Omaha, he said that he never asked Reid for special provisions for Nebraska. He asked for states to have the option to expand Medicaid themselves. He said the backlash from the Cornhusker kickback did not lead him to retire and polling showed he'd win if he'd run again. Nelson said he retired because his family wanted to spend more time with him.

"The Republicans did a pretty good job of trying to pin the tail on the donkey with me by saying things about it that weren't true," Nelson said.

While Nelson appeared sincere, I couldn't help but notice that he had just flown into Omaha from Washington, DC, the day before I spoke with him and he was headed back east the following week. Nelson is the CEO of a Florida insurance company, works for an Omaha law firm, consults for several organizations, and remains loosely involved with Democratic politics, which made me wonder just how much family time he gained by exiting office.

Republicans have been eager to blame the Cornhusker kickback for ending Nelson's career, but even political figures who worked alongside Nelson acknowledged that the health-care issue affected his popularity. Kim Robak, a political veteran who served as Nelson's chief of staff and legal counsel before Nelson appointed her as his lieutenant governor, said that had Nelson "made his vote much earlier I think it would not have been as significant . . . but all eyes were on him." Nelson's health-care deal should have benefited the state, but instead "it turned out to be an incredible black eye for him that he never ever quite lived down."

Barry Rubin, a former Nebraska Democratic Party executive director who cofounded a political consulting group with Nelson, was more direct in addressing how the health-care deal affected Nelson. He said "there's no doubt" that the Cornhusker kickback influenced Nelson not to run again. "If he voted against [Obamacare] he probably would have survived and won reelection if he ran again," Rubin said. "But I think he was willing to take the risk and knew what it meant."

Across the country, Democrats who voted for Obamacare struggled to get reelected afterward. Within a few years of the law's passage, eight Democratic senators who voted for Obamacare were defeated by Republicans. Another eight declined to run again, only to see Republicans win their seats, which is what happened in Nelson's case. The bloodbath was even worse in the House. Campaigning against the health-care law helped Republicans recapture Congress. Once again, nationalizing a personal political issue became an effective way to gain power. The conservative journalist Tim Alberta wrote that in pressuring its members to vote for the health-care law, Democratic Party leadership asked their "centrist members to walk the plank. Dozens of House Democrats were already facing stiff reelection fights; voting for the president's polarizing bill was akin to nailing shut their own coffins."[21]

It's possible that Nelson was fatigued by an increasingly polarized Congress, didn't want to have to put up with Tea Party insurgents who had no interest in making deals with moderates like himself, or wanted to make more money by going back to the private sector. Nelson thrived when he could be in the middle of a bipartisan compromise and bring earmarked funds back to Nebraska. Those days are over thanks to the polarization and nationalization of political parties. Whatever led Nelson to retire, by the time he left public office his breed of conservative Democrat was practically extinct.[22]

With the parties becoming more uniform nationally and pundits treating "moderate" and "centrist" as pejoratives, cross-aisle coalitions don't stand much of a chance with primary voters demanding partisan loyalty. The same people who cry about Washington being broken will gladly punish politicians who make compromises. People say they want to end partisan bickering, but then they vote for party loyalists. "The days of building cross-party legislative coalitions in Congress seem as outdated as Nelson's strategy for protecting his seat," concluded political scientist Daniel Hopkins.[23]

Many liberals found Nelson annoying; however, I doubt most of those people ever visited Nebraska. They don't realize, or don't care, that the only Democrats to win critical statewide elections in Nebraska's recent history are people like Bob Kerrey, Jim Exon, and Ben Nelson, who are moderate and would take a lot of heat in today's political climate for even claiming to represent Democrats. The types of candidates who have won races as Democrats in Nebraska have less incentive to run for office anymore, creating an easier path for Republicans to win.

Those who wished Nelson had been more progressive just don't seem to appreciate how much more progressive Nelson was than the alternative. Aside from securing the passage of Obamacare, Nelson voted to pull out troops from Iraq and was a key vote to repeal the military's Don't Ask, Don't Tell policy that prohibited gay soldiers from publicly acknowledging their sexual orientation. Now that he's out of office, his seat has been taken by Deb Fischer, one of the most conservative senators in the nation. It's going to be many years before Democrats get that kind of support from a Nebraskan rep. We no longer provide the incremental, yet crucial, votes that push progressive legislation through Congress.[24]

Nelson got caught in the same kind of emotional firestorm that torpedoed Heath Mello's Omaha mayoral campaign. Pro-choice activists from Washington threw Mello under the bus because he wasn't dogmatic enough for their cause. They didn't really care that the controversial ultrasound bill that Mello signed was more demanding before Mello got conservative state lawmakers to compromise. Meanwhile, Nelson got attacked by pro-life advocates for being in bed with abortionists even though Nelson had a long history of voting for pro-life causes and had tried to restrict Obamacare's abortion coverage. Both politicians were sacrificed to the partisan outrage gods.

During high school, my health improved dramatically, but my health-care politics hadn't changed much yet. My medication dosages got lowered, and for a few years I went completely off the prednisone steroid that caused my entire teenage life to feel like an extended bout of sleeplessness. At that point in my life, it was still easy to disavow big government projects like Obamacare because I didn't realize how much my medical bills cost our family. I liked that Obamacare had protections for people like me with preexisting conditions, but I didn't appreciate the government overreach.

In college, I was on my parents' insurance. They paid the monthly premiums, but I paid co-pays for doctor visits and medications. I was taken off of prednisone due to my improved health, and I only took a small dosage of azathioprine, which was pretty cheap, costing about $15 per month. My health was so good that a gastroenterologist said that it would be OK if I drank beer in moderate doses. But then I got diagnosed with ulcerative colitis. This experience affected my wallet and my political beliefs.

To combat the pain and ulcers, I was put on a drug called Lialda. Its sticker price when I got it from Walgreens was about $500 for a bottle that lasted a month. Unlike my other drugs, this one didn't have a simple co-pay.

I was told that I had to pay the costs myself until I met a deductible, and after that, the insurance would cover a portion of the drug's cost. Insurance wouldn't fully cover the drug until I hit our out-of-pocket maximum. My stomach hurt, and I was overwhelmed with financial jargon. I just wanted to get out of Walgreens and stop the cramps.

Fortunately, there were coupons online that would reduce Lialda's cost. But that required additional research, and the drug was still more expensive than anything I'd been on. I searched the web and learned that Lialda was so expensive because it still had patent protection. And then I learned about the tiers system insurance companies use to price drugs. Other drugs I took were on lower tiers because they had been available for many years, lost patent protection, and were made in generic formats that were available at low costs. Lialda was on a higher tier, which meant it cost more and wasn't covered as thoroughly. At that point, I started reading health industry trade publications and medical journals to learn more about the drug, waiting for a day when it would be cheaper. Several years later, the maker of Lialda, Shire Plc, lost a patent suit and a cheaper generic version came out, which is what I now use. According to one pharma trade publication, losing the patent suit was a "rude surprise for Shire investors who had believed the $800 million drug was safe for a few more years." As the ancient proverb goes, one pharma investor's rude surprise is another patient's joy in being able to afford live-saving medicine. The experience of figuring out how to pay for a patent-protected drug made me really sensitive about insurance shopping. I realized that compared to how preexisting conditions were treated prior to Obamacare, I was privileged to be able to "shop" for insurance at all.[25]

After college, I was diagnosed with another chronic disease—primary sclerosing cholangitis (PSC), which affects my liver and bile ducts. Now that I have a collection of lifelong illnesses, I'm really sensitive to insurance coverage. In the past six years, I've moved to multiple states and purchased insurance through employers, government marketplaces, and insurance companies' websites. Though the process of securing insurance was byzantine each time I've shopped around, I always found coverage for my conditions. Because of Obamacare's protections for people with preexisting diseases, my conditions were no longer a scarlet letter that doomed me to surrender to terrible policies, like the ones my parents had to put up with. Insurance companies had to treat me like everyone else. This meant that I could start on a more level playing field without having to be financially burdened by something entirely outside of my control.

Because my income was very low during my mid-twenties and no one who I worked for offered benefits such as paid health insurance, I qualified for a subsidy that lowered the cost of my monthly premium. The money I saved on health insurance allowed me to stick with my writing career that for years paid lousily. It's possible I wouldn't have written this book if Obamacare hadn't passed because I wouldn't have had the focus or energy to develop a strong enough resume to get a publishing contract if much of my time was spent chasing health-care costs. My experience obtaining insurance under Obamacare made me think about all of the financial sacrifices my parents made for my health that they would have never been forced to make had we lived in a country where health care is treated as a human right rather than a capitalistic enterprise. The United States is one of very few developed countries that forces its residents to make such drastic tradeoffs between their health and financial well-being.

The benefits I received from Obamacare made me reconsider other ways the government helped my life. Due to my appreciation of fiscal responsibility, after high school I wanted to go to community college because it was cheaper than a four-year university. Mom said hell no. She said I'd have a better career if I got a four-year degree and that if we filled out a Free Application for Federal Student Aid (FAFSA) we could get some financial assistance from the government that would make a university education affordable.

After filling out a FAFSA, I ended up qualifying for Pell Grants and various scholarships that were awarded to me for being a first-generation college student who was just poor enough to qualify for financial aid. Once in college, my modest background helped me get accepted to prestigious organizations such as the McNair Scholars Program, designed to increase the percentage of graduate school degrees awarded to "underrepresented segments of society." McNair received money from the federal government so that it could pay its undergraduate students to conduct empirical research. Without McNair, I'd have to volunteer to get research experience, which is a pain for kids who come from working-class homes. I wasn't smart enough to obtain a full-ride Regent's scholarship or to get accepted to fancy out-of-state schools, but I ended up receiving so much financial aid that I came out of college with lots of research experience, no debt, and a little bit of savings. This put me in a great position to start publishing right out of college. I also worked two part-time jobs during college to do my part, but the fact of the matter is that other people worked even harder than me. I came out as well as I did because I got lucky, and I got lucky because the government decided to help people in my position.

Without government assistance and some nudging from my mom, I would not have attended a university until I saved enough money to afford a bachelor's degree. Even if I would have graduated after the delayed start, my diseases would have forced me to immediately take a job with decent insurance regardless of how it aligned with my career ambitions. Without Obamacare, I probably would have used my degree to get a business job at a big company with good employee insurance, even though that career route wouldn't fulfill me. Without government programs like Obamacare and Pell Grants, diseases and debt would have crushed my American dream.

I was able to follow my dreams because government assistance enabled me to gamble on moving to New York City to pursue internships at popular magazines earning minimum wage. Despite being a hick from the sticks and the son of an "uneducated" plumber and factory worker, I published multiple books in my twenties because I could spend my free time on pet projects instead of having to take odd jobs to cover medical bills and student loans. The government helped level the playing field so that I could have some of the advantages that rich kids take for granted.

When I was younger, I would have looked at someone getting government-provided health-care as a moocher. But I don't see it that way now. Sure, part of it is that I don't like thinking of myself that way. But there's more to it than that.

All the leeching I did through receiving insurance subsidies helped stabilize my life so that I could eventually get a job in my field that pays well. And now that I have a stable income, I pay a lot more in taxes than I used to, meaning that I'm now a contributor to the system and not just a recipient of its benefits. Instead of seeing those paycheck deductions as a scourge, I like to think that some of the money I pay the government is going to people who really need it. And that they might use the government assistance like I did, to help create a more promising and fulfilling life.

While I don't think my modest success is much to brag about, and I apologize if I sound like a humblebragging know-it-all, the fact is I traded dwindling job prospects in Brainard for life as a writer in our nation's financial capital. I outearn my parents while doing something I'm passionate about. I'm certainly a nobody in the grand scheme of things, but I am upwardly mobile, which is becoming rarer in working-class towns across middle America. My high school self would tell you that I got where I am because of my determination and grit. These days, I can't help but feel that the government spending that I once saw as problematic was in fact a linchpin to my success. My accomplishments were achievable because I was fortunate enough to get help that others lack. Since I've received so much assistance from the government, it'd be hypocritical of me to denigrate others who receive help, regardless of if it comes in the form of housing, food, or a place to work.[26]

The United States was in the midst of its Great Recession as I wrapped up high school, which prompted bailouts that my friends and I hated. The way the recession was handled made most Nebraskans detest anything that came out of Washington. It all felt like an injustice that rewarded companies for having terrible business models, and it did not align with our sense of personal responsibility.

With government distrust already high, along came Obamacare. People in Brainard hated the health-care law because it increased the role of the government in people's lives, which didn't seem financially prudent with our country in such debt. Plus, the law mocked our religion and community by making Catholics pay for contraception coverage. Republicans saw an opportunity in the animus and rallied to taint the career of Ben Nelson, Nebraska's last moderate senator, by creating an abortion controversy. These events coincided with a declining share of Democrat voters in the state. Nebraska kept moving to the right after Obamacare passed.

I still have issues with Obamacare, and I know a lot of people in Brainard have trouble keeping up with rising health insurance costs. My brother Kellen, who manages a physical therapy clinic, complains that it made paperwork more complicated and that some of the law's stipulations are counterproductive. How can I totally disagree with someone who dislikes a law after it made their life more difficult? I supported Obamacare after it improved my life. Self-interest influences all of our political beliefs.

Many concerns about Obamacare are real and valid. Our health-care laws could be greatly improved, and if US politicians worked together one day instead of just yelling at each other, there might be a way for Republicans and Democrats to compromise on a justifiable solution. Repealing Obamacare without a backup plan to cover people in need and those with preexisting conditions, which is what Republicans have repeatedly attempted, is a recipe for chaos and pain.

"Republicans came up with the wrong motto, 'repeal and replace,'" Ben Nelson told me. "No, it should it be 'replace and repeal.' They got their Rs mixed up, and that's why they have struggled with it ever since and they still are."

Health insurance access will always be an important issue, even more so when health crises occur. The fragility of our health systems was laid bare during the COVID-19 pandemic. Without a law protecting preexisting conditions, the toll could have been worse. And that law might not exist today had Nelson not worked his way into the Senate with a two-point victory back in 2000.

"I've been involved in politics in some capacity my entire adult life, and I'm human enough to wonder, does it matter, especially in Nebraska, right?" said former Democrat state chair and national committeeman Vince Powers. "I remember watching Ben Nelson bust the filibuster and I said it mattered. Had Ben Nelson not got elected, over twenty million Americans in a pandemic would not have insurance."

Instead of denouncing government expenditures like I used to, my own experience forces me to recognize how government spending helps people improve their lives. Obamacare contributed to a significant decline in the number of people who are without health insurance in the United States. Between

2010 and 2016, twenty million additional people obtained health insurance. Fewer people now go broke when they get sick. In the six years following Obamacare's passage, personal bankruptcies in the United States halved, and analysts cited expanded health insurance coverage as a primary factor in reducing those bankruptcies. The law gave millions with preexisting conditions, like myself, the ability to live more freely. The way I see things now, the government is just doing its part.[27]

Health care, immigration, and abortion are key issues in Nebraska's political story, as well as my own. To really grasp why Nebraska's elected leaders have become more reactionary in these and other areas, we must examine the money being thrown at state politicians.

CHAPTER FOUR

An Undivided House Falls

On the first day of Nebraska's 2018 legislative session, state senator Laura Ebke stood up and reminded her colleagues about the state's proud tradition of nonpartisanship. Quoting from a 1937 speech by George Norris—the legendary Nebraska politician behind the state's unique nonpartisan, single-house legislature—Ebke urged her fellow lawmakers to hold positions "without any partisan political obligation to any machine, to any boss, or to any alleged political leader."

Her speech was met with applause from the floor since many state senators wanted more resistance to the partisanship that had unfolded the previous year. A political science adjunct professor who represented a district thirty miles southwest of Lincoln, Ebke had already tussled with Nebraska's Republican governor Pete Ricketts. The speech let Nebraska's power brokers know that she intended to keep confronting our well-connected governor and the Republican Party that she had affiliated with for most of her life.[1]

Like several state senators who lost their seats in recent years, Ebke is a conservative who isn't conservative enough for our governor. She grew up in a "Goldwater family" and cast her first vote for Ronald Reagan, but the party's embrace of Donald Trump, combined with Ricketts targeting fellow Republicans, appalled her. In June 2016 she switched parties and became the only registered Libertarian in the forty-nine-member legislature. "It seemed to me I was no longer welcome," she told me.

Ricketts targeted Ebke and several other senators after they voted against him on a few key items during 2015, his first year in office. To the governor's dismay, the legislature repealed the death penalty, allowed certain undocumented youth to obtain driver's and occupational licenses, and raised the state's gas tax to fund bridge and road repairs. At the Nebraska Republican Party convention in May 2016, Ricketts denounced those legislators by name and insisted that party officials elect "platform Republicans," meaning politicians who would vote exactly as the state's GOP wanted.

Ricketts donated to opponents of those who voted against his wishes. Sometimes it came in the form of $5,000 or $10,000 contributions to specific candidates. Other times he poured money into groups like Nebraskans for the Death Penalty or the Nebraska Republican Party. According to data collected by the Nebraska Accountability and Disclosure Commission, which is the state agency that enforces campaign finance and lobbying laws, Ricketts spent about $360,000 of his own money to support political causes in Nebraska during 2016. Eight of the fourteen candidates he supported in 2016 won their races.[2]

"It wasn't about party. It was about issues," Ricketts told a reporter. "Not all of our Republicans are conservatives. They lost their principled foundation. We have a more conservative, better Legislature now."[3]

With the governor's backing, ultraconservative newcomers ousted Republican incumbents. The governor's involvement in local races "made that fear of being primaried on the right a much more visible threat to people who are in the legislature," said Democrat Sue Crawford, a state senator and Creighton University political science professor.

The attacks against Ebke became unruly. The state GOP accused her of bribery because she held a public screening of *It's a Wonderful Life*. According to the GOP, not only was Ebke in trouble, but anyone who exhibited their holiday spirit by attending the movie showing was at risk of violating the law. To compete with the onslaught of attack ads, Ebke did more fundraising when she ran for reelection. When Ebke ran in 2014, she spent $81,000 on her race. In 2018 she spent more than triple that on a race she ended up losing.[4]

"It is somewhat obscene, I think, that I should have to spend $200,000 or more to win a race for a position that pays $12,000 a year," she said. "It is kind of crazy and it is concerning."

It's common for wealthy political figures to target opponents. What's happening in Nebraska to candidates like Ebke is egregious because of the state's long history of political independence.

To most Nebraskans I know, state politics is about as exciting as cleaning horse crap out of a barn. Despite the indifference to the inner workings of lawmaking, the legislature still commands respect and recognition. I remember taking field trips to Lincoln and clamoring to see museums and sports stadiums, only to get stuck in government-run buildings for much of the day. Teachers, parents, and other adults in Brainard were mostly apolitical, but they felt it important to instill in us a belief that Nebraska's approach to governing set us apart from other states.

The indoctrination carried on from elementary through high school, where my classmates and I were taught about the Nebraska Legislature's history. In 1934 about 60 percent of Nebraska voters, including nine in ten counties and precincts, voted for an amendment to create a single-house legislature, also known as a unicameral or unicam. During the fall of that year, George Norris, the architect of the unicameral, wore out his car traveling to town halls across the state to get his message out that bicameral state legislatures are too expensive and corrupt. Most of the state's four hundred newspapers ignored or opposed the unicameral. Only two papers supported it. The editorial board of the state's most influential paper, the *Omaha World-Herald*, bitterly fought the amendment. The quest consumed Norris.[5]

"He would pay his own expenses and was prepared, if necessary, to contribute to the general campaign chest," wrote Norris biographer Richard Lowitt. "Because of lack of funding, no broadcasts were scheduled. He would have to get his message across at meetings in county courthouses, city halls, and other places secured at minimal or no expense."[6]

Having to fund just *one* house with less than fifty lawmakers was a fiscally conservative move that cut down the cost and size of state government. John Norton, a Nebraska farmer who served in the state legislature and US Congress during the early 1900s, promoted the one-house system because it would save "time, talk, and money." The first unicameral session, in 1937–1938, cost taxpayers $103,000, in comparison with the $203,000 the previous session. Cutting governmental costs proved to be an attractive pitch to voters enduring the Great Depression. Another influence that drove unicameral supporters was a contempt for party politics. Norris said, "Partisanship is one of the great evils of our government, when carried into avenues and into places where, officially, there is no politics."[7]

Norris helped give the Nebraska Legislature a distinctive structure, which has made it an icon in a region that gets routinely ignored by presidential candidates, the news media, and pop culture. Nebraskans cling to it like we do to our other cultural exports. Because we're often not even considered in the national conversation, people back home *still* like to bring up the time Patrick Swayze, John Leguizamo, and Wesley Snipes stopped in Butler County to film *To Wong Foo* more than twenty years ago. Our celebrities receive more admiration than they would in more populated areas. My mom once released a handful of audible claps in a Lincoln movie theater when Nebraska native Larry the Cable Guy appeared on-screen wearing a Husker baseball hat in his B-movie comedy about health inspectors. We dip our cinnamon rolls into chili and chow down on corn-fed beef steaks with reverence as if we're taking part in a church sacrament. In villages across the state, we raise money for our volunteer fire departments by blocking off the main drag and selling Busch Light by the can that people guzzle while they sway to Garth Brooks covers. We take pride in being the only state whose electric producers are all public utilities. Politics is something most Nebraskans would rather avoid, but it's cool that we're one of just two states, along with Maine, who split out our electoral votes by congressional district. And we like to acknowledge that we have the most unusual state government system in the United States.

"Situated out on the plains, with no mountains, no natural lakes of any size, and no striking geographic features, Nebraska may seem to some an uninteresting, nondescript, run-of-the-mill backwater," wrote Nebraska author James Hewitt. "But when the focus is on the government, on the essential relationship between the governors and the governed, on the social contract whereby citizens yield some of their freedom to an entity that will aid and protect them, Nebraska takes a backseat to no one."[8]

Like the ridiculously long NCAA-record sellout streak of our university's football team or the peculiarities of a cabbage-infested, doughy Runza meat pocket, the Nebraska Legislature is a quirky homegrown cultural institution admired across the state. From kindergarten through high school graduation, I attended the same public school building that sits two blocks from my parents' house in Brainard. From there, I spent five years in the state capital, Lincoln, attending our flagship university. At both institutions, most people I encountered praised the unicameral whenever local government came up. We were taught, and believed, that the poisonous partisanship found across the country wasn't as potent in our legislature because it wasn't officially controlled by political parties.

As I started to write this book, I came to a depressing realization: the state's single-house legislature may be devoid of party labels, but it's become pretty ideological. The unicameral used to have less bickering than many other state chambers, but those days are gone. Many sources say the legislature became more partisan since Pete Ricketts became governor, but they acknowledge he's far from being the first person to inject partisanship into the body. Norris and the prairie progressives who backed the unicameral might not recognize Nebraska's current legislature.

Governors have never been poor, but extraordinarily wealthy governors have become more common in recent years. Ricketts is one of several governors nationwide to belong to a family worth billions. His father, Joe, is the billionaire founder of TD Ameritrade. Joe is known in media circles for purchasing and later shutting down the local-news websites DNAinfo and Gothamist when their employees unionized. Although he made much of his money in Nebraska, Joe lives in Wyoming to avoid income tax, and the Nebraska company that made him a fortune was sold to an out-of-state firm while his son was governor. Joe has long been a major donor to Republicans, and his sons are active in the party, too: Pete Ricketts chaired the Republican Governors Association, whose purpose is to get GOP governors elected around the nation. His brother Todd was finance chair of the Republican National Committee and supervised the fundraising for Trump's reelection campaign. Among the Ricketts family's many possessions is the Chicago Cubs baseball team.[9]

In 2006, Pete Ricketts made a bid for the US Senate. He lost by 28 percentage points to Democrat Ben Nelson despite dropping $12 million of his own money on the race and outspending Nelson. Nine years later, Ricketts swept into the governor's office on a pledge to create jobs, cut taxes, and oppose illegal immigration, which is the same platform his predecessor Dave Heineman used. Despite outspending his opponents again, Ricketts barely squeaked by in the Republican primary, winning a six-way race by 2,200 votes. In capturing 26 percent of Republican voters, Ricketts emerged from the primary with the lowest winning percentage ever for a Nebraska GOP gubernatorial nominee. After the primary, Ricketts easily cruised to victory in the general election. Once he became governor, his position, wealth, and relationships with other powerful people allowed him to influence the legislature by boosting his preferred candidates into office.[10]

State senators I spoke to were disturbed by Ricketts's alleged dark-money connections. Leading up to the 2016 elections, groups like Americans for Prosperity and Trees of Liberty made robocalls and sent postcards attacking those who voted to repeal the death penalty. The ads used false statistics about senators' attendance records, lied about voting records, and blamed candidates for tax increases that were passed by public vote.

During the 2018 elections, a Virginia-based group called the 10th Amendment Project sent mailings intended to raise hysteria over property taxes, which Ricketts and his colleagues want to lower. In one instance, the 10th Amendment Project postcards slammed a farmer running for the unicam for receiving government subsidies that, the ad alleges, lowered his personal taxes. Determining who is funding these ads is difficult due to America's deregulated campaign-finance laws, but several state senators said Ricketts is likely behind the deceptive ads. Reporting by the *Omaha World-Herald* and the campaign spending watchdog group Center for Responsive Politics showed that the treasurer of the 10th Amendment Project was also treasurer of a few other political action committees (PACs) that ran attack ads against Democrats. Pete Ricketts's father contributed a million dollars to one of these groups, and the governor's brother Todd helped these PACs fundraise. The ad agency that placed the attack ads in Nebraska radio stations also worked on Ricketts's own campaign. Shortly after those ads appeared, Ricketts's campaign manager became a senior vice president at the ad agency's parent company.[11]

"The folks who aren't getting attacked are the folks endorsed by Ricketts. It all fits together too nicely to not be coordinated," said John Hansen, president of the Nebraska Farmers Union. In a news conference at the Nebraska capitol, Hansen was more direct in pointing the finger at Ricketts. "If you're not the anointed one, you're the targeted one."[12]

Ricketts denied having ties to these groups, but most of the sources I spoke with don't believe him. Ricketts is a founder of the Nebraska chapter for Americans for Prosperity, which is controlled by the Koch brothers. The Kochs were also behind Trees of Liberty, reported Politico and HuffPost. The *Nation* reported that prior to getting elected as governor in 2014, Ricketts appeared at a summit of wealthy donors organized by the Kochs. When he ran for governor, Ricketts received donations from Koch Industries. Aside from spending directly on local races and endorsing opponents of incumbent Republicans, numerous sources said Ricketts uses his connections to other political power brokers to direct money against his targets.[13]

"His unabashed goal is to take control of the Nebraska Legislature," said former state senator Roy Baker, a registered Republican and former superintendent of a public school outside of Lincoln named after unicameral proponent George Norris. "He is very ideologically inclined rather than looking at other evidence or finding common ground on issues. . . . When you consider the amount of money the governor has and his dogma-driven agenda, it is a lethal combination."

In conversations with state lawmakers, Ricketts was described as an intelligent and disciplined person who is good with numbers and dissecting balance sheets. After his defeat in the 2006 senate race, he displayed persistence and determination, embedding himself deeper into the Nebraska GOP by becoming a national committeeman and founding a think tank as he waited eight years for the right time to run again. When he ran for governor, he showed political savvy by running an aggressive campaign and rebranding his candidacy by tweaking the topics he focused on. A few lawmakers said that he's easy to chat and laugh with when you see him face-to-face. For all his qualities, others painted a picture of reactionary vindictiveness. "Pete Ricketts, he's a nice guy," Baker said. "He's just a damn dirty politician."

Ricketts has displayed a tendency to dismiss those he disagrees with. When Nebraska author Ted Genoways won an award from the Nebraska Center for the Book, Ricketts refused to honor it, even though he hadn't even read the book, because he viewed Genoways as a "political activist." When University of Nebraska professors were honored as "admirals in the Great Navy of the State of Nebraska," Ricketts revoked the tongue-in-cheek award due to a political dustup on campus. He refused to give the Nebraska teachers union a ceremonial proclamation because the group opposed his stance on a bill about reading requirements. After Ricketts helped bring back the death penalty, the proposed date for the first execution fell on the birthday of Ernie Chambers, a state senator who fought the death penalty for more than forty years and frequently opposed Ricketts. (The execution didn't end up taking place on Chambers's birthday and the date changed eight times before it was all over.)[14]

Veteran legislature clerk Patrick O'Donnell said that Ricketts is like Trump in that he'll almost reflexively take a side without considering all the evidence. He said that most of the people the governor surrounded himself with are

unlikely to disagree with him or consider alternative options. "Pete Ricketts
is a Trumponian in more than one way," said O'Donnell, adding that he believed the governor would be flattered to be compared to Trump. "It's kind of
Pete Ricketts's way or the highway."

When Republican businesswoman Janet Palmtag ran against one of Ricketts's legislative appointees in 2020, the Nebraska GOP came after Palmtag with
radio ads and mailers that attacked her siding with "Lincoln liberals, atheists,
and radical extremists." Even though Palmtag had conservative bona fides as
former president of the Nebraska Realtors Association and endorsements from
notable Republicans like Representative Jeff Fortenberry and former governor
Dave Heineman, that wasn't enough to absolve her of the sin of running against
Ricketts's chosen candidate, his former press secretary Julie Slama. Palmtag
called the attack ads "disappointing, evil, and un-Christian." Heineman told a
reporter that GOP leaders should be ashamed of smearing a lifelong Republican and that the attacks were "despicable and disgusting." After the Nebraska
GOP sent out a flyer that featured Palmtag next to a photoshopped chain and
picture of black state senator Ernie Chambers, Heineman and former governor
Bob Kerrey cowrote Slama a letter condemning the ad as racist. Heineman and
Kerrey wrote that if Slama didn't denounce the ads, she would "risk becoming the Steve King of Nebraska," a reference to the white nationalist former
congressman from Iowa. The Nebraska GOP responded to Heineman's and
Kerrey's criticism with mockery. The party's executive director said the letter
from the septuagenarian former governors "uses all the tricks in the 'woke'
playbook" and that the criticism from the former governors was "very, very
rich." Heineman said that he was not surprised by the party's response.[15]

As one of the people defeated by a Ricketts-backed candidate and targeted
by dark money groups, former state senator Jerry Johnson believes the governor has ties to the organizations who attacked him. "If you leaned at all away
from being a total conservative, you were targeted," said Johnson, a Republican Trump voter who used to represent Brainard in the legislature. Johnson's
most notable vote against Ricketts came on the death penalty. "I cannot mor-
ally reconcile the notion that a vote of mine can result in the eventual death of
another person," Johnson said. "I campaigned on a pro-life agenda." Ricketts,
a self-described Catholic, campaigned on a pro-life agenda, but he didn't see
eye-to-eye with Johnson, or the pope, for that matter. After the legislature
repealed the death penalty, Ricketts spent $300,000 of his own money to get

the issue on the next ballot, where voters decided to bring the death penalty back. Shortly after, the state executed an inmate for the first time in over two decades.[16]

There were other times Johnson chose a different route than the one advised by the governor. According to Johnson, Ricketts pressured him to support an agriculture-focused bill. Johnson said that after he refused to vote for the bill, the senator who sponsored the bill approached Johnson on the floor. The bill's sponsor, who aligned with Ricketts on the issue, told Johnson, "If you don't support this bill, I know you are up for reelection and I'll do whatever I can so that you don't get reelected." Using a business analogy, Johnson said that the governor "has gone too far in trying to pick his own board of directors."

"This governor has got Republican senators scared," said Greg Adams, a Republican who served as speaker of the legislature from 2013 to 2015. Adams continued:

> The Republican Party in Nebraska is not what it used to be. It is not. I've sent letters to them thinking in a very arrogant way, having been speaker of the legislature, maybe the letters would make a difference. But they don't. I don't even get a response, whatever. It's not the same Republican Party that I knew. It has become too politicized. It is about gamesmanship, not about policy making. It's about money. It's not about building relationships. They have lost sight of what Republicanism really means.

In the year after Ricketts first got elected, the American Conservative Union rated the Nebraska Legislature's support for conservative causes at 35 percent. It was during this legislative session that state senators overrode the governor on the death penalty, DACA, and the gas tax, which led to the targeting of incumbent Republicans like Johnson. Just three years later, Nebraska's conservative score jumped to 71 percent. So according to one of the oldest and most powerful conservative lobbyists in the country, the unicameral's support for a conservative agenda doubled within Ricketts's first term in power. It's hard to fathom that Nebraska residents suddenly became much more conservative in a short time span. What's more logical is that the way candidates were chosen and kept in line changed.[17]

———

For nearly seventy years following the 1934 unicameral amendment, state sen-ators served as long as they pleased. In 2000, Nebraska voters approved an amendment to the state's constitution that limited state senators to two con-secutive four-year terms. Most of the sources I interviewed agreed that a pri-mary reason term limits were implemented was so that the legislature could remove Ernie Chambers, a liberal state senator who represented north Omaha from 1970 until 2008, when he was termed-limited out.

Chambers was often the sole black member of the unicameral. He's known for an outspokenness that's led to national attention when he's done things like sue God for natural disasters or compare police to terrorists. Chambers is also an expert of legislative procedures and knows how to delay and kill bills better than anybody else, according to many sources interviewed for this book. Chambers, who declined to be interviewed, was forced out for four years but was reelected in 2012 and again in 2016. Chambers was held out of office for just one term, but researchers showed that term limits had the broader effect of making the unicameral more partisan.[18]

A few years after term limits were introduced to the unicameral, political scientists Gerald Wright and Brian Schaffner found that votes in Nebraska's legislature showed consistent patterns of polarization that were akin to the partisanship found among Kansas's state lawmakers. The far right tilt of the Kansas Legislature led Thomas Frank to write his best-selling book *What's the Matter With Kansas?* in which he mocked Kansans for obsessing over wedge issues and voting against their own interests. In just a short time, the Nebraska Legislature designed for nonpartisanship had become nearly as extreme as Kansas, the poster child for right-wing experimentation.[19]

Since term limits went into effect, political parties have been much more active in recruiting candidates, said Patrick O'Donnell, the legislature's clerk since 1978. Subsequently, the kind of candidates who run now are more ideo-logical and locked into their positions. It's now rare that a passion for a given set of issues motivates candidates to run, he said. Instead, candidates run be-cause they were recruited.

"What term limits has done is it has brought so many more elections at a time and so the opportunity to influence change arises faster, so you put more effort into trying to change and so that gets more party-driven," said Republi-can Chris Langemeier, a former state senator from Schuyler who represented my district. "Your opportunity to swing Republican control or Democratic control is exposed every two years. The parties get very involved to try to sway that. And with it more party-driven, you have less independence of the Nebraska Legislature."

Five years after term limits were introduced, Nebraska elected as governor the former executive director of the state's Republican Party, Dave Heineman. As we explored earlier, Heineman pulled off a surprise victory against Tom Osborne, the popular football coach and congressman. One of the tactics Heineman used against Osborne was pushing rightward on immigration. After getting elected, Heineman exerted his influence over the legislature, according to multiple sources. In their study of the Nebraska Legislature, political scientists Seth Masket and Boris Shor wrote that Heineman was "seen as an exceptionally partisan creature with a hands-on approach to politicking."[20]

Former state senator Baker told me that at an event in Omaha for GOP officeholders and candidates during the summer of 2014, Heineman told the group in attendance that he did not subscribe to the idea that the unicameral should be nonpartisan. According to Baker, Heineman said, "Anybody who thinks Nebraska's unicameral is nonpartisan . . . that's bullshit." When I brought the subject up to Heineman, the former governor said he didn't recall that conversation. Heineman suggested that what he might have meant was that the idea that voters don't know the party of their unicameral candidates is nonsense. Baker left with a different impression. Baker said that Heineman "was pretty firm and adamant that you are crazy if you think this is not partisan."

Masket and Shor found that Nebraska's legislature rapidly became more partisan over the past decade and that political parties were overcoming the unicameral's rules that were designed to curb them. In their study of the unicameral in which they analyzed campaign finance records, observed voting patterns, and conducted interviews with insiders, Masket and Shor concluded that during the 1990s, the Nebraska Legislature had one of the lowest levels of polarization in the nation. But within ten years after introducing term limits, the unicameral was polarizing faster than any state law-making body in the nation. Voting coalitions in the unicameral used to split by particular issues, not by party. That old way of doing business got usurped by partisan politics. "I bet I was on the Republican side 80 percent of the time," said Douglas Kristensen, a Republican who served as speaker of the legislature in the early 2000s. "In today's partisan wars, I'd be a RINO [Republican in name only] because 20 percent of the time I didn't follow the party line."[21]

In her 2005 book about the unicameral, University of Nebraska journalism professor Charlyne Berens predicted that term limits would make state lawmakers less independent. State senators with less law-making experience are more likely to seek help from the executive branch. Berens said that term limits would help ensure that Nebraska's executive branch would become the most dominant branch. Political science validated her prediction.[22]

"With at least a quarter of the chamber now regularly being turned out of office, a handful of partisan actors, including the Republican governor and Democratic political operatives, have become intensely involved with recruiting partisan candidates to run for office and keeping them faithful to a partisan agenda once in office," Masket and Shor wrote. They went on to add: "The state's new legislators are increasingly being chosen for their expected adherence to party agendas, as determined by party leaders and the governor. And the donation patterns of elite campaign contributors are increasingly following a partisan and ideological pattern, suggesting that to the extent that legislators want to keep their donors happy, they will do so by voting more with their party."[23]

The adherence to party politics is on display whenever the governor fills open senate seats. For instance, the conservative state senator John Murante was elected state treasurer after running unopposed. To fill Murante's seat, Ricketts appointed a twenty-eight-year-old attorney, Andrew La Grone, who worked in Murante's office. Ricketts called his young pick "a solid conservative." The governor also appointed his twenty-two-year-old press secretary, Julie Slama, to fill an open senate seat. Ricketts told the *Wall Street Journal*, "You also have to have the right people in the Legislature, people who are going to be philosophically conservative." The GOP was more clear about its intentions in its party platform: "The Nebraska Republican Party believes in a partisan legislature as an efficient and accountable branch of government."[24]

Partisanship was already brewing in the legislature before Ricketts became governor. In some ways, Ricketts merely used his wealth to expand what his predecessors did. As state senators turn over at quicker rates and the governor influences who wins seats, basic civilities are eroding away, numerous state senators told me. Crawford said it used to be common courtesy that if people were going to run for committee chairs, they'd send a letter to every member of the legislature so that the senators knew who'd be running for each position. When committee chairs were selected following the 2016 elections, people didn't announce they were running, because the Republican majority already chose the committee heads behind closed doors. A bloc of twenty-seven voters banded together and on the first day of the session selected seventeen Republicans, one Democrat, and one Libertarian to committee chairs. A few committee chairs were awarded to Republicans who were in their first week in office.

"Some of the committee chairs were obviously unqualified to lead a committee," said state senator John McCollister, a registered Republican in Omaha. "They were freshmen, so of course they did not know how to lead a committee."

Alongside the partisan divide in selecting committee chairs, the legislature spent its first month fighting over filibuster rules. State senator Burke Harr, a registered Democrat out of Omaha, said this polarized environment altered how legislative aides and staffers choose their bosses. Many staffers work exclusively with Republican or Democratic senators. But some used to flip between working for conservatives and liberals when the person they worked for left office and a new batch of senators flowed in. Now staffers are being told that they can't ever work across party lines, according to Harr.

Harr said he also used to get deference on bills that were important to his constituents but of no consequence to his conservative colleagues. That's no longer the case. Harr presented a bill that would restrict the sale of ivory in Nebraska. Since the state isn't exactly an ivory marketplace hub, Harr said it was "an innocuous bill." But he wanted to pass it because the bill mattered to constituents of his in the Girl Scouts and Omaha's Henry Doorly Zoo. The bill was met with resistance and defeated.

"There has always been a core of four or five [state senators] that were hyperpartisan," Harr said. "But the leaders were never hyperpartisan. Now the leaders are."

Veteran lobbyist Walt Radcliffe has noticed a lot of changes in the unicameral since he began working in the legislature fifty years ago. No longer do Republicans and Democrats regularly socialize with each other outside of planned functions. He said that over the years the most effective lawmakers have been the ones who walk around the floor talking with colleagues across the aisle. Since term limits went into effect, there have been fewer senators who walk around the floor trying to make deals. Nowadays most lawmakers are either planted in their seat or are absent from the floor during deliberations.

Numerous state senators and lobbyists shared that they see lawmakers holding back—and in some cases changing their votes—because they're afraid of overstepping the governor. Instead of voting how they really feel about a bill, some lawmakers vote with the governor to avoid controversy.

"It is harder to throw the bullshit flag at the governor than it is at somebody else," Radcliffe said. "So there's a natural deference there and if people haven't been around long enough to realize that the governor isn't always necessarily right, they are going to fall in line a lot more."

After a redistricting reform bill sponsored by a GOP lawmaker passed in the legislature, the governor vetoed it. Just one more vote was needed to override the veto, which seemed possible given that five senators didn't vote the first time around. "Because of pressure from the governor, the sponsor of the bill chose not to initiate an override," McCollister said. After declining to push the legislation forward, the bill's sponsor, Senator Murante, rose within the party, gained the governor's endorsement, and became state treasurer. His vacant Senate position was filled by his former aide. As treasurer, he came under fire for not holding a public bid when he gave about $600,000 of taxpayer money to his former employer to create TV ads featuring himself.[25]

When a bill to end a ban on waiting periods before felons could vote was put in front of the legislature, it passed with just thirteen senators voting against it. The governor vetoed the bill. When the bill went back, the legislature was unable to override the veto because the number of votes against the bill increased to twenty-three. Those who changed their votes were Republicans. "I can't necessarily pinpoint if it was fear of retribution, but there isn't a logical reason why you'd have that big of a swing," said state senator Tony Vargas.[26]

When listening to people complain about the governor's influence over the state's legislative branch, it's easy for some progressives to fashion Pete Ricketts as a supervillain since they almost instinctively loathe some of his characteristics. He's a savvy businessman who comes from a family of extreme wealth. He's trying to widen his political influence to do things like defund public education. He's well-connected to the most powerful conservatives in the country. Comedian and political commentator John Oliver went so far as to mock the governor for bearing a resemblance to Lex Luthor. However, that characterization is far too simplistic.

Sociologists like to point out that those in power make rules to stay in power. Nebraska governors aren't immune to this dynamic. As I've worked on this book, I've listened to sources complain about power abuses from governors who left office long ago. In a biography about Democrat governor Jim Exon, a friend of the former governor said Exon believed "that the reason God created governors was to control the legislature." University of Nebraska–Omaha political scientist Paul Landow told me that every governor has tried to exert their influence over the Nebraska Legislature.[27]

In a 1961 study of the unicameral by the University of Nebraska School of Journalism, the majority of the surveyed state lawmakers said they appreciated not being linked to a political party because it allowed to them work independently and more freely. The governors included in the study offered a much different opinion.[28]

Most of the former governors and lieutenant governors polled said the unicameral would be better off if it became more partisan. One former governor said that the "non-partisan part of the Legislature is a weak link." Another governor said that "non-partisanship in the Legislature is a downfall for the state." The results of the survey made me think of the Bruce Springsteen lyric, "Poor man want to be rich. Rich man want to be king. And a king ain't satisfied 'til he rules everything."[29]

Ricketts operates under a different set of rules and incentives than previous governors, who neither had billionaire fathers nor lived in an era of unlimited corporate spending on political campaigns where donors could remain hidden. Legislators in today's unicameral may feel Ricketts is overreaching, but it's entirely possible previous governors would make these same moves if they had the resources to do so and the law on their side. It's feasible that Democrats would do the same thing if given the chance. Former Nebraska Democratic Party executive director Barry Rubin told me that if a Democrat won the governorship, he'd advise them to influence the legislature the way Ricketts has. "If you want to pass an agenda, then yeah, put more of your own people into office," he said.

I understand that following campaign paper trails is tedious, particularly when donors can't be tracked. Buried in statistics and legalese, the subject feels like it bears no connection to people's personal lives. But it is the glue connecting every topic we've covered. How politicians vote on abortion, death penalty, religious issues, immigration, education, and health care is influenced by who funds their campaigns and pays for attack ads. The way private and personal issues impact our lives can be affected by deep-pocketed and hidden donors from afar. When billionaires aim to strip DACA youth of their rights, they make life harder for immigrants in towns like Schuyler who are filling unwanted jobs and keeping our state's population from shrinking. When lawmakers are targeted by a self-described pro-life governor for voting against the death penalty because their Christian faith tells them its unjust, it sends a message that politicians use religion as a way to garner votes when it's convenient. When elected officials stymie health-care reforms passed by popular vote, it shows that they defer to well-financed donors over the people.

"Campaign finance is like the gateway issue to every other issue that you might care about, whether it be education or tax reform or foreign policy," said Ann Ravel, former chair of the Federal Election Committee (FEC). "Campaign finance is at the heart of all of the policy decisions that are being made."[30]

To understand the importance of campaign finance regulations, consider why they were adopted to begin with. Laws limiting political financing contributions were enacted in the early twentieth century in response to the growing influence of robber barons who bought candidates and funded political machines. At a time of growing financial inequality, these reforms were put in place to protect ordinary people's political representation. Other contribution limits came from backlash following the Watergate scandal, in which the money to pay burglars came from Richard Nixon's reelection campaign.[31]

The most notorious deregulation of campaign financing came in the Supreme Court's 2010 *Citizens United* decision. The ruling effectively stripped political spending restrictions and made it more difficult to track donors. *Citizens United* is the poster child of monied interests controlling governmental institutions, but other court decisions extended its reach. For instance, in *SpeechNow v. FEC*, an appeals court eliminated limits on how much money individuals could give to political action groups.

Nebraska's Campaign Finance Limitation Act—which opened up public funds to candidates who voluntarily agreed to predefined spending limits—got struck down in 2012 because the Supreme Court ruled against a similar Arizona law in 2011. Many of the attack ads that groups like Americans for Prosperity and Trees of Liberty launch against legislators get classified as "issue ads." Political-disclosure watchdogs say they don't have the authority to police "issue ads" due to cases like *FEC v. Wisconsin Right to Life* that ruled so-called issue ads can't be banned leading up elections, leaving PACs free to run ads right up to voting day as long as the ads don't explicitly endorse candidates. There's also the *McCutcheon v. FEC* ruling that eliminated a limit on how much money a single donor can give to candidates or political parties.[32]

Following a rash of campaign finance deregulation, the country's richest citizens poured more money into elections. The Center for Responsive Politics reported that in the 2018 election cycle, less than one-half of 1 percent of donors accounted for more than $7 of every $10 given to federal candidates, PACs, political parties, and outside political groups. Another campaign watchdog group found that in the 2012 elections, "one ten-thousandth" of Americans, or "1% of 1%," were responsible for 28 percent of all disclosed political contributions. Nebraska's governor would fall into this bucket. In the 2020 election cycle, the Ricketts family spent about $1 million on Nebraska races and political organizations. This figure doesn't include funds sent to dark money groups.[33]

"The Citizens United decision shifted the balance of power from parties built on broad consensus to individuals who were wealthy and zealous enough to spend millions of dollars from their own funds. By definition, this empowered a tiny, atypical minority of the population," wrote journalist Jane Mayer in *Dark Money: The Hidden History of the Billionaires behind the Rise of the Radical Right*. Mayer added: "Contrary to predictions, the Citizens United decision hadn't triggered a tidal wave of corporate political spending. Instead, it had empowered a few extraordinarily rich individuals with extreme and often self-serving agendas."[34]

At a time when each consecutive election is more expensive than the last, most Americans don't support unlimited campaign spending. In a 2018 poll by the Pew Research Center, more than three-fourths of adults in the United States agreed that "there should be limits on the amount of money individuals and groups can spend on campaigns." Strong support for campaign spending restrictions were found among both Republicans and Democrats. About two-thirds of Pew's respondents supported new laws to curb political spending. Given how rare bipartisan support is these days, it's encouraging to see that there are issues like this where people across the political spectrum agree on something.[35]

Unlike many other states, Nebraska places no limits on individual contributions to political campaigns. The removal of campaign finance restrictions correlates with a significant uptick in political spending. Total expenditures during Nebraska state legislative races in 2000 totaled $1.7 million, according to Nebraska Accountability and Disclosure Commission data. By 2018, that figure increased to $6.5 million. Keep in mind, these figures only include the spending that can be tracked, and the total amount spent on political ads is likely much higher due to the flood of dark money. Former Nebraska governor and US senator Ben Nelson said that what is happening to the unicameral is "sad, very sad."[36]

Other prominent politicians agree. Republican Doug Bereuter built his political career in the unicameral before becoming the longest-serving congressman in Nebraska history. Bereuter said that when he was in the unicameral, votes only became polarized when election laws were being debated or districts were redrawn. "Several of our recent governors have attempted to have a greater impact politically on the people that are elected to the legislature to advance their own agendas," he said. Unlike most of today's elected Republicans, Bereuter acknowledges that *Citizens United* was a "terrible decision" by the Supreme Court. Although Bereuter thinks that what's happening to the unicameral is a shame, he believes it's possible that Nebraska's legislature could eventually become less partisan. "It may depend on who sits in the governor's office in the future," Bereuter said.

Frank Daley, executive director of the Nebraska Accountability and Disclosure Commission, acknowledged that changes to campaign regulations make his line of work a "First Amendment landmine field." He said he'd noticed that campaigns had become more expensive and the unicameral more partisan, but that the Nebraska Legislature is still more cordial than the law-making bodies of other states. When pressed on whether he's worried the governor is dismantling the separation between the executive and legislative branches, he gave me a measured reply: "Anybody in our system can give as much money as they want to any candidate. I mean, that's just the way it is."

That's exactly the problem, according to W. Don Nelson, a veteran insider of Nebraska politics who served on the staffs of Democratic politicians like Ben Nelson and Bob Kerrey. Nelson says the courts designed campaign finance laws to benefit rich politicians: "So often in today's political world the scandal is never what's illegal. The scandal is what's legal."

The influence of money in politics is eroding the independence of lawmakers. GOP politicians have repeatedly tried to dismantle the way Nebraska splits its electoral votes. They are motivated to move Nebraska to a winner-take-all state so they can secure more votes for their national party and avoid the occasional embarrassment of a Democrat winning Omaha, like Barack Obama did in 2008 and Joe Biden did in 2020. Meanwhile, megadonors are doing their best to turn the unicam, an iconic feature of our cultural identity, into a generic assembly. Both of these dynamics are attempts to eliminate distinct features of Nebraska politics and make us more similar to every other state, which is not a flaw in the approach but the design.[37]

Court case rulings and campaign finance reports are esoteric to the people in Brainard, who just want to relax over an episode of *Wheel of Fortune* after they're done working with their hands all day. But the continued gutting of finance rules matters in places like my hometown because $10,000 here and there can have a big impact in rural districts of 35,000 people where campaigns have been, until recently, cheap. Because, unlike other states, the Nebraska Legislature doesn't have a house *and* a senate, just forty-nine people make up the state's law-making body. Deposing a few lawmakers in a small chamber significantly alters the makeup of the body while pumping Washington-like partisanship and gridlock into an institution known for being above party nonsense. The phrase "THE SALVATION OF THE STATE IS WATCHFULNESS IN THE CITIZEN" is inscribed over our Capitol's main entrance, yet much of the money influencing our elections is intentionally untraceable. Nebraska will continue to take pride in its unusual legislature, but despite what its students are taught in state history courses, the unicameral's absence of party labels is turning into window dressing.

If you step outside the Nebraska Capitol and walk up the elevated balcony on the north side of the building, you gain an unobstructed view of brick buildings that sit past a manicured promenade equipped with fountains, flags, and trimmed lawns enclosed by parking structures, government offices, and an abandoned sports arena. These buildings are part of the other notable public institution in Lincoln—the University of Nebraska. Just seven blocks separate the university and the capitol, but they're miles apart politically.

CHAPTER FIVE

Dear Old Nebraska U

After wrapping up Friday classes on a fall afternoon, political science professor Ari Kohen ventured to his office hoping to finish a little work before heading out for the weekend. When he opened his inbox, he noticed that the dean of his college and the chancellor's office had left urgent messages. They'd been contacted by the chief of staff of US Representative Jeff Fortenberry, whose district includes Kohen's employer, the University of Nebraska–Lincoln (UNL). Fortenberry's staffer Reyn Archer wanted to discuss why the professor supported vandalism. Confused by the request, Kohen quickly set up a call with Archer.

For nearly an hour, the two engaged in a bewildering and wide-ranging conversation that covered the First Amendment, university politics, blackface, vandalism, the broken windows criminology theory, elitism, and more. Most of the conversation was cordial. A few exchanges were politely contentious, and one particular passage came off as a not-so-subtle threat.[1]

Kohen and Archer repeatedly disagreed as to whether the professor was "liking vandalism." Archer brought up that there are "people who are Republicans who are offended by professors" and that "professors have been called out for denigrating individual students for saying things for supporting certain political persuasions." When Kohen asked what this had to do with him and why his bosses were brought into the issue, Archer replied that he contacted the dean and chancellor to "remind them that we live in a community and it is important to remember that faculty not condone vandalism, and even worse, violence."

The congressman's chief of staff then laid out his message more directly. "Frankly, we have a First Amendment opportunity to basically put you out there in front of everybody. And put this clearly as, 'Why is this professor liking vandalism? We can do that publicly," said Archer, as the sternness of his voice punctuated each syllable. "Would you like that? That's our First Amendment right, too."

124

What did Kohen do that was so heinous that it prompted a congressman's chief of staff to spend his day arguing with a professor and petitioning university administrators? What sort of violence was he endorsing that would offend taxpayers like my mom and dad, who support the university and send their kids there?

Kohen's sin was liking a fart joke. Bored and scrolling through Facebook on an uneventful Sunday, Kohen saw an image of a Fortenberry campaign sign that had been altered to say "Jeff Fartenbarry." For good measure, whoever desecrated the sign put googly eyes on the congressman's face. Kohen did not damage the sign himself or post the picture. He just liked it on Facebook. A Fortenberry campaign staffer screenshotted the Facebook like and shared it with Fortenberry's Washington office, which was followed by Archer's outreach to the university.[2]

Archer didn't seem to realize that Kohen recorded their phone call. Kohen shared the recording with a left-leaning Nebraska politics blog. The phone conversation found its way to YouTube. During the call, Kohen warned Archer that the "optics" of targeting a professor over a fart joke would be terrible for Fortenberry. Archer disagreed. The test got put to the public.

The zany image of the congressman with googly eyes, the silliness of flatulence humor, the idea of a politician giving a professor a hard time over the ordeal, and the bizarre nature of the phone call were too much for traffic-seeking websites to ignore. The ouroboros of digital media saw good content, and soon aggregators had news of the fiasco in the *Washington Post, New York Post,* Daily Beast, *Chronicle of Higher Education,* Associated Press, HuffPost, *Reason, Newsweek,* the Hill, Roll Call, *Raw Story,* nearly every Nebraska news source with a sizeable audience, and on TV, including comedian John Oliver's short segment about the exchange during his popular HBO show.

Kohen's conversation with Archer took place just 11 days before the 2018 elections. An entrenched Republican who is relatively popular in his district, Fortenberry easily won reelection, defeating his opponent by 20 percentage points. Perhaps the lack of serious competition freed up the congressman's staff to focus on less urgent matters like professors' Facebook habits.

The spat between Kohen and Fortenberry isn't as unusual as it might appear. The specific sequence of events in this controversy—defaced campaign sign, fart joke, Facebook like, recorded phone call, public hilarity—are unique, but the bigger issue behind the events is not. Across the United States, minor disputes at universities are getting turned into political talking points. Like so many other political trends permeating our country, Nebraska reflects the broader current. The absurdity of Kohen's incident is indicative of how politicians and political activists have become embroiled in, and in some instances empowered by, battles with colleges. Whenever I read about the most recent scuffle at my alma mater and follow people's contentious reactions to it, I contemplate if we're talking about the same university I attended, where most students didn't give a damn about politics.

My experience as a University of Nebraska student was mostly positive. Like many others, I formed many of my strongest relationships and experienced intense emotions during those formative years. During the highs, I never felt better surrounded by those I loved most. During the lows, I felt a depression unlike any other in my life, and therapy wasn't enough to pull me out of the rut. I made lifelong friends, cut myself off from people, devoted myself to church, lost my faith, developed a passion for learning, became discouraged by the inner workings of the academe, found love, got dumped. I witnessed my cherished Husker football team win three conference divisional titles only to lose each title game, leaving me in despair. I traveled to new states. I visited another country for the first time. I briefly lived in a foreign land. For better or for worse, I started having more sex . . . eventually. I formed a band, wrote the skeleton of my first book, completed a scholarly research project, racked up three majors, worked various jobs on and off campus, encountered an unfathomable amount of personal and profession rejections, and graduated without knowing what the hell I was doing. A few days after graduation, I moved to Detroit, where I still didn't know what the hell I was doing, but I at least had a job temporarily.

Through my interests in religion, grad school, sports, travel, and music, I got involved with several organizations around Lincoln. None of them were directly political, and of the groups I hung out with, only the church surfaced political discussion regularly. The only political events I ever really participated in were church-sponsored rallies. There are activists groups, partisan media companies, and state politicians who keep pushing the idea that conservative students at our university face hostility, but those fueling that story conveniently leave out how Christian events like annual pro-life rallies are openly welcomed at our school. I recall walking from the Capitol to our student union alongside thousands of pro-lifers and everyone being treated with utmost respect by university staff as we sat on campus consuming abortion speeches.

I do not claim to represent every college student in Nebraska, but if you look around you'll notice that on our campus few people run for student government, voter turnout isn't as strong as it is among older demographics, hardly any students are found lurking in the Capitol that sits next to campus unless they've been forced to venture there for class, scant attention is given to the political coverage of the university's newspaper, and students are more apt to stick in their earbuds and breeze by rowdy protestors than engage with them.

When I partied, politics very rarely came up, even during election years. When I had intimate one-on-one conversations, politics came up even less. Football, relationships, sex, money, pop culture, religion, farming, work, and speculation over the future accounted for probably 90 percent of the conversations I had with other students in social settings. Had you told me back then that I'd one day write a book about state politics, I would have called it BS and then questioned why I'd waste time on such a stupid topic.

The most vivid political memory I have of my time in Lincoln came during my freshman year. I ventured from my dorm named after Willa Cather to the student union to vote in the 2008 elections. I waited over an hour to receive my ballot because the line wrapped around the building, as many young people were energized about the possibility of the country's first black president. I did not vote for Barack Obama, but I was entertained by other people's enthusiasm. There were undoubtedly people who celebrated Obama's win as well as those dismayed by John McCain's loss, but the day after the election was just like any other on campus. I've seen the psyche of the student body affected to a much greater degree following Husker wins and losses than what transpired after the 2008 election. The election didn't feel controversial.

There were a few political controversies while I attended UNL. One occurred when Bill Ayers got invited, and then disinvited, to speak on campus. Ayers is a former leader of the Weather Underground, which was a left-wing radical group that bombed a bunch of government buildings in the 1970s as a protest against the Vietnam War. After spending over a decade as a fugitive during his involvement with the Weather Underground, Ayers earned a doctorate in education from Columbia University and became a well-known scholar. Threats of violence led the university to cancel Ayers's speech, which angered academic freedom advocates.

Another controversy came from assistant football coach Ron Brown. Brown served on several different head coaches' staffs since the 1980s and is well-regarded by fans. An outspoken and devout Christian, Brown testified against an antidiscrimination ordinance during an Omaha City Council meeting. Brown was against the ordinance because it extended protections to gay people. Many people demanded Brown be fired, including a Lincoln Public Schools board member, and the national press had a field day mocking Brown and Nebraska for being tone-deaf and outdated. The controversies surrounding Brown and Ayers were part of a tradition. Like most colleges, the University of Nebraska's long history is littered with political skirmishes.

Shortly after the university was founded, religious organizations accused it of being a godless institution. Others feared that the university would become controlled by a singular religious group. The Board of Regents combatted this fear by ensuring that the school's first faculty didn't contain more than one person from any single denomination. In college football's early days, corruption and brutality were common. Players were recruited with bribes, and the game was so violent that dozens died from their playing injuries. Nebraska's legislature introduced multiple bills in the late 1800s to outlaw football at the university, but the legislation failed when lawmakers realized that the growing enthusiasm for the sport would put a football ban at odds with voters.[3]

During World War I, the Nebraska State Council of Defense accused a dozen faculty members of disloyalty to our country and pressured the Board of Regents to hold public hearings to determine if professors were exhibiting un-American behavior. Professors who didn't support US involvement in the war were forced to resign while those who remained carried on their work in a climate of suspicion. A year after the investigation ended, one of the suspected professors suffered a mental breakdown.[4]

The university was also involved in the creation of our unicameral legislature. As I discussed in the previous chapter, the Nebraska Legislature changed from a partisan two-house system to a nonpartisan single-house system following voters' passage of a constitutional amendment during the Great Depression. The committee that drafted the amendment included multiple UNL professors. Nebraska political science professor John Senning was one of the architects of our unique state government, and he became one of its biggest advocates after the system was put into practice.[5]

When the Red Scare spread anti-communism paranoia throughout the country in the 1950s, the Nebraska Legislature passed a law that required state employees, including university staff, to sign a loyalty oath. In that environment of distrust, a few conservative and veteran's groups accused the university's chancellor of being a communist. A committee of the Nebraska American Legion investigated a professor who was suspected of teaching from a communist textbook. The American Association of University Professors (AAUP) addressed the controversy by denouncing "the validity of witch-hunts." The legion ultimately backed away from its investigation, and one of its committee members, Charles Thone, resigned from his post. Two decades later, Thone became Nebraska's thirty-fourth governor.[6]

Opposition to the Vietnam War made its way to campus, too. On the same month that National Guardsmen and police killed student protestors at Kent State and Jackson State, two thousand UNL students held a sit-in at the Military and Naval Science Building on campus. Following the sit-in, the American Legion of Nebraska stated that the university should remove protestors from campus, and a state senator demanded a list of names of professors suspected to be involved in the protest. In the next legislative session after the unrest, the unicameral passed a bill that allowed for expulsion of faculty and students who engaged in "certain activities disruptive of any public institution of higher education."[7]

In the early 1970s, UNL became one of the first colleges in the United States to offer a gay studies course. The class angered a state senator, who proceeded to introduce a bill that would make it illegal for Nebraska public universities to teach students about "aberrant sexual behavior in any form." The bill did not pass, but the class was discontinued after a semester.[8]

As you can see, many political controversies took place on the campus over the past 150 years. What stood out to me about the few politically charged events that I personally witnessed while attending UNL is that they boiled over quickly. Had I enrolled just a few years later, I'd have witnessed political clashes attached to larger issues that affect the university's ability to operate. Political snafus on UNL's campus drag on these days, and they are often about the behavior of individual students—and, in several cases, state lawmakers are throwing themselves into the muck.

The 2017 school year was supposed to be like any other, complete with sweltering heat, an overhyped football team, and a new crop of students attending their first classes. Before the leaves got a chance to change colors, an argument between a grad student lecturer and an undergraduate caught fire and sent university administrators scrambling.

Wearing a "Big Government Sucks" T-shirt, nineteen-year-old sophomore Katie Mullen stood behind a table in front of the University of Nebraska student union recruiting students to join Turning Point USA (TPUSA), a conservative group with several hundred chapters in schools across the country. TPUSA claims that it is focused on promoting limited government and rebranding free-market capitalism, but its main specialization is college culture war battles, and on that front it's been quite successful in enabling cyberbullies and generating controversies at dozens of schools, including a few in Nebraska. TPUSA's founder never attended a four-year university himself, but he believes that campus skirmishes are part of a "life-or-death fight for the future of our country and of Western Civilization" and that his organization is "exposing doctrinaire professors for what they are" with its professor watch list. He sees the leftist "infiltration" of the academe as a broader conspiracy designed to push the United States into communism. The group's donor list includes a slew of ultra-wealthy Republican donors. One of those donors has direct ties to the family of governor Pete Ricketts. In 2016 the political action group Ending Spending gave $100,000 to TPUSA, according to its IRS forms. The group's CEO was the governor's brother Todd Ricketts, and its chairman was his father, Joe Ricketts.[9]

When forty-six-year-old English lecturer and grad student Courtney Lawton saw the table for Turning Point USA, her first thought was: "Oh, hell no. I was like, not on my campus. No, no, no, no, no." Lawton hastily created her own placard in counterprotest and began shouting that the TPUSA student activist "wants to destroy public schools, public universities, hates DACA kids." English professor Amanda Gailey joined Lawton, though Gailey was less confrontational and merely held a sarcastic sign stating that she demanded to be put on the professor watch list. The argument continued. Lawton yelled that Mullen was a "neo-fascist Becky," which is a pejorative for ignorant white women. Chants of "No KKK! No NRA! No neo-Fascist USA! Fight white nationalism!" echoed in the background. Campus police arrived, but they let the protestors remain. At one point Lawton flipped Mullen off and the TPUSA rep took a photo of it. Mullen took other pictures, as well as videos of the event, which TPUSA instructs its reps to do. She shared the images with TPUSA, which posted them on social media, on TPUSA's website, and in conservative publications who find higher education problematic. Some of the publications slapped logos on Mullen's video, giving the impression they found a video of an English lecturer giving an undergrad the finger to be valuable intellectual property. The storm brewed.[10]

The entire incident lasted about as long as a college football halftime. What's striking is how no one else cared. Unlike other notable campus protests, there wasn't a group of people inciting violence through a frightening display of crowd psychology as witnessed in protests at Vermont's Middlebury College and the University of California, Berkeley. As the argument at UNL escalated, multiple students walked right through the scene unfazed as they went to study or grab a sandwich in the union. One guy breezed through on his bicycle and paid no attention to the people shouting. The video gives an impression of lonely salespeople hawking competing products in an empty parking lot.[11]

Thanks to smartphones, Twitter, and sympathetic media sources and politicians, this forgettable exchange hasn't gone away. Days after it became public, state lawmakers put the screws to the university. Conservative state senator Mike Groene, who chaired the legislature's education committee, said that the university's president has to "get his money from us, that all plays together. . . . There's a line there. You don't intimidate students." State senator Steve Erdman, a Republican farmer from the state's panhandle, called for Gailey and Lawton to be terminated. Erdman declined to be interviewed for this book.[12]

Erdman, along with Republican senators Steve Halloran and Tom Brewer, wrote an opinion article that openly questioned if UNL is hostile to conservatives and if anyone teaches English there anymore. They accused the English Department of caring more about progressive social causes than teaching their subject matter. Brewer appeared on a local conservative radio show and stated: "The biggest single issue, I think, is where they want to stress the social justice," he said. "I mean, social justice is nothing short of evil. You know, it silences free speech, it creates a toxic environment where students are afraid to share their beliefs and thoughts for fear of reprisal." Halloran arranged a photo-op with Mullen next to a TPUSA "free speech ball," which is a huge beach ball covered with provocative phrases that TPUSA urges students to roll around campus to bypass "free speech zones" that colleges have established to control where protests occur. The most legible phrase on the ball sitting next to Halloran in the photo is "fuck Antifa terrorists."[13]

UNL chancellor Ronnie Green pushed back against the senators and wrote that "the university will not be politicized and will not be used as a pawn." Green, university president Hank Bounds, and other administrators kept battling with local politicians. Meanwhile, the university's communications team kept receiving messages from parents, alumni, and internet trolls about the event, and concerned citizens wrote letters to the newspapers to voice their concerns. "I am disappointed in behavior [sic] of the students who participated in the harassment and bullying of the student," one alumni member emailed the president's office. "As a taxpayer, I am incensed that an employee of the university participated in the harassment and bullying." Other emails were more inflammatory. A few sent ominous messages.[14]

Shortly after the protest footage appeared online, the president of the anti-tax group Nebraska Taxpayers for Freedom complained to a regent about the hostility that conservative students encountered on campus. Attached with the complaint was a detailed budget analysis. "Even though the Governor and Legislature this session reduced the appropriation for the university system, we believe that there exist many additional places to whittle away at unnecessary spending," the email read. It went on: "The University of NE system is bursting at its seams with superfluous programs and bureaucrats, gorging itself on state taxpayer dollars." Suggested cuts included ending tenure, eliminating humanities and multicultural programs, removing diversity and women's studies positions, reducing benefits for university staffers, and privatizing a range of jobs ranging from landscapers to custodians. Some observers interpreted the suggested cuts as retribution intended to make the university's curriculum more conservative.[15]

The Nebraska GOP and the partisan news site Conservative Review then hit UNL with public records requests. They unearthed emails exchanged between university staffers where UNL spokespeople strategized about how to combat unfavorable press. (When a *Chronicle of Higher Education* reporter asked the former GOP chair if he tipped off the Conservative Review about the emails, the chairman hung up on the reporter.) One communications official suggested having surrogates write op-eds to local newspapers about all the good stuff the university was doing. Another suggested that they "should push harder on stories for them not related to this" and see what positive stories they could spin from their own newsroom. They were annoyed that a local reporter had the gall to write "a thumbsucker" about how tough it would be for UNL to retain support in a red state. "TPUSA is continuing to keep things inflamed with a story every day on its website regarding 'HuskerGate,' but that kind of choir-preaching stuff is generally containable," one of the emails read. "It's more concerning if [reporters from the *Omaha World-Herald* and *Lincoln Journal Star*] keep repeating the narrative."[16]

The desire of the university's communications team to try to control stories about the school isn't surprising. Public relations is about protecting an image. I've interacted with dozens of public relations managers who showed more aggression than the UNL communications staff did in those emails. Like anyone going through a tough time, UNL's communications team expressed anxiety—and that isn't a scandal.

This also wasn't the first time that the university tried to control the press. Reporters in Nebraska have told me that the university can be stifling to work with. When I was on campus, the university imposed significant restrictions on which athletes and officials we could speak with. For a class project in the journalism school, I wanted to interview the journalism dean. I was told by the dean's office that I'd have to submit all my questions in advance and stick to those questions, which is a public relations tactic that journalism professors warned us about and instructed students not to cooperate with.

Among the various regents I messaged, most ignored me, a few replied to tell me they didn't want to talk, and only one sitting regent said he would chat with me but then didn't respond to multiple phone calls. When I tried to interview Chancellor Green for this book, I was asked to send my questions in advance. When I did not give in to this demand after a few back-and-forth exchanges where I elaborated on what issues I wanted to discuss, the interview was denied. "If the process of you providing questions and us sending answers back on behalf of the Chancellor won't work, then I'm afraid we'll have to pass," was the response I received from a university spokesperson. Very few of the politicians and lobbyists I messaged during my reporting were this cautious.

When I consider the perspective of a UNL communications manager, it makes some sense why they've become gun shy about speaking openly. Amid all the emails in the open-records requests following the TPUSA incident, the university's opponents found the smoking gun they sought. "This will pass," wrote former UNL administrator Ellen Weissinger, who worked on campus for more than four decades. "But the real issue is we've got to do more to advance civility on campus. And frankly campuses have to become more tolerant and welcoming to conservative students and faculty. This has worried me for years. I don't think it is 'safe' to be conservative on our campus. Too many faculty espouse their personal political views as gospel in cases where there [sic] views have no relevance." The line about safety stuck.[17]

After it became clear that these emails would be publicized in November 2017, UNL dug deeper in damage control. In a letter to the governor, Weissinger and Bounds insisted that she was talking about "safety of ideas" and being able to openly express arguments, not physical safety. Bounds said he was "surprised and embarrassed" and that "some of the emails reflect unprofessional behavior by our employees and I apologize." Two university spokespeople whose emails were published by the Conservative Review resigned. Governor Ricketts said the "incident has highlighted concerns about the liberal bent of academia," and he urged UNL leaders to increase their efforts to "make sure conservatives feel welcome on campus." The following month, the governor sent a survey to donors that included this question: "Recently, employees of our taxpayer funded state university system have been caught bullying students for their conservative beliefs. . . . How concerned are you about this?" Given the governor's criticisms of the university and his proposed budget cuts, it isn't unreasonable to conclude that the state's top executive was testing the waters to see if highlighting the incident would open checkbooks from constituents who want to cut public education funding.[18]

Lincoln Journal Star reporters also made public records requests for messages sent between lawmakers and university administrators. The university denied the *Journal Star* but was overruled by the state attorney general. The messages painted the picture of a handful of senators hell-bent on keeping this clash going. An email from Senator Groene to the university president ended: "You will lose the fight." Senator Brewer told me that the TPUSA scandal took on a life of its own after the emails surfaced. "Things went to shit with this FOIA request," he said.[19]

The scandal continued. Nearly three hundred professors signed a letter accusing the governor and his allies of weaponizing the incident for ideological purposes. They insisted that politicians stay out of university affairs. A group of professors held a rally to defend academic freedom.[20]

To placate Nebraska politicians, the university commissioned polling firm Gallup to study the political climate across the university system. The university-commissioned study found that students overwhelmingly believed the university valued free speech. Ninety percent of polled students felt that liberals were able to freely express their views, compared to 75 percent for conservatives. Students were slightly more at ease discussing sex, religion, immigration, and race than they were politics. The poll did not find that most conservatives feel threatened on campus, as some politicians implied.[21]

Mullen and Gailey went back to their classes. Mullen met President Trump and spoke at the signing of an executive order that implored universities to protect free speech. Lawton's experience was different. She was removed from classroom teaching and her contract wasn't renewed. She secretly recorded a meeting with the chancellor where he leveled with her about the "tremendous political pressure" that contributed to her dismissal. "If we put you back in the classroom, we're going to continue to suffer damage," Chancellor Green said. "And it traces back to the incident. In every case it traces back to the incident, and the behavior in the incident. And we can't put it to bed. We just can't. We've tried."[22]

In response to what happened to Lawton, the AAUP investigated UNL and concluded that there is "little doubt that political pressure played a significant role in the Lawton case; in one sense, it is at the very heart of it." Kim Robak, a lobbyist who used to serve as the university's vice president for external affairs, told me she got the impression that the university's decisions following the TPUSA event "were being made because of political reasons, and as a result, it lasted longer and felt harsher."[23]

The AAUP determined that UNL did not give Lawton proper due process, so it censured the university. For working-class parents like my mom and dad who send their children to UNL, AAUP censures are nothing more than pointless inside baseball that they don't give a damn about. The gesture is largely symbolic, but it's considered a black eye in the academic community that can make it tougher to recruit renowned scholars.[24]

Senator Erdman pressed on. He recommended UNL admins hire the Foundation for Individual Rights in Education (FIRE) as advisors. FIRE is nonpartisan; it has defended both conservative and liberal groups who've had their free speech restricted on campuses, but it has earned the ire of left-wingers for its ties to conservative donors and for opposing certain campus reforms. FIRE found that UNL erred in terminating Lawton. FIRE researchers wrote: "It is apparent that the university views external criticism itself as disruptive, and saw Lawton's termination as an expedient route to ending that flow of criticism. In doing so, UNL defers to those 'internet trolls' the decision about who may teach at the university." When FIRE's conclusion didn't align with the Nebraska GOP, Erdman changed his tune about the group he suggested to UNL. "We thought they would be more impartial and do a better job of research, but we were wrong," Erdman said.[25]

The saga wasn't finished. Following the TPUSA dustup, the UNL Faculty Senate ousted its leader for the first time in its four-decade history. The president of AAUP's Nebraska conference resigned. The Board of Regents approved a statement that pledged the university to support freedom of expression. Senator Halloran sponsored a so-called free speech bill requiring Nebraska colleges to set free speech policies and make yearly reports to the legislature. Critics worried that because of the way the bill was written, if it became law it could give more power to politicians to police speech on campus. The bill failed to pass. Another Republican senator put forth a resolution to eliminate the democratically chosen Nebraska Board of Education and allow the governor to choose the head of the agency. That legislation failed too.[26]

Senator Erdman kept coming after the university. In a post on his Nebraska Legislature webpage, Erdman wrote that by hiring a vice chancellor for diversity, "every word spoken by White Christian conservative males at the school will be excruciatingly scrutinized against the backdrop of the new Vice Chancellor's extremist progressive worldview." He said that the Eastern part of the state—which includes Lincoln, Omaha, and the state's largest universities as well as massive amounts of farmland and numerous small towns—is a "foreign country" for western Nebraskans. While he drummed up charges of a liberal institution off its hinges, Erdman didn't acknowledge that the university's president and chancellor, as well as all eight of its regents at the time, were Republican white men. As a white man who came to UNL as a conservative Christian myself, I'm bewildered by the accusation that the school was hostile to students like me.[27]

In another post on Erdman's webpage, he made a wide-ranging list of accusations against university professors and kept redirecting his outrage to the TPUSA event. Erdman was mad about liberal bias on campuses, the AAUP censure, the UNL faculty senate ouster, and more. The theater college angered him by showing a play he found sacrilegious. "There is nothing funny about God creating Florida in the shape of male genitalia or God associating his Son with female genitalia, yet these statements describe actual lines from the play," the senator wrote.[28]

The farmer turned lawmaker wasn't finished. He said that "certain extremist, left-wing professors" keep harassing Mullen, the student activist with TPUSA. Erdman said that chemistry professor Gerard Harbison "continuously trolls Mullen online, leaving creepy and negative messages" and that "Mullen's death is exactly what [Harbison] wants." Erdman said this is indicative that UNL professors can do whatever they want, including threaten and harass students. Harbison's headshot was embedded at the end of the post.[29]

Harbison told a reporter at the campus newspaper that his only interaction with Mullen came through a few tweet exchanges. He said that Erdman's death threat claim from satiric song lyrics he shared on Facebook in September 2018, a month prior to Erdman's post. The post stated that a "junior Nazi" will "soon be underground." Harbison said the reference was to a known white supremacist on campus, not to Mullen.[30]

The chemistry professor also took issue with being labeled as a "left-wing extremist" by Erdman. Harbison, a registered Republican, used to run a blog called The Right-Wing Professor, and he has sponsored many conservative groups on campus over the last few decades, with the most recent being a student group promoting Marco Rubio's presidential run. Harbison was active enough in conservative politics that years ago anonymous bloggers mocked the professor for "injecting right wing conservative politics into his non-political scientific classes." The bloggers joked that Harbison's idols are Rush Limbaugh and Barry Goldwater and that the professor is "often seen online complaining about the Democratic Party, pathologically blaming them for every personal problem he has."[31]

Harbison asked Erdman to retract the post, and when that did not happen Harbison filed a lawsuit against the senator. Court documents revealed that Erdman tried to publish his screed in a small weekly newspaper, but the editor declined to run the article because the editor thought the comments about Harbison were inaccurate. Harbison declined to comment on the lawsuit, which is still pending.[32]

When universities are wielded as a wedge issue, things can get out of hand.

Some politicians who attack colleges don't really care if the university officials that they tag as extremist liberals are actually registered Republicans, which was the case with Harbison as well as the university's president, chancellor, and regents. It might seem silly for a congressman's chief of staff to bully a professor over a Facebook like, but that behavior makes more sense when you recognize that higher education is an easy political target.[33]

No matter what they did, university administrators were bound to anger people in this fight. Conservative activists and their associated press outlets who see universities as liberal enemies weren't satisfied when the lecturer they targeted didn't have her contract renewed. Free speech advocates and academic associations criticized the university for dismissing the lecturer and caving to political pressure. State senators, the governor, and activists opposed to the public financing of higher education kept the political heat on and dangled the possibility of budget cuts. This all happened while parents and alumni expressed concerns of liberal bias, nasty messages flooded university officials' inboxes, multiple individuals lost their jobs, lawsuits were filed, and various groups commissioned independent investigations into what transpired during a twenty-minute dispute between two students. Along the way, this minor dustup transformed into a litmus test as to whether conservative parents can trust their own state universities. The *Chronicle of Higher Education* called it a "proxy war for the future of campus politics."

"As the university becomes this constant source of controversy, over time it wears people down," said Amanda Gailey, a UNL professor who joined Lawton's protest and was subsequently targeted by TPUSA. "It wears down university administrators. It wears down lower-level administrators, who get impatient and develop policies to prevent these kind of things from happening. It wears down employees. One of the consequences of that event on campus is it has had a widespread chilling effect on faculty talking about controversial issues in class."

Back in 2017, the Board of Regents chairman told the *World-Herald*: "Gawd, this is a story that just won't go away." He proved to be more correct than he probably realized.[34]

The TPUSA incident was not the only political skirmish to happen on a Nebraska campus during this time. For Nebraskans who were already skeptical of how our universities operate, a handful of publicized incidents could give the impression that they're becoming more radical. Another way to view these events is that external groups have become more active in patrolling what happens at higher-ed institutions.

As we'll explore later, a Nebraska chapter of the far left political activist group Antifa brought attention to a UNL student who supported white supremacy. Local Antifa members also exposed another UNL student, a former campaign staffer for Governor Ricketts, who posted hundreds of racist and anti-Semitic messages in anonymous chatrooms. The governor distanced himself from the former staffer, whose main job responsibilities involved overseeing interns' phone calls and putting up yard signs. Antifa used the incident to clamor for broad social justice reforms and a reorganization of the Republican Party. "The only acceptable course of action is for Governor Ricketts to fire everyone on his staff, repatriate this land to the indigenous people it was stolen from, then resign in disgrace," according to Antifa.[35]

Sports were politicized, too. Following in the footsteps of Colin Kaepernick, the former 49ers quarterback who hasn't played in the NFL since his widely publicized protests against police brutality, a few Husker football players kneeled during the National Anthem played before a 2016 contest. Emails sent to university administrators showed that some fans and alumni supported the players' protest. Unfortunately, others expressed their disapproval with racist remarks.[36]

Michael Rose-Ivey, a starting linebacker who participated in the protest, addressed the situation with a powerful speech made before members of the local press. He said:

As we looked at what has been going on in this country the injustice has been taken place primarily against people of color and we all realize there is a systematic problem in America that needs to be addressed. . . . We did this understanding the implications of these actions, but what we didn't expect was the enormous amount of racially hateful comments we received from friends, peers, fans, members of the media and others about the method of protest. While you may disagree with the method, these reactions to it further underscore the need for this protest and gives us just a small glimpse into the persistent problems of race in this country and the divisive mentality of some Americans.[37]

Governor Ricketts said the players' protest was "disgraceful and disre-spectful." Ricketts said he would meet with Rose-Ivey to discuss the player's concerns. That meeting never happened. Rose-Ivey said that he canceled his talk with the governor because he didn't want to be used as a political prop.[38]

Regent Hal Daub, a Republican who served in Congress and as Omaha's mayor, also criticized the players. Daub warned the university's president in an email that the kneeling controversy "could have legs in this conservative state." In an interview with the *Lincoln Journal Star*, Daub was quoted saying that the protesting players should be booted off the team. Daub later denied that comment but held firm in his criticism. Husker beat writers opined that the pressure created by Ricketts and Daub would make it more difficult for Nebraska to recruit coveted out-of-state athletes. Thankfully for Husker play-ers, their coach had a stronger respect for the First Amendment than the re-gent or governor had. "It was the right thing to do—because it's *their* right," former Husker head coach Mike Riley told reporters after he was asked if his players should have approached the situation differently.[39]

The political controversies weren't limited to my school. TPUSA activists at Creighton University, a Jesuit school in Omaha, generated several scuffles that momentarily received attention from right-wing news sources, though none of these events led to action by Nebraska lawmakers. But the state GOP couldn't entirely resist sticking its nose into the Catholic university's business. The Nebraska Republican Party's executive director publicly advocated that Creighton rescind its commencement speech invitation to Bob Kerrey, the war hero and businessman who went on to hold Nebraska's highest offices in the 1990s. The GOP said that Kerrey shouldn't be allowed to address the grad-uating students because he was a "pro-abortion advocate." Creighton needed to "take a stand for their pro-life values," and barring a Democrat from speak-ing was one way it could do so. Kerrey, who lost a leg fighting for his country and whose son graduated from Creighton, backed out because he didn't want to become a distraction. No bishop or church official demanded action from the school. The group that demanded that Kerrey be shut down was the same one claiming that universities don't respect free speech.[40]

When my brother graduated from college, Republican Doug Bereuter spoke at the commencement. Nobody made it controversial. When I grad-uated, Democrat Ben Nelson was the scheduled speaker. Again, no contro-versy. The day I graduated, I could not have cared less about who spoke on stage. "I don't want to sit here all day," I told local TV reporters that day after they stuck a camera in my face to fill airtime. "I want to go home, watch cartoons, and eat pizza." I suspect that most Nebraska college students want to zip through their graduation ceremony so they can get on with their lives. Regardless of what students' opinions are, political operatives have partisanized these events. These days, inviting a former governor to speak on graduation day can mire a university in an abortion scandal.[41]

Ostensibly, Nebraska is governed by a nonpartisan lawmaking body and its universities are designed to train and empower its workforce, but lately they feel like two opposing forces. Even if you don't follow state politics or care much about higher education, the battles between members of these powerful institutions affect the state financially and politically. These fights aren't encouraging for working-class Americans who rely on public education.

From kindergarten through college I went to public schools, which is a common trajectory in my family. Had I been forced to pay more for my education, it would've been more difficult to overcome career obstacles. Whenever I see people like my high school baseball coach share Facebook memes that say that schools are no longer places of education because they've become liberal indoctrination centers, I think about how an affordable education at the University of Nebraska made it possible for me to achieve upward mobility and how the university's renowned medical center saved my liver from failing. Like so many others from small towns, I left the state after college. People in my position are becoming less likely to be present at the local bar to provide our viewpoint when bad news about the university comes up. Parents, already mad that few young people come back to support their shrinking towns and that they're paying a lot more tuition to get their children a shot at entry-level jobs than they did a generation ago, fill the information void with politicians and news sources who tell them what they want to hear.

If you want to know how Tom Brewer feels about government oversight, look no further than the buffalo head in his office. The state senator wanted to mount the head of a buffalo that his daughter shot. Those overseeing the Capitol wouldn't let him stick the animal directly to the wall of his legislative office. Brewer thought their rule was stupid. So he created a seven-foot-tall metal contraption with a thick border and a hollow center, giving the appearance of a massive picture frame. He stuck the buffalo's head to the structure and rolled it up against the wall so that it appears that the animal head is mounted.

Items in Brewer's office reflect his unusual past. On the day I met with him, he wore a black polo shirt from a sovereign native youth leadership group, which is a reminder that Brewer grew up on a reservation and is the state's lone Native American state senator. The Kevlar vest Brewer wore when he got shot in Afghanistan sits on a shelf, where visitors can note its missing chinks. A knife that was given to Brewer by a Gurkhan man who saved his life sits atop a cabinet. The rifles and pistols in his office denote his time in the military as well as his success in sharpshooting contests. Thirty-nine medals hang in honor of his enthusiasm for marathons. A TPUSA "Big Government Sucks" emblem slapped to the side of his aide's desk indicates that once in power, Brewer got behind the organization giving the state university hell.

On an overcast Friday afternoon in 2019, the day before the Huskers kicked off yet another dismal football season, I spoke with Brewer for a few hours in his office. When I asked him what it's been like to work with the university as a state senator, he pulled out a large white three-ring binder stuffed to the brim with files. The cover of the binder read "UNL" in bold black letters. A tab within the binder was labeled "free speech" and contained news articles and emails about the TPUSA incident and subsequent AAUP censure. While I dug deeper into the files, Brewer pulled out a second binder with UNL's name on it. Within the second binder were pictures of campus protestors. One protestor held a sign that said, "Pro Death Pete Fetus Fetishist." I gazed at the binders and listened to Brewer's gripes about the university.

Brewer said that too many professors are behaving like activists. He launched into stories about how university employees came after him. After a school shooting, a UNL professor who advocated for gun control delivered the Second Amendment–loving Brewer a Barbie doll covered in fake blood. Brewer told me that a professor once showed up at his office wearing a wire. The implication was that the professor was trying to goad Brewer into saying something inflammatory that could be recorded and used against the senator, which would be a mirror version of TPUSA's tactics. He took issue with how the university pressures state lawmakers to obtain funding. "The university can be kind of bullies when it comes to their budget," Brewer said. "If they don't like what's going on, they simply autodial to all the alumni, then the alumni light you up and chew you out. So, I didn't like their tactic there."

The three senators—Brewer, Halloran, Erdman—most critical of the university came into office in 2016. Two of them beat out incumbent Republicans who Governor Ricketts targeted after they voted against him. Aside from bickering with university officials, this trio has another thing in common: they want to lower taxes. "It angers me that the government has the audacity to tax a person's income in the first place," Brewer wrote in a newspaper op-ed. He added: "You don't cost the government money—the government costs you money!" When I asked Brewer if his election opponent, Al Davis, was unfairly targeted by his own party for voting with his conscience, he replied: "If you vote to increase taxes, you are a fair target."[42]

Brewer and other state politicians have tapped into Nebraska's long animosity toward taxes and government-sponsored programs. One of the primary reasons why Nebraskans voted against statehood in the mid-1800s is because they feared that joining the union would increase their taxes. According to historians James Olson and Ronald Naugle, during the Great Depression Nebraskans approved the adoption of a single-house legislature because they "found the idea of a more efficient and economical government appealing, especially if it meant a reduction in taxes." Throughout the twentieth century, Nebraska governors who raised taxes didn't win reelection.[43]

The property tax is the most visible tax, and it has been a subject of political debate throughout state history. Nebraska farmers are facing tough times and landowners are struggling with property taxes, so taxation and government spending has once again become a predominant political issue. Unlike surrounding states, Nebraska doesn't receive proceeds from legalized marijuana or gambling to offset tax pressure. If the state is to take action to reduce the tax revenue it receives, something will have to give—and it's likely that spending will get cut. Education is one of the first items on the chopping block.[44]

"The only money that's out there that many of the budgeters feel they can cut is higher-education funds," said University of Nebraska–Kearney chancellor Douglas Kristensen, a Republican who previously was the longest-tenured speaker in the unicameral's history when he served in the legislature. "That's the reason it has become politicized. It's the largest remaining pool of discretionary spending for the state."

Bob Krist, a former Republican state senator who ran for governor as a Democrat in 2018, said that the TPUSA incident became such an ordeal because it "got mixed up in a fight for money from the university itself." In the legislative session leading up to the TPUSA incident, it was reported that Nebraska had a projected $895 million state revenue shortfall. Krist, who was chair of the legislature's executive board at that time, said he was part of a meeting with Ricketts, state budget personnel, and university officials and lobbyists where Ricketts asked university president Bounds: "How far can I cut before you have to raise tuition?" When Bounds came back with a response, the governor cut Bounds's proposed figure even lower, according to Krist. "All of that is happening, then all of the sudden we have this event on campus," Krist said. (Bounds resigned from the presidency about two years after the incident between Mullen and Lawton, and while he never directly cited the TPUSA saga as cause for his departure, numerous state senators and lobbyists told me that they believe continual pressure from politicians contributed to his decision to leave. Bounds did not respond to my interview requests.)[45]

Like Ricketts, Brewer is a big supporter of property tax relief. Brewer wants to phase out state income taxes and eliminate social security taxes. He told me that he's "not going to hold a grudge" against the university and its budget over the TPUSA saga. But later in our conversation he gave me the impression that he hasn't entirely let his anger toward the university go:

> When it comes time to vote yay or nay on the university budget, and you've got a bad feeling in your gut that they're not doing what they ought to be doing, there very well could be consequences that they don't want and they don't need. . . . They're going to have to make hard decisions between defending their professors or dealing with less money in their budget. We don't have to deal with this. And if you don't want to take action, we'll do the only thing we can do, and that's really all we can affect is the budget of the university.[46]

Laura Ebke, a conservative former state senator who served on the legislature's education committee, said it isn't coincidence that the lawmakers who pressed for cuts to the university budget also wanted to lower taxes. One idea circulating at the time was that if you take away money from the university, then you could funnel more money into property tax relief. "When things like [the TPUSA incident] happen at the university, they make for a good punching bag," Ebke said.

When education becomes a political football, the public university system does what it can to protect its existence as one of the largest items of the state's budget. In an effort to secure its funding and clout in the legislature, the university continues to hire former state senators as its chief lobbyists. Between 2015 and 2019, the University of Nebraska spent three-quarters of a million dollars on lobbying, according to government watchdog group Common Cause. Just three other organizations in Nebraska spent more than the university on lobbying during that timeframe. "The university is still very good at maintaining its political posture," said lobbyist Kim Robak, who once was a finalist candidate for the university's presidency.[47]

When budget shortfalls have loomed, governor Ricketts and allies of his in the unicameral have proposed cutting the university budget. This isn't the first time that lawmakers have targeted the university. In the late 1800s, the legislature and university couldn't agree on how much funding was needed to finish erecting a new campus library, so the partially constructed building sat untouched for two years before the two institutions finally compromised and completed construction. Amid the Great Depression, the legislature attempted to reduce spending by discontinuing the university's teachers college, cutting the salaries of professors, and withdrawing from collegiate accrediting agencies that required high, and expensive-to-maintain, standards. The university fought back and maintained its programs but was forced to compromise on a million-dollar budget decrease.[48]

Democrat Jim Exon pressured the legislature to reduce the university's budget when he was governor during the 1970s. During Exon's tenure, the university sued the governor, which culminated in a court case wherein the Nebraska Supreme Court ruled that the Board of Regents was the university's ultimate governing body. When Democrat Bob Kerrey was governor during the 1980s farm crisis, he also called for a tightening of the university budget. One of the programs Kerrey proposed cutting was the pharmacy school where he had obtained his degree.[49]

What's different now than in the past is that today political discussions about the university today are more likely to be about cultural conflicts stirred by national activist organizations. Another difference is that in the past, support for higher ed wasn't as split down party lines. Throughout the latter part of the 1900s, Republican governors and influential state senators advocated for higher education and protected the university from cuts. The Republicans who controlled state politics when I was a kid had a different set of priorities than today's lot.[50]

Among politicians, there's been a diminution of support for higher education over the past twenty years, Kristensen said. "That's primarily due to
legislators who don't have broad long views," he said. "They come in with a
term-limited view. 'We're going to come in, get our punches in, do what we
can do, then we're out.' Well, the university is a long-term investment. It's
been there a long time and will be here for a long time. We hire thousands of
people, we have thousands of students, there's always going to be something
you can pick at and complain about. . . . It has become fashionable to take
swipes at higher education."

With the TPUSA saga behind it, the university still dealt with state lawmakers picking at the institution. On the floor, legislators debated ideas such
as, why did the university waste so much money keeping the football stadium's security lights on? Despite these criticisms, and the occasional cut in state
funding, the university maintained strong enough support in the legislature to
protect its budget. Prior to the coronavirus recession, the university's budget
was relatively stable.[51]

Between 2010 and 2019, state appropriations to the university, as well as
the university's total revenues, increased slightly higher than the low national
inflation rate. The percentage of university revenues that come from state appropriations dropped by about 1 percentage point between 2010 and 2019. In
1989, the year I was born, state appropriations accounted for two-fifths of the
university's funding, about double the portion they account for today. But the
trend of less reliance upon state aid was part of a national phenomenon that
developed before Ricketts was elected.[52]

Between 2000 and 2012, the share of revenue for public research universities that came from state appropriations was nearly cut in half nationwide. According to a 2019 study by the Pew Charitable Trusts, Nebraska postsecondary
institutions (which includes state and community colleges in addition to the
public university system) received 27 percent of their funding from the state,
which is 3 percentage points higher than the national average. Put another
way, there were thirty-four states whose higher-ed institutions relied less on
state aid than Nebraska's did.[53]

Nebraska is still a state that supports public education. But politicians have
criticized our schools in recent years, and universities aren't the only ones
under attack.

In most states, local property taxes account for about a third of public K–12 education funding, but in Nebraska they account for closer to half. Nebraska relies more heavily on property taxes to fund education because the state provides a smaller share of school district funding relative to other states. Because more than half of Nebraska's public schools are in rural areas, these forces put farmers and other landowners in a tough bind. Due to higher transportation costs and a lack of economies of scale, most states provide a disproportionate amount of money to rural schools. In Nebraska, rural schools receive a smaller share of state funds than their number of students would indicate. For every $4 that local rural school districts raise in tax revenues, they receive $1 from the state. According to one nationwide study, Nebraska's rural education funding gap is the largest in the country.[54]

Nebraska's school funding formula takes into account a district's needs and resources before the state distributes aid. One of a school district's main resources is its property values, and its needs are determined by its number of students. So rural school districts with lots of taxable property but few students are viewed as having high resources and low needs, which blocks them from receiving state aid, said Greg Adams, a Republican former legislature speaker who now lobbies for Nebraska's community colleges. That's why more than two-thirds of the state's school districts don't receive any state equalization aid.[55]

Public K–12 schools in Nebraska have become more dependent on property taxes over time. This is partially because land values have risen significantly. Considering that 92 percent of Nebraska's land is occupied by farms and ranches, rising farmland valuations had a significant impact on the state's tax dollars. Rising land values also increase a school district's resources, which results in less state aid. Between 2008 and 2018, the average cost per acre of Nebraska farmland more than doubled. While the Great Recession was unfolding, the prices of commodities like corn soared, which increased farmland earnings and drove up the market value of land. Additionally, the Federal Reserve lowered interest rates to encourage people to borrow money during the recession. And some investors, looking for safe investments after risky securities tanked the economy, parked that money into land. Commodity prices have dropped significantly from their peak, but interest rates remain low and ag land values haven't come down much yet. This has created a dynamic where land values and property taxes have increased even if landowners' incomes have fallen.[56]

Another reason why local property taxes have shouldered the education funding burden is because the state isn't doing its part to funnel money back to school districts, according to Nebraska Farmers Union board member and former state senator Al Davis. "I was on the revenue committee," he said. "It wasn't really revenue; it was really about tax exemptions and tax credits." Lynn Rex, executive director of the League of Nebraska Municipalities, agreed: "The Nebraska Legislature, over a period of years, granted one tax break after another."

Tax breaks have pros and cons. Consumers don't pay a sales tax on most groceries in Nebraska because progressive lawmakers fought to eliminate food taxes, which they argued hurt the poor. Davis himself sponsored legislation that gave volunteer firefighters an income tax break. Tax breaks can genuinely benefit constituents, but each exemption reduces the amount of revenue coming into the state, and some of the cuts primarily benefit the well-to-do. When Nebraska repealed its estate tax and lowered its inheritance tax, it effectively gave a tax break only to those who were rich enough to afford an estate. To prevent companies from moving, Nebraska provided generous tax breaks to the state's largest corporations, including some to TD Ameritrade, the company that made the governor's family extraordinarily wealthy.[57]

"You would sit there year after year and give away the tax base," said Adams, who served on the legislature's education and revenue committees. He continued:

It was one of those "damned if you do, damned if you don't [situations]." Because taxes were getting high in Nebraska, rather than lower them, we shot holes in the base. . . . Whoever was in front of us at the altar of testimony on any given day—tanning salons, zoo admission, or whatever—we just granted them an exemption. If we're going to have substantive tax reform in Nebraska, what we have to do is broaden the base and lower rates. But the politics behind that is an inferno.

Determining what should and should not be taxed is complicated. Taxation trade-offs prompt larger debates about what types of services the state should fund. The circumstances that placed the school funding burden onto property taxpayers are not simple. Instead of addressing the complexity of this situation, Governor Ricketts borrowed the language of President Trump and derisively referred to public K–12 institutions as "government schools." He called them the biggest spenders of public funds and insinuated that they're contributing to rising property taxes. The idea that local school districts are carefree spenders doesn't align with my experience of attending the same public schoolhouse for thirteen years. During that time, I saw schools around us drop programs so they could stay afloat as long as possible before an inevitable school merger crushed their town. When our school's longtime third grade teacher retired, our fourth grade teacher got tasked with teaching all the third and fourth graders simultaneously for an entire year. Her pay certainly did not double after picking up twice the work.[58]

Perhaps Ricketts came to a much different conclusion because his educational experience isn't like that of working-class Nebraskans. He did attend a public high school in Omaha, but it was one of the most affluent in the state. His high school had its own school district separate from Omaha Public Schools. The legacy of that arrangement dates back to a pre–*Brown v. Board of Education* decision fueled by integration anxiety. Some folks in Omaha's well-to-do west side were so opposed to having black neighbors that they didn't even want Bob Gibson, a black man from Omaha who became one of the greatest baseball players of all time, to live near them. After high school, Ricketts attended the University of Chicago, one of the most prestigious private colleges in the world. Not long after getting his diploma, he joined his father's online stock trading company and climbed the ranks to become an executive in the multibillion-dollar business. From his vantage point, maybe state support for public education isn't so critical.[59]

School district spending growth is already limited to 2.5 percent per year, and Nebraska ranks forty-ninth in its share of K–12 funding coming from state government. But that's not enough for Ricketts and his colleagues, who want to reduce taxes and put further restrictions on educational spending.[60]

Sändra Washington, a Democrat who serves on Lincoln's City Council, was angered when Ricketts referred to public K–12 as "government schools." It is fine for the governor to advocate for lower property taxes and to want to cut school funding, but she felt that he wasn't being very direct about his intentions. "I want us to have a real budget conversation instead of just a political stump speech," Washington said. "Tell me, what is it that you think the state of Nebraska shouldn't be paying for?"

Ricketts has embraced the school choice movement, which hasn't been able to catch on in Nebraska. That's because coming after public schools directly is a hard sell in our state. A recent poll of rural Nebraskans showed that two-thirds had a lot of confidence in the state's public schools. It is easier to criticize educational institutions when they're approached from a culture war angle.[61]

There are numerous reasons why colleges have become a reliable target for conservative politicians who want to trim taxes by cutting their budgets. University administration costs are growing. Tuition is increasing. Returns on degrees are diminishing. Politicians who have a problem with the state of higher education can point to the never-ending supply of stories about sensitive university administrators, ideological professors, and overparented students gone berserk to help sway voters their way. Most faculty politically lean left compared to the general population, which is another cudgel used against universities. And there's been a growth of well-funded organizations opposed to publicly financed higher education who are savvy with social media, which extends anti-university messages. This is happening when many rural states are struggling to retain young workers who will power their future economies.

Making matters more acrimonious, across the country we can easily spot examples of individual students, progressive activists, professors, and university administrators who demonstrate an inability to see outside of their social bubble, thin-skinnedness, a preference for political correctness to the point of advocating censorship, unwillingness to be exposed to ideas that make them uncomfortable, and a fetish for regulation of anything they dislike. In their popular book *The Coddling of the American Mind*, psychologist Jonathan Haidt and FIRE president Greg Lukianoff found that campus speaker disinvitations and the desire for students to be protected from ideas that make them uncomfortable really took off in 2013. That's the year that Generation Z students arrived on campus and is coincidentally the same year I graduated. The individuals who value safetyism over intellectual inquiry do not represent most people on campuses, but there are enough liberals wielding half-baked academic concepts to forcefully protest petty grievances that they provide right-wing publications with inexhaustible programming. So when news outlets like Fox News would rather ignore the latest Trump administration scandal, thanks to the ubiquity of smartphones and social media they can fill their segments with cherry-picked disputes, like the incident between Mullen and Lawton at UNL. This territory is so well-covered in numerous books, TV programs, documentaries, and news articles that I'll stop myself from elaborating here out of consideration of boring readers.[62]

One of the perks of working at a public university is being afforded a level of free expression that many corporate employers would not tolerate. University of Nebraska employees have used this freedom to advocate for many issues they believe in. They absolutely have the right to do this. But when a teacher or researcher does something like berate a student for their views or spray fake blood on the steps of an NRA lobbyist's home, they do Fox News' work for them.[63]

"I would like to grab some of those professors by the neck and say, 'You are your own worst enemy,'" said former state senator and University of Nebraska lobbyist Lee Rupp, who was incensed by how long the controversy from the TPUSA incident lingered.[64]

Most Nebraskans probably won't care about the technicalities of how the First Amendment applies to employees of public institutions when they read stories about professors run amok. They also probably won't care that these stories aren't very newsworthy in and of themselves and that the momentum behind these stories is generated by opportunists. Instead, a populace that already leans conservative continually intakes the message that the university is operated by left-wing extremists. The image of the liberal English instructor shutting down a young conservative student became their key metaphor for academia. Meanwhile, a group of state lawmakers uses the university in a crusade against liberalism.

Earlier, we mentioned how Husker coach Ron Brown protested a city ordinance over gay rights. Like the argument that unfolded between Lawton and Mullen, the fallout from Brown's protest showed that free speech can get contentious and nasty. After Brown's episode, I noticed that a lot of liberals who claim to value free speech wanted him gone. In their view, Brown didn't have the right to express his beliefs publicly. After the TPUSA episode, I noticed that a lot of conservatives who said they valued free speech wanted Lawton off campus. In their view, the English grad student didn't have the right to yell at the conservative undergrad. The fallout from these controversies shows that many people think the First Amendment only applies to their allies. If people really valued free speech and stopped letting their partisan views guide their

anger, they'd see that both Brown and Lawton, as well as the kneeling football
players and the former UNL students who expressed distasteful views, should
be allowed to speak.

Lawton received good reviews from her students, and she wasn't let go
because of anything relating to job performance. She did not deserve to be
terminated for practicing a nonviolent protest, and the university ultimately
infringed on her First Amendment rights. She did, however, present conservatives with a perfect villain. "They were out trolling for liberals," Lawton told
NPR. "And they got a live one on the line with me."[65]

University professors have become an easy target for far-right groups
because some members of the academe have become liberal to the point of
self-parody. Again, the examples of this are so plentiful, and have been recalled in multiple volumes, that I have nothing new to add. This trend affects
UNL. It's apparent in an interview Lawton had with NPR's *This American
Life* wherein she implied that all Trump supporters are fascists. Under this
definition, most parents of UNL students could be classified as fascists. And
if you recall, Lawton called Mullen a "Becky." In case you are confused as to
why this particular name is an insult, Lawton, who is white herself, explained
that a "Becky" is really "a white woman who weaponizes her whiteness and her
white privilege." This explanation would baffle almost everyone in Brainard,
including UNL grads who live there. Conservatives are logical for believing
that a person needs to spend several years in an academic setting to learn how
to think that way. Highly educated liberals are less likely than people without
high school degrees to be exposed to political disagreements. This bubble explains why Democrats' perceptions of what views Republicans hold become
more inaccurate with each degree they earn. In some ways, people are becoming less attuned to reality with each additional degree they earn.[66]

Throughout the TPUSA scandal, there was a lot of insincere posturing,
which is par for the course for TPUSA given that its chief creative officer is a
former journalist who got fired numerous times for plagiarism. To say that
its videos are selectively edited would be an understatement. But the idea that
professors are usually liberal is not just a fantasy that TPUSA and conservative
lawmakers have.[67]

The Higher Education Research Institute at UCLA found that each year
they do their survey, fewer professors describe themselves as moderate. Professors are now five times more likely to describe themselves as liberal than

conservative. In the humanities and social sciences, the imbalance is worse: liberals in those departments outnumber conservatives by a factor of ten. Compared to their own students, professors are about 30 percentage points more likely to call themselves liberal. A study published in *Econ Journal Watch* found that social science professors are about twelve times more likely to register as Democrats than Republicans. Another study from a Harvard symposium, which included community college teachers as well as professors at liberal arts universities, found that faculty were slightly more likely to be moderate than liberal. This study showered higher levels of moderates because community college teachers were more likely to be moderate or conservative than their university counterparts. But the study still showed liberals outnumbering conservatives by a ratio of more than 4 to 1. (The media industry, especially the New York area where I work and where many media jobs are located, suffers from these same biases, which contribute to how out of touch the press has become for most people.)[68]

Political affiliation is much different among the general population. In its survey of US adults, Gallup continues to find, year after year, that the percentage of people who identify as liberal is lower than those who describe themselves as conservative. Like conservatives, moderates also outnumber liberals by about 10 percentage points. Regarding political affiliation, Democrats and Republicans are pretty even.[69]

Because most university teachers are required to have advanced degrees, and people with advanced degrees are more likely to be liberal, it's unrealistic to expect professors' political affiliations to entirely mimic the general population. There is likely a self-selection effect where liberals are more apt to choose the professor lifestyle, which is something that can't be controlled. Any regulation of professors' political beliefs would infringe on their liberty and probably spur unintended consequences that could create their own set of problems. There is also a sordid history of people in power trying to pressure teachers to adhere to certain beliefs. When one lawmaker recently tried to regulate the political affiliation of university staff, he wound up looking like a fool.

In 2017, Iowa Republican state senator Mark Chelgren proposed a bill that required public universities to implement a hiring freeze until the number of registered Democrats and Republicans in faculty positions were nearly even. He said that his own experiences with liberal professors during his college days inspired his bill. Chelgren was confident that "any student that goes to any university anywhere in the United States of America has experienced intimidation for their conservative political views." His legislation never made it to the floor, and First Amendment advocates said that the proposal was unconstitutional. The proposed bill still spawned much press coverage. Chelgren changed his biography on the Iowa State Republicans website after reporters revealed that his "degree in business management from Forbco Management school" was really just a course he took from a company that operated a Sizzler's steakhouse franchise. According to an Iowa Republican spokesperson, Chelgren's degree was "kind of like Hamburger University at McDonald's." Chelgren also once compared preschool to Nazi indoctrination and proposed a bill that would structure professor tenure like a reality TV contest in which students could vote their least favorite professors off campus. He didn't seek reelection.[70]

When professors' political leanings are so far left of the people who send their children to college, it can create tension. University leaders are doing themselves a disservice if they don't see this as an issue worth addressing. From the point of view of many parents in towns like Brainard, the TPUSA incident was symbolic of what they view as a bigger problem in academia. Such incidents and perceptions don't earn universities any favors with conservative taxpayers.

There is still support for the university throughout the state, but polls indicate that the perceived importance of college education has declined in rural Nebraska. Some of this sentiment is part of a national current where Republicans have become more likely to view higher education negatively. This isn't surprising if you've sat through a few rounds of $2 Busch Lights at small-town bars west of Lincoln and Omaha. The first round usually starts with a friendly comment about Husker football or with bohunks comparing how many hundredths (pronounced "hunnerds") of an inch of rain they received last night. If you bring up the state of higher education, someone will probably let loose after a few rounds.[71]

They go off about colleges brainwashing their children to denounce religion and reduce social interactions into us-versus-them situations that pit oppressors against victims based on whoever claims to belong to the least marginalized group. They say that professors and other leftists view people as groups instead of individuals. That academics don't believe in agency or self-responsibility, but rather in the idea that entire ethnic groups should think and act the same way. They say that professors are training our young to view mere words as violence. They blame universities, the media, and politicians for creating a culture where people can't even say what they feel anymore. They complain that beliefs they've held for ages are suddenly considered hate speech that can't be expressed aloud. Anyone who speaks up gets canceled. Anyone who questions the liberal cause of the day gets labeled a bigot. Trigger warnings, microaggressions, safe spaces, toxic masculinity, white fragility, intersectionality, cultural appropriation, and other academic hobbyhorses are just gobbledygook created by liberals who want to deflect debate and assert control over society through shame. Political correctness and social justice are their schemes designed to shut you up. Liberals get their rocks off at being offended, and this is instilled in people at the academe.

Of course, many rural Nebraskans aren't so critical of higher ed. Brainard's saloon is named Husker Bar, and in it you'll find people who proudly sent their kids to the state university, which they still see as a quality and affordable education. Many people in Butler County recognize that the university isn't simply a liberal money hog. I grew up with people whose parents recognized that the university is a major employer in our state and helps drive Nebraska's economy. But those who are critical of higher ed have become more vocal about it, and the popularization of fringe leftist concepts has only made these discussions more annoying.

Another thing to consider is that the worst excesses of campus liberalism, in many cases, are not generated by professors and don't benefit professors. In some instances, professors have been victims of reactionary liberals. There have been several widely reported cases where agitated students and clumsy administrators have enabled smear campaigns and silenced academic freedom without due process. Student newspapers have been another target of leftist outrage mobs. For decades, journalists and professors have been boogeymen for the conservative movement. But the reality is more complicated, as witnessed by the reporters and teachers who have been denounced by leftists for probing uncomfortable topics.[72]

There are legitimate debates to be had about campus politics and faculty members' political affiliation. In a highly cited academic article, a group of social scientists wrote that in the field of psychology, the "lack of political diversity can undermine the validity of social psychological science via mechanisms such as the embedding of liberal values into research questions and methods, steering researchers away from important but politically unpalatable research topics, and producing conclusions that mischaracterize liberals and conservatives alike." While there is debate to be had, many of the people leading this conversation are disingenuous about their intentions. When politicians attack universities, voters should consider if their elected officials are trying to push an ulterior motive. Pundits who receive checks from corporate-backed, anti-taxation think tanks should be viewed with caution when they launch tirades about the liberal indoctrination of American universities, which coincidentally end in pleas for reducing public funding. Organizations like TPUSA, which exist to inflame animosity against universities, are just hucksters who are really good at leveraging little spats to generate controversy and anger people. The group's "professor watchlist" is an attempt at intimidation.[73]

Another area that deserves legitimate debate is the university's budget and how much taxpayers should support it. It isn't preordained that the university automatically deserves a significant budget increase every time appropriations are given. When tax revenues are restricted, particularly during economic downturns, maybe it makes sense for the state to allocate less funding to higher education and more to other state agencies that focus on health care, local government, child welfare, roads, or other services. Then again, there are fine arguments to be made that investments in higher education will grow our economy and pay off. Either way, if we are going to run our state government effectively, these discussions shouldn't be led by trivial altercations.

Parents, educators, and students can discuss among themselves and come to their own conclusions about what it means when higher education is primarily carried out by individuals who lean liberal. Although I believe universities and students would all benefit from having teachers with more political diversity, in my own experience most professors were very professional and didn't let their own beliefs dictate their teaching. In most classes I took at the University of Nebraska, politics never came up. When it did, professors respected those who they disagreed with. There were exceptions where professors let their biases creep in, but they were rare.

Like so many young people, I became more liberal during my college years. A conservative firebrand would proclaim that I was indoctrinated by university leftists. I found professors to be much less persuasive than conservative pundits make them out to be. I clearly believe in the mission of colleges and find them to be valuable, otherwise I wouldn't publish a memoir with a university press. I enjoyed many of my professors, but none of them really influenced my beliefs greatly. Instead, what affected my beliefs to a much greater degree were life experiences. In Brainard, I wasn't exposed to many new ideas, and most of the people I knew looked and thought alike. When I was in high school, I spent much more of my time playing sports and creating movies with my friends than I did in researching social issues. These things changed for me when I left home. My political beliefs evolved over time, so it is too simplistic to attribute any changes to a single event. However, several things I went through nudged me in a new direction. Many of these experiences, which I have gone over in other parts of this book, happened in college.

I became less rigid in my pro-life stances after I continued to research and question Catholic doctrine, a devout woman I dated broke my heart, and I was recommended an incendiary book in the confessional. Plus, a priest I loved got kicked out of the priesthood, church scandals proliferated (including some in our backyard), and I found love again with a woman who is pro-choice.

I became more supportive of immigration reform after I interacted with immigrants regularly, instructed them, learned from them, lived with them, and formed relationships with them.

I became more accepting of gays after I became friends with several gay people, I reexamined my own sexual hypocrisies, and I saw one of my best friends flourish and grow in confidence after he came out to me.

I became in favor of more government assistance programs after I received the government's help to pay for school, which improved my life and helped me start a successful career.

I became in favor of health-care reform after I became seriously ill and my family grappled with how we'd pay for something we had no control over for the rest of our lives.

These experiences were driven by life circumstances, not professors. My views changed because of what I was exposed to, not what I was prevented from hearing.

When I went to UNL, the worst politics I experienced were internal. I'd structured most of my undergraduate career as a resume-builder to get into graduate school. That's why I worked in multiple research labs and wound up with several majors while taking 50 percent more credits than I needed to graduate. Because I was a first-generation student on Pell Grants, I got accepted into the McNair Scholars program, which boosted my grad school odds and allowed me to get paid for conducting research. I ultimately chose not to apply to graduate school. One of the things that turned me off was witnessing petty politicking and passive-aggressive behavior. I saw feuds that weren't kept in check or dealt with openly and properly. A professor beloved by students was denied tenure, and from our view, the denial occurred because he was personally disliked by department heads. One professor that I was close with shared a story that occurred at a college outside Nebraska, where the college wanted to sack a tenured professor but couldn't do so directly, so it eliminated the prof's subdepartment in retaliation. Another irritant was that the overburdensome bureaucrats running the Institutional Review Board made academic research unappealing.

These issues personally bothered me, but they weren't exerted by outside forces and they didn't threaten the university's ability to operate. Things have changed in recent years as free speech debates and political controversies snowballed. In Nebraska, as in other states, state politicians and college professors find themselves pitted against each other as they spend an inordinate amount of time fighting over minor scandals that get blown out of proportion. In the particular incident involving a TPUSA organizer at the University of Nebraska, almost everyone who physically came across the protest that day ignored it and went about their own business. Although young people today have developed a more restrictive view of free speech than their predecessors, there are scores of students on campuses today who defy the stereotype of pampered young adults hungering for protection from ideas they dislike.[74]

The Husker basketball team provided an encouraging example of how to handle an on-campus political controversy.

Around the same time that activists opposed to higher education were ginning up outrage over an argument that unfolded in front of the UNL student union, liberal activists ignited a separate controversy by outing a white nationalist. Left-wing group Anti-Fascist Action Nebraska disclosed that UNL student Daniel Kleve was part of the neo-Nazi organization Vanguard America. Kleve attended the infamous Unite the Right rally in Charlottesville, Virginia, that left one civilian dead and dozens injured in an event that many consider to be the most blatant display of white supremacy our country has seen in decades.

Part of the rally took place at the University of Virginia, which made it one of the most heinous political events to ever occur on an American campus. In a YouTube video, Kleve boasted, "I am the most active white nationalist in the Nebraska area." He opined that the government should have stopped Martin Luther King Jr. and that our nation's founding fathers didn't care about the opinions of Mexicans and black people. He went on: "Trust me, I want to be violent. Trust me. Really violent."[75]

Once Kleve's comments became publicly known, some people, particularly politically active leftists, demanded his removal from campus. University administrators condemned Kleve's statements, but they did not punish Kleve because they determined that his speech was protected by the First Amendment. "UNL unequivocally said yes, having a violent, armed neo-Nazi on campus isn't an issue for them," cried the anonymous militants at Antifa Nebraska after they didn't get their desired outcome. The Nebraska Left Coalition bemoaned that "UNL refuses to take any action whatsoever, endangering the entire student body and surrounding community."[76]

The controversy over Kleve and his white nationalism simmered just as the Nebraska men's basketball team was gearing up for the heart of its Big Ten schedule. Several hundred students held a rally in front of the student union in protest of Kleve. Tim Miles, then head coach of the basketball team, attended the rally and told reporters that his players, who heralded from seven states and four countries, were "extremely troubled" by the situation. Basketball players and coaches decided to make a simple statement against Kleve and his white nationalistic allies by wearing black-and-white shirts during pregame warmups that stated "Hate Will Never Win." The women's basketball team wore similar shirts. Their message caught on.

A glowing round of media coverage followed the basketball teams' protest. Surely the favorable attention was a godsend for university officials battling politicians over the TPUSA saga. The T-shirts became popular enough that the university's multicultural center began hawking them. Within days, more than a thousand students attended a "Hate Will Never Win" rally on campus, which is an impressive figure given how politically apathetic most Huskers are. "We are here as family," said guard Evan Taylor. "This is about us having love and respect for each other."[77]

Unlike several political activists discussed in this chapter, the basketball players didn't: weaponize partisan news sources to attack their opponents, demand censorship, foment division, urge officials to create new rules, or call for the heads of the people they disagree with. Instead, they drowned hateful ideas with their uplifting message. The players used their own free speech to win over supporters. No administrative regulation was needed. Kleve left the university on his own, and he never gained a following. Unlike other provocateurs who rely on campus speech disinvitations to market themselves, Kleve was unable to portray himself as a free-speech champion who was censored by university officials. "Instead of making this student a martyr and a victim, he's being made into an afterthought," wrote the *Journal Star* editorial board.[78]

The basketball players and students rallying against hate showed that when individuals band together, they have the power to shape political events in their communities. This bottoms-up approach was more effective than the top-down tactics that administrators used to try to control the stories being written about their school. In Nebraska, where most elected officials are loyal to the Republican Party and Democrats struggle mightily, the best chance to advance progressive causes is through everyday people.

CHAPTER SIX

Democratic Disarray and Hidden Progressivism

With my friends out pounding Natty Light–filled keg cups and showing off suggestive costumes, I was stuck in the basement of the University of Nebraska's journalism school a few days before Halloween, pouring over voter registration data for a class project. It quickly became clear to us amateur analysts that Bob Kerrey, one of our most famous alums, would lose the 2012 Senate race the following week regardless of his past popularity and unique résumé.

Kerrey's ties to Nebraska progressive politics began at birth. Pregnant on the eve of America's baby boom, Kerrey's mother couldn't reserve a maternity room at Lincoln's overcrowded Bryan Memorial Hospital. So the hospital's staff moved her to an offsite estate, where she delivered her baby boy in the former home of the hospital's namesake, political firebrand William Jennings Bryan.[1]

After serving as a US Navy SEAL and losing part of a leg in the Vietnam War, Kerrey earned a Purple Heart and Medal of Honor. Coming back to the states, he opened a series of restaurants and fitness centers and became a self-made millionaire. He bolted onto the Nebraska political scene in the early 1980s, defeating incumbent Republican governor Charles Thone in a tight race. As a divorced governor, Kerrey met the actress Debra Winger when she was in Lincoln filming *Terms of Endearment*, which won the Academy Award for Best Picture in 1984. The two began dating, and one of the most famous actresses of the day frequently stayed in Lincoln with the governor during their relationship. Few, if any, Nebraskans found it controversial that Kerrey was shacking up with Winger. The owner of a used car dealership in Lincoln told the *Washington Post*, "More people would rather have Debra Winger stay in the governor's mansion than Bob Kerrey."[2]

Kerrey was well liked as a governor, boasting a 70 percent approval rating. While other Nebraska governors appeared stiff in front of the press,

Kerrey embraced his sardonic wit. When a reporter asked him how his date
with Winger went, Kerrey replied: "Fluff up your pillow and dream about it."
Kerrey was no party loyalist and worked well with Republicans. He irritated
Democratic Party officials when he appointed a Republican attorney general.
He surprised Nebraskans when he didn't seek a second gubernatorial term.
Kerrey later parlayed his name recognition to win a US Senate seat in 1988, defeating his Republican opponent by 15 percentage points. He ran again in 1994
and soundly defeated another Republican opponent by 10 percentage points.
Most people expected Kerrey to run for another term, but he mystified the
political class by stepping away from politics and announcing: "I feel my spiritual side needs to be filled back up." In the early 1990s, an eager and energetic
Kerrey ran for president of the United States. During his failed presidential
run, a political consultant who worked on Kerrey's 1988 Senate campaign told
Rolling Stone that Kerrey "is the kind of guy who will piss in the wind just to
see if he'll get wet."[3]

Kerrey advocated for government spending cuts and approached his job
from a business point of view. He also supported some progressive social
causes. In 1996 Kerrey was one of just fourteen senators to oppose the Defense
of Marriage Act (DOMA), which legally defined marriage at the federal level
as being between one man and one woman. DOMA stayed in place until it was
struck down by US Supreme Court decisions in 2013 and 2015 that expanded
gay marriage rights. When Kerrey voted against DOMA he stated that gay
couples "are not hurting us with their actions, in fact they may be helping us
by showing us that love can indeed conquer prejudice and hatred." That comment might seem rather dull to today's progressive reader, but Kerrey took a
bold stance for a red-state politician of the 1990s.[4]

It's remarkable now that someone like Kerrey could be so popular in Nebraska. He's pro-choice and religiously agnostic. He voted for an assault weapons ban and supported gay rights. He's also fiscally conservative and known in
Capitol Hill for his bipartisanship. He once called fellow Democrat President
Bill Clinton an "unusually good liar." He earned the nickname "Cosmic Bob"
because of his unorthodox philosophical beliefs of sometimes voting on the
right and sometimes voting on the left.[5]

Despite how popular he once was, Kerrey was a statistical long shot to
take Nebraska's open Senate seat in 2012. After running through the numbers, my college classmates concluded that barring a complete screw-up by

his Republican opponent, Deb Fischer, Kerrey stood little chance to win. Since Kerrey's previous run for office, in 1994, Nebraska had added 96,000 registered Republicans—and only 4,000 Democrats—to its voter lists. In 1994 Kerrey's Democrats controlled 40 percent of the electorate. By 2012 they had dwindled to 32 percent of the state's voters. The number of registered independents about doubled during this time, to 20 percent of voters, but that didn't help Democrats.

"The number of independents has grown dramatically, but many of them in Nebraska are closet Republicans who prefer to maintain the façade that they are independents," University of Nebraska political scientist John Hibbing told our class. "Independents in this state tend to break heavily for Republicans, meaning the party registration numbers underestimate Republican strength."

Another university political scientist added: "Kerrey has a great résumé that would be hard to duplicate, even in fiction, but it isn't selling because people are thinking, 'Well that's great, but you're a Democrat and I'm a Republican.'"[6]

Kerrey told me that the 2012 race was more difficult than his other campaigns because people had become more accustomed to voting down party lines. Throughout the 1980s and 1990s, Kerrey received about 20 percent of Republicans' votes. This time, he received just 4 percent of the Republican vote. "They just didn't vote Democratic," he said. "And with Obama at the top of the ticket, people were really anti-Obama and anti-Obamacare."

Kerrey had the experience and name recognition advantage. He had the backing of politicians like Chuck Hagel, celebrities like Steve Martin, and one of the richest people in the world in fellow Nebraskan Warren Buffett. (Although Buffett's father was a congressman and he has an enormous amount of wealth, Buffett usually doesn't get active in Nebraska politics. Buffett maintains no official relationship with the Democratic Party even though he sporadically fundraises for Democrats. His daughter, the philanthropist Susie Buffett, has been more active in political endeavors, but much of her effort and donations get directed to education projects, like the one that gave me and thousands of other working-class Nebraskan kids scholarships.) None of that helped Kerrey. Fischer walloped Kerrey by 16 percentage points. The resounding defeat sent the message that moderately liberal politicians had gone out of style in Nebraska, just as the Huskers' option offense had.[7]

"When that happened in 2012, I said something's changed," said Chris Rodgers, a Democrat county commissioner in Omaha. Rodgers told me Kerrey's large margin of defeat made it clear that "it's just a whole lot harder" for moderate and liberal candidates to win in Nebraska than it used to be.

With the numbers stacked against him, it's curious Kerrey chose to run at all. He'd been out of politics for more than a decade and settled down in New York City, where he married former *Saturday Night Live* writer Sarah Paley and served as president of the liberal arts college the New School. His time at the New School became tumultuous after *60 Minutes* ran a report that called into question what happened during Kerrey's time in Vietnam. A member of Kerrey's SEAL team, Gerhard Klann, told reporters that their group rounded up and killed Vietnamese women and children who they feared would alert enemy soldiers. Klann said that Kerrey ordered the killing. Kerrey and other members of his team denied these accusations and recalled the events differently. "I did not have to give an order to begin the killing," Kerrey wrote, "but I could have stopped it and I didn't." Following the report, paparazzi staked out Kerrey's residence, and students at his affluent school launched attack websites and held rallies near campus where protestors held placards displaying the mugshots of people they called war criminals. One placard featured Kerrey's face slotted next to Henry Kissinger's. Protestors at the university continued to haggle Kerrey, and the faculty senate handed him a vote of no confidence. Eventually he quit. Heralded as a war hero, successful as a local business owner, beloved as a governor and senator, Kerrey momentarily dealt with more public outcry as a private citizen in New York than he had in Lincoln when he was the most powerful man in the state. A major part of this is due to the press in New York being much more unrelenting than it is in the heartland.[8]

So when Kerrey decided to run for office again he put himself back in the spotlight and became a target. Kerrey's opponents repeatedly tagged him as a carpetbagger, which is convenient considering that Republican Nebraska senators like Ben Sasse and Chuck Hagel spent years outside the state before coming back and running for office. But unlike Sasse and Hagel, Kerrey filed late, and he hadn't been back in Nebraska for a few years before he ran. The carpetbag label got extra miles in this campaign because, to many Nebraska voters, New York City is a scourge. To give you an idea of how NYC is perceived by some in the rural Midwest, the end scene of *Terms of Endearment* is illustrative of life and art imitating each other. Kerrey was dating the star of the movie, Debra Winger. In the scene, Winger's character is a frustrated Nebraskan housewife on her deathbed. But she still finds energy to mock her philandering professor husband over his desire to live in New York City.

At a restaurant behind the lobby of a Greenwich Village boutique hotel where Jack Kerouac once lived, I asked Kerrey why he bothered campaigning in Nebraska when he realistically stood little chance of winning and he'd expose himself to vociferous attacks. Kerrey wore round thin-rimmed glasses and a fitted light blue checkered shirt popping out of his fleece. At this point in his life, Kerrey looked more like a well-dressed grandpa than a strapping man courting starlets. We were wayward sons for discussing Nebraska politics in what people back home view as enemy territory.

"I just felt like I had an obligation to try," Kerrey told me. "I had no illusion; I knew it was going to be hard." When I suggested that changes in voter registration likely doomed the effort from the start and pressed Kerrey on what he was searching for and who he had an "obligation" to, he seemed mildly annoyed by the questioning and gave an exhausted look, before replying "myself."

As bad as Kerrey's 2012 defeat was, things have only gotten worse for Nebraska Democrats. Kerrey lost by about 16 percentage points. In the three Senate races in Nebraska since then, Democrats lost by 31 points on average, and neither candidate came as close as Kerrey.

"The Democratic Party is in complete disarray in the state of Nebraska," former US senator and defense secretary Chuck Hagel told me.

It's telling that in the 2020 Senate election, Ben Sasse had a Republican primary challenger before any Democrat officially launched a campaign. The candidate that ended up winning the 2020 Democratic primary, Chris Janicek, was a baker originally from David City, the town where I was born. Janicek's greatest political claim to fame had been finishing second in a Democratic primary two years earlier. He had never won an election for public office before.

About a month after winning the primary, Janicek torpedoed whatever tiny chance he had at competing with Sasse. In a group text message, Janicek's campaign staff conversed about copyedits of a post they were working on.

Janicek dictated a message into this phone that he just had an argument with one of his female staffers. The message went on: "Do you think the campaign should spend some I'm [*sic*] getting her laid. . . . It will probably take three guys I want one for the mouth the ass in the va-jay-jay. Thoughts?! money." Janicek followed up: "Spend some money on getting her laid. Siri must be having a heat stroke!"[9]

Janicek immediately apologized within the group text, but the damage had already been done. The staff member filed a harassment complaint. The Nebraska Democratic Party demanded that Janicek withdraw from the race and cut him off from party resources such as voter file data. Multiple newspaper editorials called for him to drop out. Many Democratic candidates and officers individually called for Janicek to step down, which he resisted.[10]

After the party asked Janicek to leave the race, the Democratic candidate for Nebraska's Third Congressional District sounded off. Keep in mind that the Third Congressional is so conservative that Republicans often take 70 percent or more of the vote and sometimes the race is uncontested, which leaves it ripe for fringe challengers. The only time in recent history that Democrats ran competitively in that district was when Jane Kleeb's husband, Scott, captured 45 percent of the vote in 2006. In 2020 Mark Elworth ran unopposed in the Democratic primary to become the party's nominee. Elworth had previously run in Iowa and Nebraska races for the Libertarian and Legal Marijuana Now parties, so he wasn't a standard Democrat.[11]

On his Facebook page, Elworth unleashed a series of unhinged posts. He accused Democrats of engaging in a "witch hunt" when they asked Janicek to step down. He repeatedly accused chair Kleeb of backing another candidate in the district, David Else, who Elworth claimed opposed gay rights and legal marijuana. He shared a screenshot of a text message between himself and Else where Else stated that he believed marriage is between a man and a woman. The exchange was difficult to read because in the upper left-hand corner of the screenshot, there was an active Google maps navigation widget covering Elworth's reply wherein he talked about someone's wife being a "Victoria Secrets model." Elworth called Kleeb a "really bad narcissist" and a "bigot" and shared an exchange between himself and Kleeb wherein Kleeb replied to his series of texts with, "Do not contact me."[12]

The Janicek and Elworth episode was embarrassing for the party, and it wasn't the first time in recent history that a candidate made the party look unstable. While the Blue Wave was turning red seats blue during the 2018 midterms, Nebraska had a different experience. Its Democratic Party ran a Republican state senator for the governor's race because nobody else emerged as a viable candidate. The state's GOP treasurer and attorney general both ran unopposed. To be fair to Nebraska Democrats, they had an attorney general candidate at one point. But that guy dropped out after getting slapped with a felony for strangling his eighty-two-year-old father. After that, nobody stepped up to fill in.[13]

"From a political scientist's perspective, that seems like malpractice," said Ari Kohen, a University of Nebraska political science professor. "Democrats have a more difficult time raising money than the Republicans; that makes it very difficult to recruit someone to run statewide. Knowing the financial support will not be there in the same way it is for your opponent, you know you are running uphill, so why put yourself through a race like that that?"

Kim Robak, a former lieutenant governor turned lobbyist, flirted with the idea of running on the Democratic ticket for US Senate, but decided not to because she didn't see a path to victory. She said: "We just don't have the resources. I can't tell you how many times people have said 'you should run, you should run.' Well, I can't raise that amount of money."

Robak's experience is emblematic of the problems facing Nebraska Democrats. The party suffers from having too few serious candidates. It struggles to recruit well-connected Democrats because they don't see the point in dropping everything in their lives to run a race they're almost bound to lose. The cycle becomes self-fulfilling.

Former governor Dave Heineman said that the inability to hold competitive primaries is one of Nebraska Democrats' biggest problems. Heineman knows a thing or two about building parties. As executive director of the state's GOP, he helped Nebraska Republicans become a juggernaut. His adeptness at reading the party's base helped him pull off one of the state's biggest political upsets ever when he defeated Tom Osborne in the gubernatorial primary. Once he became governor, Republicans became even more dominant statewide.

In the Nebraska GOP, it's not unusual for four, five, or even six candidates to run for governor. Democrats are lucky if they field one viable candidate. "If you have a contested primary you gotta get organized, you gotta get volunteers on board, you gotta raise the money, you gotta get your message out,"

Heineman said. "If you don't have a contested primary . . . you get no coverage in the primary; no one knows your name coming out of your primary if
you're uncontested. So I think it puts them at a disadvantage and it puts us at
a big advantage by having gone through a competitive primary. You either get
better or you're not going to win."

Nebraska Legislature clerk Patrick O'Donnell told me that part of the
reason Democrats have a short bench is because Democrat governors didn't
do a good job of building up the party while they were in power. When Jim
Exon was governor during the 1970s, he helped build Nebraska's Democratic
Party, which paved the way for Democrats to win senate and governor races
throughout the 1980s and 1990s. But the Democratic leaders who followed
Exon weren't as active in building up their party.

Republican governors have been much more effective at party building.
When governors are involved with the legislature to the point of expelling
people from within their own party for not being loyal enough, they create a
cult-of-personality power dynamic. On the other hand, being inactive with
state lawmakers doesn't help emerging candidates elevate their position.

John Cavanaugh, a Democrat who represented Omaha in Congress during
the late 1970s, said that throughout state history Democratic governors hav-
en't been party builders, and they've often built their own campaign structures
instead of relying on their party. Cavanaugh is quite familiar with Nebraska
Democratic Party history. Over multiple generations, his Democratic father,
uncles, siblings, and children held various elected positions. "We haven't had
a situation really where [Democrat governors] were actually interested in running the party," he said. "They mostly wanted it to stay out of the way." In
some ways, this is true at the national level as well, seeing that Bill Clinton
and Barack Obama have been criticized for letting state parties' infrastructure
crumble while they were in office.[14]

A few Democratic officials I spoke with took offense at the notion their
party has a short bench. They claim the issue isn't a lack of talented candidates.
Rather, the problem is convincing qualified people to run for higher office
when the state's voter registration and fundraising trends aren't in their favor.
"You have to say to yourself, 'If I run, can I win? Do I want to give up what I've
got here?' . . . Let's say you're a state senator, you're doing great," said former
Democrat state chair Vince Powers. "Do you want to run when you look at
the numbers?"

Whether the problem is a lack of viable candidates or that good candidates are out there but can't be convinced to run, the end result is the same—Democrats lose. As Robak demonstrated, it's difficult for Democrats to convince candidates to run when they're planning on getting outspent. According to Nebraska Democratic Party chair Jane Kleeb, the amount of money the state party received from the Democratic National Committee (DNC) dwindled from $25,000 a month to $2,500 a month after Barack Obama became president and Howard Dean no longer ran the DNC. The state party now receives $10,000 per month from the DNC, which is an improvement but still below previous levels. Kleeb's chair position is unpaid.[15]

"The national party for the last ten years has literally treated state parties as if they are out on their own, rather than this is a national party and the state parties are the basic infrastructure that we have," Kleeb said. "A major culture shift needs to happen at the national level on how they view and treat state parties. Is that beginning to shift? Yes. Is it where it needs to be? Not even close."

For too long, Democrats in Nebraska ignored rural areas and failed to consistently show up and make their case, Kleeb said. Politicians would parachute into town the month before an election and ask for people's vote, and that strategy never paid off. Democrats might see a bloodbath in the heavily Republican area of western Nebraska, but by not visiting small towns they help perpetuate the image that they don't care about folks there.

"When you ignore state parties, you don't have financial resources to then compete in very difficult districts," Kleeb said. She continued:

So your party gets smaller and smaller until you no longer even have events in the remote rural areas of the state. This is not just a Nebraska issue. If you talk to any red state Democratic Party chair, they will tell you that for the last ten years, they have been living on very slim margins and they are lucky if they have a paid chair and maybe have one or two staff members. That is a national party issue. The DNC, the DCCC [Democratic Congressional Campaign Committee], all of those national party organizations currently raising millions of dollars, instead of funding a bunch of staff in DC or a bunch of consultants, they should be putting money in to the state parties where the rubber hits the road, where you are the one recruiting candidates and convincing them that they actually have an infrastructure to win. . . . When you have people in these national organizations who have never lived in a red state or in a small town, they have the stereotypes of a red state and a small town and so they give up on us. They don't even think twice about it. They get sidetracked with whatever coastal race they are focused on.

Even where Democrats are clustered in Nebraska, it's been a struggle promoting the party. Nearly 40 percent of the state's Democrats reside in Douglas County, which includes Omaha. For context, about 30 percent of all Nebraskans live in Douglas County, making it the state's most populous county. Despite having a higher share of Democrats than the rest of the state, the Douglas County Democratic Party had just $13,000 in its bank account in 2016 when Crystal Rhoades became chair of the county's Democrats. Rhoades said that "isn't enough money to help anybody with anything." The county office's coffers have filled up some since then, but they aren't where they need to be in order to thoroughly fund party-building tactics such as direct mailings, digital advertising, voter registration initiatives, and campaign events.[16]

In elections for governor and US Congress, Nebraska Democrats get crushed more often than not. The only race where they're regularly competitive is in the state's Second Congressional District, which includes Omaha. The past five elections in the second district have been decided by just a few percentage points, and in 2014 Democrat Brad Ashford won before ceding power to the GOP two years later. Kara Eastman represented the Democrats in this district in the 2018 election and ran another tight race. According to Eastman, she was supported by national Democratic groups like the DCCC, but they ended their funding at an inopportune time. She said that two weeks before the election, these groups diverted their money elsewhere.

"The party pulled support at the end, but we found out that's because they felt like they had the seats they needed to win [control of the US House], which is a shame," Eastman told me. "I do feel like Nebraska has been abandoned by the party. . . . We're just really not on the radar for national politics too much, and that needs to change, especially on the Democratic side."

Another issue for Democrats is that the rural-urban divide has become a focal point of our national politics, which isn't unique to the United States. Statistics show that rural areas tend to be more conservative and cities tend to be more liberal. Bob Kerrey said that part of the reason Democrats in Nebraska struggle much more now than they did when he was in office is because the party "has become much more of an urban party." But even in Omaha, the state's biggest city, Democrats aren't really winning in Nebraska.[17]

Registered Democrats do win state legislative races and down-ballot races on the county board and city council in Omaha, but Republicans are winning in these areas too. Omaha's mayor is a Republican who rode to victory after her Democratic opponent got sucked into an abortion controversy. In the congressional district that Omaha belongs to, Democrats held power for just two years since 1995. And that Democrat was a former Republican. Many Democrats who I interviewed were quick to blame their party's ills on Republicans who gerrymander and suppress voter turnout, but when the losses are so frequent and routine—and occur across a multitude of political bodies that all have their own distinct geographical boundaries—Democrats should spend more energy figuring out what they need to change in order to win instead of blaming others when they don't.[18]

Like in most states, each consecutive census shows that a higher share of Nebraskans are living in cities. Over two-thirds of Nebraska's ninety-three counties lost population since 2000. Brainard is lucky because it is the site of a consolidated high school that keeps the town alive. Our school's enrollment has decreased some since I went there, and they now play eight-man football after going down a class size. But the school is far from closing and that's because its enrollment is propped up by other towns who now ship their kids to Brainard because they lost their own school. Those towns haven't been so fortunate. Across Nebraska, I've witnessed small towns lose their schools and sense of hope as population loss, blight, meth, and business closures set in. Once the school goes, you can feel the decay accelerate. It bites your face like a midwinter Great Plains wind gust. This issue is personal to rural voters. If Democrats can develop a plan to help these schools survive, they will find sympathetic ears.[19]

"What is happening in many small towns—the devastating loss of educated and talented young people, the aging of the population, and the erosion of the local economy—has repercussions far beyond their boundaries," wrote husband-and-wife sociologists Patrick Carr and Maria Kefalas in their study of midwestern brain drain. "Put simply, the health of the small towns that are dotted across the Heartland matters because, without them, the country couldn't function, in the same way that a body cannot function without a heart."[20]

Increased urbanization should benefit Nebraska Democrats, but it hasn't. Despite the growth of Nebraska's urban population, the state's number of registered Democrats keeps shrinking. One reason for this phenomenon is that hordes of young people with college degrees keep leaving the state. I am one of them. And so is my roommate who grew up in south-central Nebraska and attended the University of Nebraska only to become a doctor in the Bronx. The American small-town way of life we experienced in our youth is crumbling in part because people in our position keep leaving it behind.

My roommate and I are part of a broader trend. A study of US census data showed that between 2006 and 2010, Nebraska ranked thirty-fourth in the rate at which it lost people with college degrees. Between 2011 and 2015, Nebraska ranked forty-forth in this metric. The brain drain, coupled with the state having one of the lowest unemployment rates in the nation, contributes to what area business leaders call a "workforce crisis" where companies cannot locally find enough people with degrees to fill open jobs. The problem appears to be getting worse, which doesn't bode well for the Democratic Party that relies on votes from young people with college degrees.[21]

I left home for a better career opportunity, which is the type of cliché found in corporate brochures. I wanted to write books, but I needed to bulk up my experience and résumé before anyone would give me a contract to do so. Fresh out of college, the lure of internships and fellowships from Crain's, *Esquire*, and Deadspin were too good to pass up. The stipulation with those jobs was that I had to move eastward.

Taking those jobs helped me secure writing assignments for more major newspapers and magazines, which in turn helped me get a contract for my first book, which helped me get a deal for my second book, which helped me convince the University Press of Kansas that this book was worth publishing. There are many writers in Nebraska who are more talented and successful than me, but due to the way that the country's largest media companies structure their workforce to operate in just a few select cities, anyone in my profession (sportswriters excluded) who stays in Nebraska has an uphill fight if they want to gain recognition. It's notable that most of the very successful writers who are originally from or currently live in the state have lived elsewhere at some point in their lives, usually because a job pulled them away.

Paradoxically, if I never left the state to work for well-known media firms, I don't think a respectable publisher would've been interested in a book I authored about Nebraska politics. Had I never left I probably wouldn't have had interest in writing one, either. I didn't truly grasp how polarized our country was and how politically self-reinforcing my hometown was until I lived in an area opposite of it, which made me reexamine my assumptions.

Because no one in my immediate family had lived outside the state, I initially felt uneasy about moving so far away. I enjoyed Nebraska's quietness, the friendliness of its people, the joy of riding my bike down a crushed-rock trail through unincorporated villages dotted along the prairie, the regularity of Huskers football on Saturdays and church get-togethers on Sundays, and the ease of finding my way around familiar places. "Such accessories, and the dust and the winds and the ever-calling train whistles, add up to a 'home town' that is probably remembered with nostalgia by those who have left it, and that for those who have remained, provides a sense of roots and contentment," wrote Truman Capote in his blockbuster book *In Cold Blood*, which tells the story of how a rural Kansas family fell victim to murderers.[22]

As hard as moving was, technology made it easier. I never had an internet-enabled phone when I lived in Nebraska, but that changed in New York because of the constant demands of my digital media job. My smartphone made it more difficult to tune out work, but constant access to social media and messaging apps helped me stay in touch with friends and family. To keep tabs on what was going on back home, I read the *Omaha World-Herald* or *Lincoln Journal Star* on my phone whenever I got stuck on the subway. Apps made it easier to book cabs or flights when I felt the need to return home. They also made it easier for me to find new apartments whenever my relationships with the rotating cast of strangers that I lived with frayed. During my first five years in New York, I lived in six different apartments with a combined eighteen roommates, not including the Airbnb guests who stayed illegally or the hidden roommate in one apartment that I found out about a week after I had moved in. I also didn't have an address for months at a time because, after getting fed up with the overcrowded places in my budget, I'd travel and stay with people I knew while storing my few possessions in friends' closets. It was the millennial equivalent of living in a suitcase.

Technology reduces resistance for mobility and makes it easier for a kid from the heartland to relocate to a coastal city. It also contributes to self-reinforcing social divisions. Instead of being a left-of-center kid in Nebraska, where I'd respectfully disagree with my conservative friends over a few Bud Lights as we called into question each other's assumptions, I became just another moderately liberal young guy living in New York City who hung out with people who shared many of the same beliefs. When I was a high schooler in Nebraska I was so strongly against illegal immigration, partially because I didn't really know any immigrants or witness their experiences, and since everyone around me was so intent on shipping undocumented people away, my beliefs on the matter were never scrutinized. My thoughts about immigration changed after I formed relationships with immigrants. Likewise, I'm probably developing biases right now that I'm not conscious of. My biases are further fueled by the disproportionate number of New York media people I follow who are very active on social media and who tend to perpetuate the same opinions among themselves (and antagonize anyone who dares disagree) with such an intensity that I ponder if they belong to a community-wide hive mind like *Star Trek*'s Borg. I'd be challenged more thoroughly if I hung out with conservatives more often in New York, but I haven't met all that many conservatives in New York. I didn't have politics in mind when I moved. But with thousands of people in similar positions making similar moves, the cumulative effects of these migrations are consequential.

"As people seek out the social settings they prefer—as they choose the group that makes them feel the most comfortable—the nation grows more politically segregated—and the benefit that ought to come with having a variety of opinions is lost to the righteousness that is the special entitlement of homogeneous groups," wrote Bill Bishop and Robert Cushing in their influential book *The Big Sort: Why the Clustering of Like-Minded America Is Tearing Us Apart*, which concludes that the United States became more polarized because people increasingly decided to move to neighborhoods that align with their beliefs and lifestyles. They added: "Like-minded, homogeneous groups squelch dissent, grow more extreme in their thinking, and ignore evidence that their positions are wrong. As a result, we now live in a giant feedback loop, hearing our own thoughts about what's right and wrong bounced back to us by the television shows we watch, the newspapers and books we read, the blogs we visit online, the sermons we hear, and the neighborhoods we live in."[23]

In Nebraska, the continual loss of young college-educated people, like myself, who tend to lean further left than the rest of the state, reduced resistance for the GOP as it marched ever rightward. This has been the case throughout the Midwest, which has suffered worse population losses than any other US region since the turn of the century. With the Democratic share of voters declining, the feedback loop keeps telling the majority who vote for Republicans that they're on the right side.[24]

What ails the Democratic Party in red states such as Nebraska could fill the pages of multiple books. It's s a pick-your-poison situation. The reasons for the downfall are many, and they're not mutually exclusive. When I asked some of the state's most recognizable political figures about the topic, their answers were all over the place. There's no silver bullet or single soundbite that can concisely and definitively explain the problem away. Everyone has their theories; some are self-serving.

Republicans blame Democrats for focusing on identity politics and giving up on white rural voters. Democrats blame Republicans for weaponizing identity politics and turning people against demographic groups. Democrats and moderate Republicans blame the gutting of campaign finance restrictions and the increasing amount of untraceable corporate money used to boost far-right candidates into power. Republicans and moderate Democrats blame the national Democratic Party for being too dogmatic about abortion rights and for veering too far left, which makes Democrats mostly unelectable in red states. Progressive Democrats blame gerrymandering and voter suppression. Progressives also said that voters are tired of "Republican light" centrists and that the reason state Democrats are in a hole is because they never tried to distinguish themselves from the Republicans. Moderate Democrats said that Nebraska Democrats are adopting a losing strategy by running more progressive candidates who aren't aligned with most voters' values.

Sources across the political spectrum acknowledged that brain drain, an aging population, a perceived push for secularization among the Democratic Party, partisan voting splitting rural-urban lines, and Democrats' inadequate local political infrastructure and shortage of competitive candidates who are willing to run combine to make it more difficult for Democrats to win in Nebraska. Polarization in media and social media news sources were also commonly cited.

Another issue is that Democrats can't seem to get on the same page. In a system with just two major parties, conflict is common within parties. The coalitions that make up our large and evolving nationwide parties are at times at odds with each other. Sometimes it seems like there is as much fighting within the parties as there is between them. Throughout our state's history, these internal divisions have cost both Republicans and Democrats elections.

For example, the moderate Republican governor Nobby Tiemann was defeated by Democrat Jim Exon in 1970 because Tiemann was weakened by people within his own party. Conservatives came after Tiemann because he restructured the state's finances by implementing income and sales taxes, which allowed the state to increase state aid to K–12 schools, expand its public university system, and establish a department of economic development. During the 1970 GOP primary, Tiemann barely defeated a far-right candidate who opposed taxes and open housing for racial minorities. Tiemann failed to win over conservatives, and many Republicans went on to support Exon, who ran to the right of Tiemann. Republican infighting and the bruising primary contributed to Tiemann's defeat in November. When asked about his defeat years later, Tiemann remarked that he "didn't spend enough time kissing Republican leadership butt."[25]

Inner turmoil within the Republican Party surfaced again with the Tea Party movement. Republican Lee Terry represented Omaha in Congress for eight consecutive terms before losing in 2014. That year, Terry won a close primary despite significantly outspending his more conservative opponent. Competitive primaries can strengthen parties, but in Terry's case, the attacks from within his party were more like self-sabotage because they continued after the primary ended. Numerous Democrats and Republicans that I interviewed said that the opposition from very conservative Libertarians and Tea Partiers weakened Terry, which contributed to his loss to Democrat Brad Ashford in November. Terry voted with his party 92 percent of the time but was still considered too moderate for far-right purists. Terry told me that a week before the general election, he met with one of the Tea Party activists who was frequently critical of him and asked why the far-right contingent seemed more willing to put a Democrat in office than reelect Terry. "They said, 'Well because what we'll do is we'll beat you. And then we can go back and beat the Democrat the next time,'" according to Terry. And that's what ended up happening when Ashford was defeated by Republican Don Bacon the following election. "That just pisses me off that it worked out the way they said," Terry said.[26]

Every once in a while Republicans eat their own, and there are people within the GOP dismayed with its leadership, but while working on this book the past few years, I noticed a bigger division in the state Democratic Party than the Republican Party. With Republicans, the governor and his associates have a firm grip on power. They have a large influence over who runs and wins in the Nebraska Legislature. Lawmakers loyal to the party are springboarded into new positions of power, such as state auditor and treasurer. Once a legislator leaves for a new office, the governor appoints someone to fill the vacancy. Those appointed are a new generation of party loyalists in their twenties, whose qualifications include being employed either by the governor or by the person they're replacing. To keep people in line, the governor, or groups connected to his family, wields his/their financial resources to support a primary candidate who challenges fellow Republicans who vote against the governor. This strategy may seem calculated and off-putting, but it's legal. Another way to view it is as an effective way to retain power.[27]

On the rare instances that a Nebraska Republican in office actually challenges their party, the state GOP tells them to leave. State senator John McCollister is a lifelong Republican who has deep ties to the party. His father was a Republican congressman who represented Omaha during the 1970s. McCollister was also executive director of the Platte Institute, a conservative think tank founded by Governor Pete Ricketts. These credentials weren't enough to save him from his own party's wrath.

Following a wave of mass shootings in the summer of 2019, McCollister took to Twitter to call out President Trump and the Republican Party for promoting falsehoods and enabling racism and violence. McCollister's thread went viral, and he appeared on a litany of TV news programs. "I don't accept the mandates of today's GOP because MOST of these ideas weren't EVEN part of our original tradition," McCollister said in one social media post. "Republicans didn't always hate public schools. Republicans didn't always try to bludgeon unions. Republicans didn't always ignore scientists. Republicans used to fight corruption, not promote it. Republicans used to follow the constitution." His criticism angered people within his party.[28]

Tom Brewer, the Republican state senator at odds with the university and who chaired the legislature's government affairs committee, told me that

McCollister is now "one of the more disliked senators in the body." Brewer accused McCollister of bringing more partisanship to the legislature. He said that McCollister lost political capital by pitting himself against his party. Brewer stated: "I guarantee if John McCollister has a bill that comes before the government committee, it will likely be at the bottom of the pile, not at the top of the pile. And I think there are a number of committee chairs who feel the same way." The executive director of the Nebraska Republican Party went a step further. He sent a statement to McCollister that read: "I am happy to send a change of voter registration form along to his office so he can make the switch officially and start, for once, telling the truth to voters in his district."[29]

The *Lincoln-Journal Star* editorial board wrote that the GOP's response gave the impression that "As if orthodoxy, loyalty and groupthink must triumph over independent inquiry for someone to be a member of an organization . . . any questioning of the standard bearer is apparently anathema to Nebraska's GOP leadership. . . . Attempting to kick a sitting state senator out of the GOP, merely because he disagrees with what he sees, illustrates that only those who pass an ideological purity test are welcome within the tent is petty beyond belief—and a repudiation of its past." This inflammatory partisan-driven exchange occurred within the same Nebraska Legislature that I was taught to be nonpartisan.[30]

McCollister quickly became a media darling, and liberals who've never been to Nebraska thanked him online for his bravery. But McCollister made these comments knowing they wouldn't affect his odds of retaining office. He won reelection in 2018, and because the Nebraska Legislature has term limits, he'll be out of the body in 2022 regardless of how popular or unpopular he is. "The risk to me is minimal," McCollister said. "We don't have a caucus system in Nebraska, and I term out in three years, so I think I won't pay a big political price." It's telling that no Nebraska Republican lawmakers with something to lose are making similar stands. "I'd like to see some moral outrage from some of our Republican officeholders," McCollister said. "The silence is deafening."[31]

On the Democratic side, divisions are more apparent. When I asked Preston Love Jr.—a political activist out of North Omaha who has held positions within the Nebraska Democratic Party and worked on campaigns for nationally famous politicians like Jesse Jackson and Harold Washington—why there is so much division among Democrats, he chuckled and said that "the answer requires a social psychologist."

With Democrats, there's been a push to replace the centrist old guard with more liberal candidates. This is a national trend best viewed through local examples. Nationally, the split in the party became very visible when Bernie Sanders challenged Hillary Clinton to represent the Democratic ticket in the 2016 election and supporters of his refused to support Clinton after she won the nomination. These tensions haven't disappeared. A writer in the *New York Review of Books* wondered if the 2020 elections will become a "schismatic turning point that proved that the divisions were beyond bridging" for the Democrats. The party's rifts run all the way through lowly populated conservative states like Nebraska. The differences in Democratic factions were noticeable down to the locations where sources suggested I interview them.[32]

I met Ben Nelson at the corporate law firm he works at. The place was full of older men in stiff suits. A parking garage sat beneath the building. Leatherbound books and thick wooden desks filled the office. While we talked, the only discernible sound in the background was the drone of an air ventilation system. The surrounding neighborhood had more cul-de-sacs than my GPS knew what to do with. Across the road was a strip mall where the best place to eat was a Panera Bread imitator. If you're a centrist politician who prefers working with businesses, it's a great place to do work.

When I met Kara Eastman, we grabbed a table at a hip coffee shop in Omaha's historic Dundee district. The other people in the shop included guys with visible tattoos hiding long hair under stocking hats and women sporting simple chic looks. Fliers for free birth control, art exhibitions, living room concerts, socialist zines, and local farmer's markets adorned the place. While we talked, cups clanged and patrons talked over jazz records. A few blocks down the street there were music clubs and an artsy theater with films shown in select cities. If you're a progressive candidate who prefers working with liberal grassroots partners, it's a great place to do work.

Eastman surprised many people when she won the 2018 Democratic primary for Nebraska's Second Congressional District. Eastman was relatively new to the Nebraska political scene. The only elected position she'd held was being a board member of Metro Community College. Her primary opponent, Brad Ashford, had been on the Nebraska political scene for ages. Ashford is a former Republican who represented two different districts in the Nebraska

Legislature between 1987 and 2015. He switched parties and gave the Democrats a victory in the Second Congressional District in 2014 before he lost the seat to Republican Don Bacon in 2016.

Things got awkward when the DCCC put Ashford on its "Red-to-Blue" list during primary season. Matters got more heated at a Nebraska Democratic Party fundraiser that took place about a year prior to the 2018 general election. To stir up donors' excitement, the Nebraska Democratic Party invited out-of-state Democratic figures like South Bend, Indiana, mayor Pete Buttigieg and Michigan congresswoman Debbie Dingell. During the event, Dingell told the crowd that they need to help put Ashford back in Congress. The remark offended some in attendance.

"Because [state party chair Kleeb] brought in a surrogate and had them stand up in front of the entire state Democratic Party fundraising dinner and stump for Brad [Ashford] when Kara [Eastman] was sitting in the room, because she did all of those things, that created a lot of tension," former Douglas County Democratic Party chair Crystal Rhoades told me. "The county party ended up forming our own federal committee so that I could do candidate-neutral vote-by-mail, site cards, all those things the [state] party should be doing. It really created a very clear line."

Aside from heading Douglas County Democrats, Rhoades also serves on the Nebraska Public Service Commission. And her husband was Eastman's campaign manager in 2018. Rhoades hasn't been shy about criticizing Kleeb. The chair of the state party and the head of the Democratic Party in the state's biggest county clearly didn't see eye-to-eye.

Rhoades accused Kleeb of "sabotaging" Eastman, being "divisive and the reason the state party has struggled to recruit and elect Democrats," improperly sharing Democratic Party data with external groups, cutting Eastman's campaign off from a critical Democratic voter database, telling Douglas County donors that giving money to their county's party was illegal, and "jeopardizing every single [Democrat] candidate in [Douglas] county." Kleeb said that Rhoades notified donors of the environmental activist group Kleeb cofounded, "telling them not to donate to us because of me," and that Rhoades went on a "rant" about "what an awful person I am." Kleeb wrote that Rhoades's "behavior is out of control and we can't just turn the other cheek anymore" and went on to endorse a candidate running against Rhoades for county chair. After Kleeb endorsed Rhoades's challenger, the *World-Herald* reported that Rhoades supported a behind-the-scenes effort to remove Kleeb from her chair position. Rhoades declined to run again for county chair in 2020.[33]

Rhoades stated that Kleeb "grabs a person of color as a token for her photos. Then she leaves without doing a thing to actually help." Following the token comments, Precious McKesson resigned as the Democrat African American representative for Douglas County and criticized Rhoades for her treatment of women of color. In response, Rhoades apologized for offending McKesson and her colleagues. (Former Nebraska Democratic Black Caucus chairwoman Chelsey Gentry-Tipton took to Facebook to back Rhoades and criticize Kleeb and McKesson. Gentry-Tipton wrote that McKesson "knows EVERYTHING about Jane Kleeb and her corruption and she is attacking Crystal Rhoades in efforts to help Jane destroy Kara Eastman's campaign. SHE IS A TOKEN.")[34]

During a 2018 state central committee meeting, Nebraska Democrats passed a nonbinding resolution that state and county party chairs shouldn't take sides during primaries. That resolution didn't calm the tension. Preston Love told me that he suggested getting the Douglas County and state chairs together so that they could work their problems out and start helping each other. "Man, they told me to go to hell," Love said. "They didn't want to get together and work it out. They didn't want to be in the same room."[35]

When I asked Rhoades in 2018 why Kleeb, whose job is to get Nebraska Democrats elected, would possibly want to sabotage a rising candidate, Rhoades replied: "For [Kleeb], it was really about wanting to maintain and have more control. Wanting to be able to say that the state party was an active player in the campaign. Beyond that I don't really know. I think it was an exercise in trying to exert power. I don't know; other than that, I have no idea. I haven't had a conversation with Jane Kleeb in months."

I talked to Eastman two days before she publicly announced she would run again in 2020. Eastman stopped short of listing infighting as a roadblock to her campaign, but she said that there was "favoritism" in the party when she ran in 2018, "which is too bad." This issue could crop up again in future elections.

"The party is changing, and change is always hard," Rhoades said. She continued:

There will be people who want it and people who don't, and that causes sort of a natural divisiveness. Right now the party is going through a crisis of what are we, who are we, what are we going to become. . . . My frustration is that once the voters have spoken, the party needs to fall in line. This is something Republicans do that Democrats don't. . . . Once [Republicans] have their nominee, they have their nominee, and everybody rallies behind them. If there is a lesson to be learned for us, that's what it is. That's what we need to do, always, is get behind our nominees.

Veteran lobbyist Walt Radcliffe said that intraparty squabbles have always been around, but they usually occur behind closed doors. Part of the reason Nebraska Democrats publicly infight more than Republicans lately is because Democrats are more frustrated with one another due to their constant losses. "You know, winners don't usually fight," he said.

Democrats in red states like Nebraska tend to be idealistic, said former state Democrat chair Vic Covalt. To defend their status in a group that is statistically disadvantaged, they tend to demand that the party elevates their preferred candidate and are reluctant to compromise. "It is just one of those natural things—the minority party will always be a little bit self-destructive in its pursuit of the perfect over the good," Covalt said. He added: "There are a lot of problems with people in their little fiefdoms and their little egos, and they're clinging to losing positions after they lost. That's a real problem. You got to get over that if you're going to win."

Barry Rubin, a former Nebraska Democratic Party executive director turned lobbyist, talked at length when I asked him what's hindering Democrats in Nebraska. Over lunch on a December afternoon that wasn't that bad out after the wind died down, he shared that Democrats have to become more willing to support candidates that they don't always agree with. He felt that Democrats care too much about being right and not enough about winning. Regarding infighting, Rubin said that "the Democratic Party here in Nebraska is famous for circular firing squads" and that the arguments that occur at party meetings turn potential candidates off while encouraging "crazy people" to become active. "It's like an island of misfit toys." He took issue with national organizations like the Democratic Legislative Campaign Committee (DLCC) that refused to support Nebraska state senators financially because they couldn't take credit for a "win" if they got someone elected to a nonpartisan body. He griped about people active in the Nebraska Democratic Party "who care more about coming to four central committee meetings a year than finding a candidate to run for dog catcher or for county council or mayor."

Megan Hunt, a progressive small business owner out of Omaha who is the first openly LGBT person elected to the Nebraska Legislature, didn't go as far as Rubin in her criticism but did acknowledge infighting. She said that it's in the nature of Democrats to resist authority figures. Democrats who dissent and critique the leaders in their party think they're helping by challenging the powers that be. Instead, what happens is the party becomes less unified. Her response was illustrative of how many liberals think. She said:

> I am just kind of an independent-minded person. I don't really need a party to tell me what to think or how to believe. I think we would really benefit if we had more unity in our party. I think one thing about Democrats is just, psychologically, by nature, we're just a little more resistant to authority. We have to get talked into a good candidate. Whereas, I feel with Republicans you can't talk them out of a bad candidate. With Democrats, we will be in party meetings and don't come to an agreement. But Republicans, on the other hand, they follow the leader. You know of course that's something I love about being a Democrat and that's something I love about the party. But I don't know if that's getting us wins in elections.

Former congressman Cavanaugh shared a similar theory explaining the Democrats' lack of cohesion: "We're not a party-driven party. We're individual driven."

Disputes among Nebraska Democrats long predate the feud between Kleeb and Rhoades. Before Kleeb became Democratic chair, her predecessor withdrew from the position amid party turmoil. Back in the 1960s, there was a split in the party over a failed attempt to oust its entrenched national committeeman. After Nebraska became a state in 1867, its first seven governors were Republicans. A big reason why Republicans controlled state politics at that time was because Democratic leaders like J. Sterling Morton and George Miller divided their own party and couldn't reconcile their differences. "The Democrats have rarely been able to get along in Omaha," Robak said.[36]

Intraparty divisions surfaced in the summer of 2017 after a left-wing activist opened fire during a practice for the congressional baseball game for charity in Virginia. The gunman wounded Louisiana Republican congressman

Steve Scalise and several others. Following the shooting, Nebraska Democratic Black Caucus chairwoman Chelsey Gentry-Tipton commented on Facebook that she had trouble feeling sorry for Scalise because he showed a "complete disregard for human life" when he pushed "pro NRA legislation."[37]

Kleeb asked Gentry-Tipton to resign, but that did not transpire. Phil Montag, then cochair of the Nebraska Democrats technology committee, went to a private home in Omaha to discuss the matter with Gentry-Tipton. Montag told reporters that he wanted to console Gentry-Tipton over the backlash her posts provoked. In an effort to empathize, Montag ranted that he hated Scalise, whose "whole job is to convince Republicans to fucking kick people off of fucking healthcare." For good measure, Montag added, "I'm fucking glad he got shot."[38]

Gentry-Tipton and one of her friends secretly recorded Montag and tried to get him to publicly state his support for Gentry-Tipton. Montag was told he had twenty-four hours to comply. Following this exchange, Gentry-Tipton's friend leaked a truncated, edited version of Montag's rant to an online news source and the story took off. Kleeb immediately fired Montag. And the Nebraska Democratic Party Black Caucus unanimously voted to remove Gentry-Tipton from her position.[39]

"When Phil [Montag] says what he said, man oh man, that's on him; I want nothing to do with that," Love said. "But we've got to figure out within the party how to better work together. The Democratic Party, nationally, state and locally, needs to be inclusive not only statistically, but in reality."[40]

The lack of cohesion among Democrats, combined with the Republicans' dominance of Nebraska's elections, gives the impression that the Cornhusker State is more conservative than any other place in the United States. Democrats win so few high-profile races in the state that when I chatted with Public Service commissioner Rhoades in 2018, she let out a subdued laugh when she referred to herself as the "highest-ranking Democrat elected in the state of Nebraska." However, Nebraska is not a monolith. Progressivism flows throughout the state in a way that is obfuscated by party politics.

The Ogallala Aquifer is a treasure. It's a massive freshwater source that sits under Nebraska and a few nearby states. Farmers like my nephews, uncles, and cousins rely on for it irrigation. I relied on it for drinking water, bathing, and more. For the past decade, the aquifer has been the subject of an ongoing political battle between environmentalists and a foreign oil corporation. The controversy is over whether TC Energy, formerly known as TransCanada, has the right to build its Keystone XL pipeline to push crude oil from Canada through Nebraska.

As of this writing, the pipeline is caught in a legal quagmire due to pressure from environmental operatives like Jane Kleeb, who helped lead the fight against the pipeline. TC Energy has met resistance and legal challenges in other states, but Nebraskans have been particularly active in blocking it. Nebraska landowners sued TransCanada over its use of eminent domain, which was followed by the oil company filling its own slew of land ownership lawsuits. A Nebraska farmer sold some land along the pipeline's proposed route to the Ponca Tribe of Nebraska, adding another legal barrier for the pipeline. Nebraska activists have been opposing Keystone XL for a decade, and challenges to the pipeline have snaked through Nebraska's courts, Public Service Commission, and governor's office. The pipeline remains in limbo, and both sides keep fighting.[41]

The people protesting the pipeline in Nebraska belong to a politically diverse coalition of conservative farmers and ranchers, Native American tribes, and liberal environmentalists. Protests against the pipeline included community events ranging from an anti-pipeline tractor pull, a concert featuring Neil Young and Willie Nelson, and a pumpkin-carving session near the governor's mansion to stunts like planting Ponca corn and building a barn covered in solar panels along the pipeline's route. Nebraska football fans even opposed the pipeline. When a TransCanada ad aired on the big screen during a 2011 contest, boos filled the stadium. The school promptly ended its sponsorship deal with TransCanada the following week.[42]

Mary Pipher, a Nebraska author and environmental activist who helped organize protests against the pipeline, said:

> One of the ways we had as much luck as we did with Keystone is we didn't frame it in political terms. We worked with Nebraska language and kept framing it in ways that were extremely non-ideological, like we had water festivals and pumpkin parties against the pipeline. We never used any progressive language. We didn't even use the word "environmentalist" or "climate change." We talked about protecting Nebraska's heritage. It was totally intentional. . . .

At first, when we got these Republican farmers and ranchers working with us, we were stunned. But we really figured out a way to craft our work in non-ideological terms.

Showing a flair for environmentalism isn't anything new for Nebraska. In 1872, Nebraska City was the first community in the country to celebrate Arbor Day. That tradition continues as Nebraska expands its renewable energy output. I felt Nebraska's powerful winds whenever I rode my bike in Brainard against punishing drifts or watched tornado clouds form above our house. Some people are trying to take economic advantage of these conditions. According to a study by the wind-power trade group American Wind Energy Association, when calculated on a percentage basis, Nebraska led the country in wind energy growth in 2018. Nebraska's been ranked as the windiest state in the country by the Department of Energy, so there's more room for expansion there.[43]

Nebraska has a tradition of being progressive about energy. It's the only state in the nation whose electric utilities are public entities. The main difference between municipal-owned and corporate-owned power is that when a town controls its own utilities, the town is free to use income from its utilities as it sees fit whereas investor-owned utilities send money profits back to shareholders. Municipal-owned entities are also less prone to jack up rates during an energy shortage or manipulate the market like energy corporations did to California during its 2001 power crisis. Nebraska's electric rates are about 15 percent cheaper than the national average, and Nebraska has cheaper rates than most of the states it borders.[44]

"I don't think Nebraskans really see public power as being progressive even though it is," said Omaha Public Power District board member Janece Mollhoff. "I don't think that the majority of Nebraskans really see it as progressive as much as they see it as a driver of the ag economy. Because really, without affordable power in our rural areas, to run all of those center pivots and all of the farming operations, it would be more difficult for us to have a thriving ag economy without public power."

In 1885 the Nebraska Legislature granted municipalities the power to control their local electric and water services. Private power companies said this was tantamount to socialism, but Nebraskans proceeded anyway to wrestle control of their energy away from corporations. Crete became the first in the state to feature a municipality-owned power plant. Schuyler followed soon after. This was a century before Latin American immigrants transformed Schuyler. "The state's traditional Progressive political bent, and its mistrust of big business, would make it the fastest-growing public power state in the nation during the first twenty years of the 1900s," wrote Don Schaufelberger and Bill Beck in their history of public power in Nebraska.[45]

Public power found its greatest advocate in US senator George Norris. From the massive Kingsley Dam in western Nebraska, to the Tennessee Valley Authority, Norris's fingerprints are all over several ambitious power projects. His crusades helped keep public power a fixture in Nebraska. (Near the end of Norris's political career, the father of comedian Johnny Carson managed a Nebraska public power district.)[46]

Advocating for public power wasn't Norris's biggest Nebraska project. That honor would go to his influence on our unique legislature. Removing party labels from the ballot allowed moderate and progressive candidates to make inroads in a conservative state.

"It does benefit progressives and independents in Nebraska that we don't have partisan ballots," said state senator Hunt. "It is a good thing to have our party affiliation off the ballot because then people really evaluate us on our positions on issues instead of our parties. I think there are more races on the ballot that should be nonpartisan in our state."

The absence of party labels helps facilitate bipartisan alliances, which is what happened when unlikely coalitions came together to ban the death penalty, pass a bill that allowed DACA youth to obtain driver's licenses, approve a gas tax increase to fix damaged roads, stop voter ID proposals from gaining momentum, and push back on the governor's effort to cut funding for the state university system. Some state lawmakers paid the price for overriding Ricketts—they were drummed out of office after being defeated by far-right candidates he helped bankroll. What's remarkable isn't that the deep-pocketed Ricketts overcame some opposition; it's that the he faced plenty of resistance in a state where Republicans have so much power.[47]

"It's only because of the difference in the folks who are elected by that system, and the way that the legislature is organized, that Nebraska has a record of semi-progressive legislation," said Drey Samuelson, a Nebraska native who worked for several Great Plains Democrats, including Tim Johnson, Tom Daschle, and Bob Kerrey. "There is no analog of similar resistance to a

Republican governor in another red state, believe me. And the difference is that the Nebraska election system elects moderates who want to make government work, rather than right-wing radicals who are happiest when it does little or nothing."

Aside from the Nebraska Legislature, across the state there are nonpartisan elections for city councils, power districts, and mayors. Schuyler's current mayor, Jon Knutson, is a registered Democrat, and he was recommended for the position by the town's previous mayor, a registered Republican. Both said removing party labels from their office helped them get things done and work with people from other parties. Knutson is a supporter of the immigrant Dreamers in his town, and he said that as a Democrat, he probably wouldn't have gotten elected if his party were listed on the ballot. While politics lurks all around in offices, church pews, homes, university campuses, and government institutions, partisan bickering doesn't have to. It's questionable why down-ballot races like county commissioner or sheriff include political affiliation at all.

Another area where Nebraskans have pushed progressive initiatives is through ballot measures. The ability to change government policy through a ballot measure isn't anything new—it was through this method that our nonpartisan one-house legislature came to be. But it's become a more common tactic. In 2014, the state voted to raise the minimum wage, in 2018 voters passed Medicaid expansion, and in 2020 Nebraska capped payday loan interest rates. These campaigns were successful even though Nebraskans continue to elect GOP officials who oppose raising wages and expanding healthcare access. Likewise, Nebraskans voted overwhelmingly for Donald Trump, who made immigration restrictions a key part of his platform and slashed the number of refugees coming into the country after he got elected, yet for a number of years before Trump came into office Nebraska welcomed more refugees per capita than any other state.[48]

"If you ask people to vote for things that might be in their own interest, and you explain the issue to them in one paragraph on the ballot, they will vote for the thing that is good for them," said political science professor Kohen. "But you can't ask them to give up their party affiliation."

The authors of *The Big Sort* put it this way: "Political party affiliation had more to do with social identity than ideology. Choosing to be a Republican or a Democrat reflected a way of life."[49]

Other ballot measures that progressive operatives are considering include lowering the voting age to sixteen, extending the nonpartisan open-primary election system to more statewide elections, giving redistricting power to a nonpartisan group, and legalizing medical marijuana. Financing ballot measures is expensive, and there have been—and will continue to be—conservative victories through them. However, ballot measures have helped liberals pass several laws, and that's an opportunity they rarely have when nearly every significant officeholder in the state is a Republican.[50]

Another effect of ballot measures is that they can reduce resistance among elected officials who oppose the issue being passed. When Tom Brewer first ran for state senate, one of the key planks in his conservative platform was "stopping government overreach," and he vowed to fight programs like Obamacare and Medicaid expansion. When Medicaid expansion made the ballot, he called it a "terrible idea" that is "really going to hurt a lot of people who utterly depend on this program." He bemoaned that other programs would get cut in order to pay for it. His tone changed after voters passed it.[51]

"I don't know that there is any death and doom over the deal as far as the budget," Brewer said as we chatted inside his uniquely decorated office. "There are folks who need help, and [Medicaid expansion] will probably go a ways toward helping them. . . . I'm still not a huge fan, but I'm also realistic that it's what the people want, and we need to represent the people and so we will make the best of it. We will figure out how to pay for it and we will get 'er done."

Brewer's comments indicate how ballot measures can influence hardened critics by sending a clear and public message what voters want. They aren't a cure-all, but they can be used to pressure elected officials to be more flexible. Another feature of ballot measures is that they can be leveraged to increase voter turnout. A study in *American Politics Research* shows that each additional ballot measure increases turnout by about 1 percentage point, with that figure being higher during midterms. This might not sound like much, but recent history shows that Nebraska Democrats need all the help they can get in getting people to the polls.[52]

It's possible that Democrats will one day stop the bleeding and start winning again in states like Nebraska. That likely won't happen soon. But that doesn't mean liberals in the heartland should accept defeat and despair. The environmentalists fighting Canadian energy companies, humanitarians welcoming refugees, nonpartisan state lawmakers putting principle over party, apolitical mayors protecting their most vulnerable constituents, and activists pushing ballot measures that increase health-care access and wages for people on the margins all have something in common, and they lay out a pathway for those aching for change. They show that even in a Republican-dominated state, progressives who are willing to work to advance certain issues outside the unrelenting rancor of contemporary partisan politics can get the job done.

Conclusion

When I think about Brainard, I like to recall all those summer days I spent with friends while my parents worked. Before I started fixing air conditioners each summer with my dad in sixth grade, I spent most of my summertime however I pleased. My older brother was supposed to keep an eye on me, but he didn't give a damn if I went to the pool all day by myself, started a pickup basketball game, or played video games with our neighbors. He had his interests and I had mine, and we were allowed to go our own way just as long as we eventually came home, which is how we liked it. In Brainard, you don't have to lock your doors, there's next to no traffic, and most people feel a sense of comfort from knowing everyone else in town. The unsupervised freedom I experienced as a child is at odds with what I see when I walk my dogs in Brooklyn, where I witness parents helicoptering over their children and pets-who-substitute-as-children, as they shuffle them from one activity to the next.

I felt so free in the streets of Brainard that I didn't fully realize how isolated we were. I was lucky to have a good group of friends who I played sports and created home movies with, which kept me busy. Others find small-town life to be suffocating. People get bored and drinking becomes a way of life. Some feel judged for their otherness and can't wait to leave. Accessing mental health services becomes more difficult the farther you live from a city, which is a huge problem given that the Centers for Disease Control and Prevention found that suicide is most common in rural areas.[1]

When I was roaming Brainard's wide streets, I didn't recognize that politically divisive issues were taking hold in rural America. The perception that rural residents have of being separated from the rest of the country has become a source of power for politicians. In small towns, where there are few social clubs and traditionalism is revered, it's common for people to turn to their church for a sense of purpose and community. The church taught me to respect life and instructed me to live selflessly, but it also politicized abortion to the point that many voters only care about that one issue. This leads people in Brainard to vote for pro-life candidates who offer them nothing else but moral outrage.

When the town that you spend all your time in is full of white people and has no immigrants, you begin to view undocumented laborers as law-breaking deviants who worsen our nation. In this context, building a wall along the Mexican border doesn't seem so asinine. Like many midwesterners, I was taught that living modestly and self-reliance were virtues. And because I was always one degree away from knowing anyone I had a personal interaction with, I was unfamiliar with anonymity. An appreciation for fiscal constraint combined with distrust of the outside world led me to oppose big government. Politicians have leveraged this sentiment to target public institutions and lower taxes for their wealthy backers.

Since leaving Brainard, each time I move I land in an even bigger city. Along the progression from Brainard to Lincoln to Detroit to New York City, I've come to see things differently. When you see single moms without much community support struggling to hold everything together and when you befriend people who openly support abortion rights, it becomes harder to demonize pro-choicers; I now see gray in areas where I used to see only black and white. When you establish personal relationships with immigrants, they become much more than distant law breakers, and you realize that their humanity is every bit as valid as your own. When you develop chronic illnesses and find yourself spending an inordinate amount of time navigating through various states' health exchanges on a low budget, you wish like hell the government could step in and make it easier. My perceptions wouldn't be what they are if I stayed in my hometown and neglected metropolises.

Armed with well-financed campaigns and a Democratic Party that likes to get in its own way, Republicans gained power in Nebraska through these emotions. Our state has become so dominated by a single party that our politicians can obey their organization more than their constituents without facing repercussions. The lack of a legitimate challenge means that elected Republicans don't have to compromise or moderate their votes to placate more voters and temper tribalism. The loyalty that our officials have to their party is reflected by voters passing ballot measures that our elected leaders oppose. Because the parties have become more nationalized and polarized, many Nebraskans continue to identify with, and vote for, Republicans even if they disagree with the party's various positions because they feel the GOP is still a better alternative than the Democratic Party, which they see as being too far left.

Where you live doesn't automatically pigeonhole you into a political affiliation. I know liberal hippies from Butler County and cultural conservatives from New York City, but they are rare exceptions. The correlation between where you live and what party you vote for has only grown stronger, and it's hurting our country. When I watched the Huskers win multiple football national titles during the 1990s, Republicans and Democrats had the same level of support in rural counties, according to the Pew Research Center. Since then, Republicans increased their voter representation in rural counties nationwide by about 10 percentage points as Democrats' share fell. Likewise, Democrats made gains in cities while Republicans lost votes there. GOP governors and senators who lose in Nebraska's cities still win easily statewide thanks to rural voters who overwhelmingly back Republicans and turn out at higher rates than urban voters. "Population density now predicts partisanship," wrote Princeton sociologist Paul Starr in a book review about the growing urban-rural divide. In other words, the partisanship afflicting Nebraska is best viewed as a microcosm for our current national crisis.[2]

Like Nebraska, many states now effectively operate under the power of a single party, making compromises rarer. As we examined throughout this book, during my lifetime Nebraska's political representatives have taken a single-sided hard turn to the right. What's happening in Nebraska, and in many other states throughout the country, will continue after our sitting president is gone. Ballot splitting and moderation have vanished as we've become a nation of disaffected voters. But after dividing time between Brainard and New York City, I've learned firsthand that people's party registration doesn't determine their ability to care for one another. If we're really going to combat the extreme ways that geography affects politics, then we're going to have to put more effort in interacting with people who live in neighborhoods unlike our own. People in towns like Brainard might become less anti-immigrant if they got out of town more often and spent some time developing a familiarity with how immigrants live and work in other parts of the state and country. People in cities who support gun restrictions out of a sincere desire to reduce violence might better appreciate rural conservatives' adulation for the Second Amendment if they spent time on a farm hunting predators that threaten to destroy crops and livestock. These are just a few of the many ways that we might come to know each other's perspectives a little better.

When you become more familiar with someone, it becomes more difficult to demonize them based on their political opinions. The disgraced Republican strategist and Fox News CEO Roger Ailes was very successful in helping presidents and congressmen get elected by wedging people against each other. But when Ailes used his fortune to try to influence local politics near his home in New York's Hudson Valley, he couldn't even get a county supervisor elected. The reason Ailes failed locally is that division politics don't work when scaled down because people know their neighbors too well to fall for it. In a country as large as ours, it is impossible to know everyone. But given the misperceptions Democrats and Republicans have about each other, we can certainly make some progress in becoming more familiar with those whom we disagree with.[3]

We should listen to the stories of people whose lives are shaped by environments that we're unfamiliar with. But becoming more familiar with people whose views differ from our own is just one part of the solution. If we're going to get over the crazy state of partisanship, then we're going to need better media habits. Spending less time on social networks couldn't hurt. Neither could investments in civic education. There are lots of little things we could individually do to better understand one another. But a "kumbaya" moment is unlikely right now, and our polarized state can't be conquered through a little bit of peace, love, and understanding. We need structural changes to how our politics function.

When a single party dominates an area, its politicians don't have to compromise their party's position or moderate themselves. This has contributed to Nebraska's one-sided rightward shift. Single-party rule also makes it easy for those in power to squash attempts to reform the system. Nebraska has some of the most lax campaign finance laws in the country, and those rules are unlikely to change if they benefit current officeholders. As we've examined, Nebraska's governor used his immense wealth to push his preferred legislative candidates into office. The lawmakers he's picked have been more apt to oppose expanded health-care access and public education, which voters tend to support. The governor also vetoed efforts to restructure redistricting by shutting down a bill that was sponsored by a fellow Republican.[4]

Our political systems need retooling if we're going to lessen the perils of hyperpartisanship. Now, partisanship isn't necessarily a bad thing in and of itself. Partisanship can boost voter turnout and drive people to work on campaigns and engage in public discourse. But at the extreme level we're seeing, partisanship is closing minds and intensifying people's animosity while making it difficult for elected leaders to compromise on anything.[5]

It's difficult to achieve bipartisan support these days, but one thing that most Republican and Democrat voters agree on is that there's too much damn money in politics. Campaign finance deregulations, most notably *Citizens United*, have benefited the rich at the expense of the rest of us. We need laws that give us more clarity into who is paying political candidates.[6]

Gerrymandering is another issue that has led us to a frenzied political atmosphere. Gerrymandering has always existed, but it's become more egregious with advanced data analytics software. This isn't something that applies just to Republican officeholders. Any party in power will be tempted to draw boundaries that favor themselves. Maryland Democrats gerrymandered their districts so badly that their tactics were challenged in the Supreme Court.[7]

The problem of gerrymandering is reflected in the heightened number of districts that result in landslide victories. Some states are pushing back against gerrymandering by putting redistricting in the hands of independent nonpartisan committees. There's no way to entirely eliminate bias from influencing how districts are drawn, but places that took this power out of the hands of politicians were rewarded with more competitive elections.[8]

We also need to rethink how we choose candidates. For anyone who thinks we cannot change the status quo out of reverence to traditionalism, consider that in the early days of our nation only white landowners could vote, people couldn't directly vote for senators, and voters received their ballots from partisan newspapers that encouraged them to support the same party in every race. Future historians will probably view the way we vote for candidates today as highly arbitrary. Nebraska's own unique legislature is evidence that tweaking political institutions can improve government and benefit citizens.[9]

In most elections today, even down-ballot races, candidates are effectively nominated by a small group of hyperpartisan voters who turn out in primaries and caucuses. This is happening while an increasing percentage of voters register as independents, which usually cuts them off from participating in how candidates are chosen. Candidates who are really popular among their party's zealots don't necessarily have broad appeal. In a US Senate race the Tea Party activist Christine O'Donnell beat former Delaware governor Mike Castle in the Republican primary, only to lose decidedly to her Democrat opponent. Yet polling showed that Castle, who didn't make it out of the primary, was more popular than either candidate offered on the general election ballot.[10]

To reduce the chances that fringe candidates are chosen, more elections could utilize open primaries, which allow people to vote for any candidate regardless of their voter registration. In this scenario, registered Democrats can vote for Republicans, and vice versa, which could lead to less extreme candidates being picked because politicians would need to appeal to various types of voters (and not just those from their party) if they want to advance. In open primaries, the two candidates with the most votes advance to the general election, which can lead to elections where the two final candidates are from the same party. Theoretically, open primaries could reduce partisanship, but the evidence is mixed.[11]

Another candidate nomination process that municipalities are testing is ranked voting. In this system, instead of being presented a binary choice, people rank multiple candidates on their ballot. This system gives politicians less incentive to attack each other because getting second-place votes from your opponent's base is still beneficial, which reduces some of the nastiness in elections. Like open primaries, ranked voting could theoretically reduce partisanship, but it's in an experimental stage and the evidence isn't clear yet. Open primaries and ranked voting aren't a cure-all, but these and other reforms are worth considering given how many people are dissatisfied with the way our leaders are chosen today. Polling shows that just over one-fourth of US adults are very confident that their party's nomination process is fair.[12]

Political parties could also do their part to ensure that geography doesn't predict people's votes. I suspect that Republicans would win more votes in the cities if they were more open about criminal justice reform and less hostile about immigration. The perception that Republicans want to gut social services and public institutions also doesn't help them in dense areas.

On the other hand, Democrats will have to change what they talk about if they want to gain rural supporters. Despite what happened with the Cornhusker kickback, with the right messaging, there's an opportunity for Democrats to win some rural voters with health care. Rural America has a severe shortage of doctors, and its hospitals keep closing, creating a terrible recipe for an aging population. Accessing mental health services is challenging for people living far from cities. A lot of rural folks say they prefer small government, but they're wise enough to realize that for-profit health-care enterprises aren't serving them well. Also, the continual closure of small-town schools, international trade wars, and the continual lack of broadband are all hurting rural economies. Democratic candidates should ask themselves if there is anything they can do about these issues.

Compared to economic positions, cultural issues are a tougher sell for Democrats in small towns. Whenever an emotional cultural issue surfaces during a campaign, Democrats are tempted to avoid the issue altogether. This approach is understandable considering that being dogmatic about abortion rights can mobilize urban voters but doesn't resonate in the countryside. As tempting as it may be, avoiding issues entirely comes across as weak.

Abortion will remain difficult for Democrats to navigate in rural areas, where identifying as pro-life is in vogue. But on issues like immigration, Democrats would have better luck appealing to voters in small towns if they addressed the issue by tying their message back to the struggles of the working class. Old-timers who used to earn a living wage at the local packing plant become resentful after their wages drop and benefits disappear. People in towns like Schuyler and Fremont, Nebraska, get mad at the migrant laborers who fill the poorly paid and dangerous jobs at their former employers. I don't deny that xenophobia exists in rural Nebraska. But Democrats should aim to redirect that ire at the corporations who, through consolidation and union busting, drove wages down so far that the only people who will take their jobs anymore are the people they recruit from other countries eager for a new life. A 2019 poll of rural Nebraskans showed that three-fourths of respondents believed that businesses who bring employees to the country illegally should be penalized. The number of people who believed these businesses should be punished was 10 percentage points higher than the number of people who said that undocumented workers should be deported. Purity tests and wedge issues will continue to hinder Democrats in sparsely populated regions, but if Democrats can keep debates focused on issues that affect local economies, they have stronger material to work with.[13]

Another thing that gives me hope is, as toxic as our politics have become, there are many people who care more about values than in identifying with a particular group. Sometimes voters support lousy candidates or repressive policies because of their ignorance, not their maliciousness. That's a crucial distinction because malicious voters are lost causes but ignorant ones can become better informed and persuaded. Over the past twenty years, the percentage of Americans who support gay marriage has roughly doubled, which is a remarkable change in public opinion in a short time span. If our country was truly full of bigots with hardened hearts, this type of shift wouldn't be possible. Malice may motivate a lot of political messaging, but I'm not convinced that it motivates most voters.

Shortly before this book went into final production, I called my mom. Per our usual conversations, I told her how my fiancée and our hounds were holding up in Brooklyn. Mom then rambled about recent property sales and weddings they just got invited to. She mentioned that she talked to some of my high school classmates at the bar the other day. The conversation was as bland as ever. But then she said, "We're going to go vote at the legion tomorrow in the Democratic primary." I asked if she meant Republican. She hadn't misspoken. She and Dad had been Republicans since the 1970s, long before I was born. When I realized my parents had really switched parties, I nearly shit my pants, which would have been unfortunate because I was quarantined in my apartment and the coronavirus made it difficult to obtain toilet paper. I asked mom why they changed parties. Because her hearing is shot, she had the phone volume all the way up and Dad overheard me. Dad shouted so that Mom's phone would pick it up: "It's because of Trump, and I even voted for the jackass."

My parents don't represent all conservatives, and becoming a Democrat isn't a virtue, but I believe there are many more like them who are open to changing how they vote when the party they've belonged to disappoints them. Fixing our partisanship issue will require us to change several things. We need to reform our own habits, the financing of campaigns, the selection of candidates, and the issues that political parties focus on. Most folks aren't happy with our political situation. Trump didn't create the mess we're in; he just benefited from it, as will other opportunists in future elections. Politics is clearly important, but there is much more to our country. Our society doesn't appear so dire when you look at how people help each other during trying times.

––––––––––

Judging from the ratio of Bud Light to Busch Light, Brian Healy knew the mystery fridge belonged to him.

The fridge surfaced after extreme weather hit home. Blizzards, large temperature swings, and dramatic air pressure fluctuations culminated in one of the worst floods in Nebraska history, leaving ice chunks big enough to square dance on scattered over the plains. The March 2019 flood killed people, destroyed farms, ruined homes, wrecked military bases, and devastated towns. During the chaos, Nebraskans risked their own lives to save strangers, protected endangered species, temporarily retrofitted schools to accommodate the needs that damaged post offices and daycare centers ordinarily provided, and banded together to rebuild what they could and assist those in most need. Governor Ricketts honored these people as heroes. For all the things lost in the flood, hope was not one of them.

Which brings us to Healy's fridge. On a cloudy spring Sunday afternoon a few days after the rain stopped, the denizens of Butler County went out to clear debris from their property. Kyle Simpson noticed a strange black box sitting next to one of his trees. When he got closer, he realized it was a fridge. To his delight, it was full of Anheuser-Busch products. Even better, the beers were cold. Simpson and his buddy guzzled a few brews and laughed about it. They posted pictures to Facebook, and their friends started sharing their posts. Three-and-a-half miles upstream, Healy logged on and recognized that the fridge in the photos is the same one that went missing from his storm-damaged cabin. Healy connected with Simpson, who reunited him with his appliance. "At least they can have their refrigerator full of beer back, minus a couple," Simpson said.[14]

Stories that emerged from the flood, like the one about the magic beer fridge, show that Nebraskans are resilient and care for one another. Democrats should take notice. Not only does ignoring these voters do a disservice to working-class constituents, but it's poor strategy, too. Democrat Senate minority leader Chuck Schumer insisted in 2016 that for every blue-collar voter lost in the Midwest, Democrats would pick up two in the suburbs. That didn't pan out.[15]

Whether Nebraska elects Republicans or Democrats doesn't determine the goodness of its people. Life will go on, crops will get sold, football games will be lost, beer will get drunk regardless of who is in office. However, if our country is to find political sanity during an era of intense polarization and perpetual shenanigans, then we must bring back some balance to areas where single-party rule breeds intense partisanship. Our national crisis can't be solved all at once, but there's plenty of room for incremental progress in middle America. The people out here don't give up on each other, and neither should politicians.

Notes

Introduction

1. Alexander Marquardt and Brian Vitagliano, "Six Months in, Nebraska Voters Say They're Sticking with Trump," CNN, August 2, 2017.

2. William Robbins, "Democrats Focused on Farm Crisis in Midwest," *New York Times*, February 16, 1986; Jane Kleeb, *Harvest the Vote: How Democrats Can Win Again in Rural America* (New York: Ecco, 2020), 26–33; Brian Mann, *Welcome to the Homeland: A Journey to the Rural Heart of America's Conservative Revolution* (Hanover, NH: 2006), 119; Cory Haala, "'There Exists a Conservative Veneer': Terry Branstad, Chuck Grassley, and the New Right's Capture of Republican Politics in Iowa, 1976–1986," in *The Conservative Heartland: A Political History of the Postwar American Midwest*, edited by Jon Lauck and Catherine McNicol Stock (Lawrence: University Press of Kansas, 2020), 217–219.

3. Jim McKee, "Lancaster Becomes Lincoln with Nebraska's Statehood," *Lincoln Journal Star*, November 12, 2016; James Olson, *J. Sterling Morton* (Lincoln: University of Nebraska Press, 1942).

4. George Norris, *Fighting Liberal: The Autobiography of George Norris* (New York: Macmillan, 1945), 288.

5. John Yang, "Senate Passes Bill against Same-Sex Marriage," *Washington Post*, September 11, 1996; B. Drummond Ayres Jr., "Political Briefing; Drawing a Battle Line at a Rally for Unity," *New York Times*, July 20, 1998; "Hagel: Iraq Growing More Like Vietnam," CNN, August 18, 2005; Eric Boehm, "What the Heck, Ben Sasse?," *Reason*, March 14, 2019.

6. Don Walton, "Hagel, Kerrey, Nelson Join Appeal to Senate to Protect Democracy," *Lincoln Journal Star*, December 11, 2018; Aaron Sanderford, "A Perversion of Equal Justice': Nebraska GOP Condemns Mueller Investigation," *Omaha World-Herald*, June 18, 2018.

7. Perry Bacon, "The Republican Party Has Changed Dramatically Since George H. W. Bush Ran It," FiveThirtyEight, December 1, 2018, https://fivethirtyeight.com/features/the-republican-party-has-changed-dramatically-since-george-h-w-bush-ran-it/.

8. Ken Rudin, "On This Day in 1986: Nebraska Gov Race First to Have 2 Women," NPR, May 13, 2009.

9. James Olson and Ronald Naugle, *History of Nebraska*, 3rd ed. (Lincoln: University of Nebraska Press, 1997), 373; Adam Breckenridge, "Nebraska State Government," in *Nebraska Government and Politics*, edited by Robert Miewald (Lincoln: University of Nebraska Press, 1984), 8.

10. Maddie Sach, "Why the Democrats Have Shifted Left over the Last 30 Years," FiveThirtyEight, December 16, 2019, https://fivethirtyeight.com/features/why-the-democrats-have-shifted-left-over-the-last-30-years/; Lydia Saad, Jeffrey Jones, and Megan Brenan, "Understanding Shifts in the Democratic Party Ideology," Gallup, February 19, 2019, https://news.gallup.com/poll/246806/understanding-shifts-democratic-party-ideology.aspx; "Many US Voters Say Parties Moving Too Far Left, Right, Quinnipiac University National Poll Finds: Health Care, Race Relations Outweigh Economy," *Quinnipiac University Poll*, August 24, 2017, https://poll.qu.edu/national/release-detail?ReleaseID=2483; Tess Bonn, "Nearly Half of Independents Say Democratic Party Leans Too Far Left: Poll," the Hill, July 31, 2019, https://thehill.com/hilltv/what-americas-thinking/455574-nearly-half-of-independents-say-democratic-party-is-too-far-left.

11. Sam Pimper, "Krist Looking to Take Governor Seat in 2018," *Columbus Telegram*, August 17, 2008; Roseann Moring, "Attorney General Candidate Steps Down Amid Strangulation Charge; Democrats Plan a Replacement," *Omaha World-Herald*, June 25, 2018.

12. Ross Benes, "Our Intern Really Needed a Makeover. We Gave Him One. Here's What Happened," *Esquire*, July 2, 2014.

Chapter 1. Pro-Life License Plates

1. "Teen Birth Rate by State," Centers for Disease Control and Prevention, https://www.cdc.gov/nchs/pressroom/sosmap/teen-births/teenbirths.htm, accessed December 10, 2019; Karen Kaplan, "There's Another Type of Rural/Urban Divide in America: Teens Having Babies," *Los Angeles Times*, November 16, 2016.

2. Robert Wuthnow, *The Left Behind: Decline and Rage in Rural America* (Princeton, NJ: Princeton University Press, 2018), 123.

3. Erin Andersen, "Catholic Bishop Tells Women to Abstain from Yoga," *Lincoln Journal Star*, May 22, 2015; Robert McClory, "Book Tells Nebraska's Catholic Horror Story," *National Catholic Reporter*, June 18, 2014; Dennis Coday, "Bishops' Conference Releases 2015 Abuse Audit Report," *National Catholic Reporter*, May 20, 2016; "Report Singles Out Lincoln Diocese," *Lincoln Journal Star*, February 27, 2004; Bob Reeves, "Lincoln Diocese Alone in Not Allowing Girls to Be Altar Servers," *Lincoln Journal Star*, March 23, 2006.

4. Paul Hammel, "Paid Family and Medical Leave Bill Appears Doomed in Nebraska Legislature," *Omaha World-Herald*, March 19, 2019; "State Senator First in Nebraska History to Nurse on Legislative Floor, Staff Says," 10/11 KOLN/KGIN, January 22, 2019.

5. Alexis Grenell, "White Women, Come Get Your People," *New York Times*, October 6, 2018; Wendy Doniger, "All Beliefs Welcome, Unless They are Forced on Others," *Newsweek*, September 9, 2008; Jonah Goldberg, "Feminist Army Aims at Palin," *Real Clear Politics*, September 13, 2008, https://www.realclearpolitics.com/articles/2008/09 /feminist_army_aims_at_palin.html.

6. Danielle Kurtzleben, "POLL: White Evangelicals Have Warmed to Politicians Who Commit 'Immoral' Acts," NPR, October 23, 2016; Heather Timmons, "Trump Shifted from Pro-Choice to Pro-Life Only as He Planned a Presidential Run," *Quartz*, May 20, 2019, https://qz.com/1623437/trump-shifted-from-pro-choice-to-pro-life-as -he-planned-a-presidential-run/; Melina Delkic, "How Many Times Has Trump Cheated on His Wives? Here's What We Know," *Newsweek*, January 12, 2018; Tierney McAfee, "Inside Trump's History with Playboy as It Preps to Make White House Correspondents' Dinner Debut," *People*, April 27, 2018; Eliza Relman, "The 25 Women Who Have Accused Trump of Sexual Misconduct," *Business Insider*, October 9, 2019; Tim Alberta, "Social Conservatives Are 'Over the Moon' about Trump," Politico, April 26, 2017, https://www.politico.com/magazine/story/2017/04/26/donald-trump-social -conservatives-215073.

7. Jonathan Haidt, *The Righteous Mind: Why Good People Are Divided by Politics and Religion* (New York: Random House, 2012); David Campbell and Robert Putnam, *American Grace: How Religion Divides and Unites Us* (New York: Simon & Schuster, 2010).

8. Joshua Stewart, "Catholic Parish's Bulletin Says Democratic Voters Are Doomed to Hell, Clinton Is Satanic," *San Diego Tribune*, November 2, 2016.

9. Tim Murphy and Bill Bishop, "Largest Share of Army Recruits Come from Rural/Exurban America," *Daily Yonder*, March 3, 2009, https://www.dailyyonder.com /largest-share-army-recruits-come-ruralexurban-america/2009/03/03/.

10. Mary Rezac, "Being Pro-Life Never Used to Mean Being Republican," *Catholic News Agency*, April 12, 2016.

11. Jennifer Latson, "What Margaret Sanger Really Said About Eugenics and Race," *Time*, October 14, 2016; Arizona Women's Heritage Trail, "Margaret 'Peggy' Johnson Goldwater," https://www.womensheritagetrail.org/women/PeggyGoldwater .php, accessed April 10, 2019; Gloria Feldt, "Convictions to Action: Lessons from Margaret Sanger," *On the Issues Magazine*, https://www.ontheissuesmagazine.com /2010winter/2010winter_Feldt.php, accessed April 10, 2019; Kate Scanlon, "The Republican Congressman Applauded by Planned Parenthood," Daily Signal, July 29, 2015, https://www.dailysignal.com/2015/07/29/the-republican-congressman-applaud ed-by-planned-parenthood/; Randy Moody, "The Truth about Republicans' Link with Planned Parenthood," *Arizona Daily Star*, January 22, 2016; Linda Hirshman, "Sandra Day O'Connor and the Fate of Abortion Rights," *Los Angeles Times*, February 28, 2016; Alice Schroeder, *The Snowball: Warren Buffett and the Business of Life* (New

York: Bantam, 2008), 642; Ann Marie Wambeke, "Politics Makes for Strange Bedfellows: Republican Feminists Fight for Abortion Rights in Michigan, 1968–1982," in *The Conservative Heartland: A Political History of the Postwar American Midwest,* edited by Jon Lauck and Catherine McNicol Stock (Lawrence: University Press of Kansas, 2020), 116–127.

12. Charles Pallesen and Samuel Van Pelt, *Big Jim Exon: A Political Biography* (Lincoln: Infusionmedia, 2012), 176–225, 303.

13. "Democrat and Pro-Life?," *America,* September 24, 2012, https://www.ameri camagazine.org/issue/5151/signs/democrat-and-pro-life; Reid Wilson, "Anti-Abortion Democrats Fading from the Scene," the Hill, October 4, 2017, https://thehill.com /homenews/campaign/345231-anti-abortion-democrats-fading-from-the-scene; Carter Sherman and Alex Thompson, "Where Have All the Pro-Life Democrats Gone?," *Vice News,* January 23, 2018, https://www.vice.com/en_us/article/yw5j9x/where-have -all-the-pro-life-democrats-gone; Daniel Hopkins, *The Increasingly United States: How and Why American Political Behavior Nationalized* (Chicago: University of Chicago Press, 2018), 137.

14. Robert Wuthnow, *Red State Religion: Faith and Politics in America's Heartland* (Princeton, NJ: Princeton University Press, 2012), 268.

15. Don Walton, "Legislative Online Sales Tax Decision Bigger Than It Looks," *Lincoln Journal Star,* June 24, 2018.

16. "Seven Themes of Catholic Social Teaching," United States Conference of Catholic Bishops, http://www.usccb.org/beliefs-and-teachings/what-we-believe/cath olic-social-teaching/seven-themes-of-catholic-social-teaching.cfm, accessed June 10, 2020.

17. Kevin O'Hanlon, "Neb. Rep. Says Abortion Divides GOP," Associated Press, July 11, 1998.

18. Email with CARA, August 13, 2018; Rachel Pokora, *Crisis of Catholic Authority: Faith and Power in the Diocese of Lincoln Nebraska* (St. Paul, MN: Paragon House, 2013), 154.

19. Hopkins, *The Increasingly United States,* 3.

20. "Sasse Condemns Virginia Governor's Late-Term Abortion Comments," Fox News via YouTube, January 31, 2019.

21. Ken Burns, *Prohibition,* PBS documentary, 2011.

22. W. Bradford Wilcox and Samuel Sturgeon, "Too Much Netflix, Not Enough Chill: Why Young Americans Are Having Less Sex," Politico *Magazine,* February 8, 2018; John Gramlich, "5 Facts about Crime in the U.S.," Pew Research Center, January 3, 2019, https://www.pewresearch.org/fact-tank/2019/10/17/facts-about-crime-in-the-u-s/.

23. Kelsi Martin, "Home Office to Retire with TV Host," *Wahoo Newspaper,* June 26, 2014, https://www.wahoo-ashland-waverly.com/news/local/featured/home-office -to-retire-with-tv-host/article_2bc130d4-fc9a-11e3-b578-001a4bcf887a.html.

24. Faye Fiore, "Clinton Visit Better Never Than Late, Nebraskans Say," *Los Angeles Times*, December 8, 2000.

25. Roseann Moring, "Nebraska Democrats Resist Litmus Test on Abortion," *Omaha World-Herald*, December 8, 2017; Roseann Moring and Henry Cordes, "Bernie Sanders Campaigning for Heath Mello Was 'A Colossal Mistake,' UNO Professor Says," *Omaha World-Herald*, May 12, 2017.

26. Daniel Marans, Laura Bassett, and Ryan Grim, "Omaha Mayoral Candidate Under Fire for Anti-Choice Past Vows to Protect Reproductive Rights," HuffPost, April 20, 2017, https://www.huffpost.com/entry/omaha-mayoral-candidate-under-fire -says-he-would-never-do-anything-to-restrict-access-to-reproductive-health-care _n_58f8e868e4b018a9ce590a84; Clare Foran, "Is There Any Room in the 'Big Tent' for Pro-Life Democrats?," *Atlantic*, April 27, 2017; D. D. Guttenplan, "Why Was Heath Mello Thrown Under the Bus?," *Nation*, April 24, 2017; Heath Mello speech, uploaded to Facebook by Sofia JW, April 24, 2017.

27. Reid Epstein and Natalie Andrews, "Democrats Reload for Georgia Runoff, but Party Divisions Remain," *Wall Street Journal*, April 19, 2017; David Nir, "Daily Kos Statement on Withdrawing Endorsement of Heath Mello," Daily Kos, April 20, 2017, https://www.dailykos.com/stories/2017/4/20/1654645/-Daily-Kos-statement-on-with drawing-endorsement-of-Heath-Mello; Lindy West, "Of Course Abortion Should Be a Litmus Test for Democrats," *New York Times*, August 2, 2017.

28. Moring, "Nebraska Democrats Resist Litmus Test on Abortion"; Graham Vyse, "Why Democrats Are Debating Abortion Yet Again," *New Republic*, April 26, 2017.

29. Vyse, "Why Democrats Are Debating Abortion Yet Again"; Laura Bassett, "Democratic Party Draws a Line in the Sand on Abortion Rights," HuffPost, April 21, 2017, https://www.huffpost.com/entry/democrats-tom-perez-abortion-rights_n_58fa 5fade4b018a9ce5b351d; Jane Kleeb, *Harvest the Vote: How Democrats Can Win Again in Rural America* (New York: Ecco, 2020), 140–141.

30. Kevin Cole, "Omaha Man Spends Thousands of Dollars to Fix Potholes the City Won't," *Omaha World-Herald*, April 17, 2017; "Pro-Life Dem Running for Mayor of Omaha," Fox News, May 9, 2017; Caroline Kelly, "Democratic Attorneys General Group Will Only Endorse Candidates Supporting Abortion Rights," CNN, November 18, 2019.

31. Moring and Cordes, "Bernie Sanders Campaigning for Heath Mello was 'A Colossal Mistake.'"

32. "Local Candidate Survey 2017," Nebraska Right to Life; Emily Nitcher, "Planned Parenthood Supporters Rally at State Capitol after Vote that May Defund Organization," *Omaha World-Herald*, March 30, 2018; "Our Next Mayor Health Mello Shares His Vision, Vote May 9," Nebraska Democratic Party, April 22, 2017, https://ne-braskademocrats.org/blog/our-next-mayor-heath-mello-shares-his-vision-vote-may -9/; Becky Yeh, "Nebraska Governor Strips Planned Parenthood Funding in New Budget," *Life Site*, April 6, 2018, https://www.lifesitenews.com/news/nebraska-gover

nor-strips-planned-parenthood-funding-in-new-budget; Joanne Young, "Nebraska Could Be Headed toward More Restrictive Abortion Law," *Lincoln Journal Star*, May 20, 2019; Guttenplan, "Why Was Heath Mello Thrown Under the Bus?"

33. "Presidential Vote of Catholics," Center for Applied Research in the Apostolate, https://cara.georgetown.edu/presidential%20vote%20only.pdf, accessed August 13, 2018; Gregory Smith and Jessica Martinez, "How the Faithful Voted: A Preliminary 2016 Analysis," Pew Research Center, November 9, 2016, https://www.pewresearch .org/fact-tank/2016/11/09/how-the-faithful-voted-a-preliminary-2016-analysis/; Frederick Luebke, "Time, Place, and Culture in Nebraska History," *Nebraska History* 69 (1988): 150–168; John McGreevy, "Catholics, Democrats, and the GOP in Contemporary America," *American Quarterly* 59, no. 3 (2007): 669–681.

34. Pope Leo XIII, *Rerum Novarum*, May 15, 1891; Lisa Fullam, "Benedict Calls for 'Redistribution of Wealth,'" *Commonweal*, December 19, 2011.

35. Don Walton, "Nebraska Unveils Specialized 'Choose Life' License Plates," *Lincoln Journal Star*, November 27, 2017; Emily Nitcher, "Planned Parenthood Unveils 'My Body, My Choice' License Plate," *Omaha World-Herald*, December 29, 2017; "'Choose Life' License Plate Design Unveiled," *Southern Nebraska Register*, December 1, 2017; Abortion Access Fund Inc. website, February 18, 2017.

36. D. D. Guttenplan, "A Leader of the Keystone Opposition Talks about Building Progressive Coalitions in Red America," *Nation*, August 8, 2017.

37. Roseann Moring, "Nebraska Democrats Take Platform to the Left on Abortion, Guns and Health Care," *Omaha World-Herald*, June 26, 2018; Kleeb, *Harvest the Vote*, 143–144; Hopkins, *The Increasingly United States*, 228.

38. Briana Boyington, "See High School Graduation Rates by State," *U.S. News & World Report*, May 18, 2018; Howard Hawks, "NU Cuts Not a Recipe for Economic Growth," *Omaha World-Herald*, January 16, 2018.

39. Rachel Zoll, "Dinesh D'Souza: Why Did He Resign from King's College?," Associated Press, October 19, 2012; David Jackson, "Author Calls Obama 'Grown-Up Trayvon,'" *USA Today*, November 26, 2013; Dylan Byers, "Dinesh D'Souza Indicted for Campaign Finance Fraud," Politico, January 23, 2014, https://www.politico.com /blogs/media/2014/01/dinesh-dsouza-indicted-for-campaign-finance-fraud-181784; Jack Hunter, "D'Souza's 'Kenyan Anti-Colonial' Distraction," American Conservative, December 17, 2012; Astead Herndon, "A New Film Compares Democrats to Nazis and Trump to Lincoln. At This Screening, It Was a Hit," *New York Times*, August 17, 2018.

40. Rod Dreher, "Msgr Kalin & #MeToo Conservatives," American Conservative, August 1, 2018; Rod Dreher, "Lincoln Diocese Comes Clean on Abuse," American Conservative, April 2, 2019.

41. Steven Ertelt, "Right to Life Will Oppose 'Pro-Life' Democrat Ben Nelson," Life News, December 14, 2011, https://www.lifenews.com/2011/12/14/right-to-life-will -oppose-pro-life-democrat-ben-nelson/; Damon Linker, "Why Is the Women's March

Excluding Pro-Life Women?," the Week, January 18, 2017; Charles Camosy, "Democrats Could Destroy the GOP—if only They Would Welcome Antiabortion Liberals," *Washington Post*, March 21, 2016; "Europe's Abortion Rules," BBC, February 12, 2007; "Abortion Laws Vary Significantly Across the EU," *France 24*, May 25, 2018, https://www.france24.com/en/20180525-abortion-laws-vary-eu-ireland-malta-poland-termination; "Abortion Bans at 20 Weeks: A Dangerous Restriction for Women," NARAL Pro-Choice America, January 1, 2017.

Chapter 2. A Soccer Town

1. Richard Wood, *Survival of Rural America: Small Victories and Bitter Harvests* (Lawrence: University Press of Kansas, 2008), xvi, 8; Dirk Chatelain, *24th and Glory: The Intersection of Civil Rights and Omaha's Greatest Generation of Athletes* (Omaha: Omaha World Herald, 2019), 87–88; Michael Broadway, "From City to Countryside: Recent Changes in the Structure and Location of the Meat- and Fish-Processing Industries," in *Any Way You Cut It: Meat Processing and Small-Town America*, edited by Donald Stull, Michael Broadway, and David Griffith (Lawrence: University Press of Kansas, 1995), 22.

2. James Olson and Ronald Naugle, *History of Nebraska*, 3rd ed. (Lincoln: University of Nebraska Press, 1997), 188–189; Donald Hickey, *Nebraska Moments: Glimpses of Nebraska's Past* (Lincoln: University of Nebraska Press, 1992), 97–98; Frederick Luebke, *Nebraska: An Illustrated History* (Lincoln: University of Nebraska Press, 1995), 64.

3. Jim Kasik, "What It Means to Be a Schuyler Warrior," *Schuyler Sun*, May 2, 2017; "Schuyler Central High School Sports Racism," News Channel Nebraska, Rose Valenzuela via YouTube, May 15, 2017.

4. Joe Dejka, "Test Scores at Schuyler Central Don't Make the Grade," *Omaha World-Herald*, July 8, 2018; Joe Dejka, "Work of $4,000-a-day Consultant at Struggling Nebraska Schools Shows Promise, but Some Question Cost," *Omaha World-Herald*, January 15, 2019.

5. "President Busch Discusses Comprehensive Immigration Reform in Nebraska," White House Archives of President George W. Bush, June 7, 2006, https://georgewbush-whitehouse.archives.gov/news/releases/2006/06/20060607.html; "Bush Promotes Immigration Reform in Omaha," *Lawrence Journal-World*, June 8, 2006.

6. Jennifer Ludden, "Hastert Takes Stern Immigration Stance," NPR, June 21, 2006, https://www.npr.org/templates/story/story.php?storyId=5501782; Laura Meckler, "Former Speaker Haster Calls for Immigration Overhaul," *Wall Street Journal*, January 30, 2014; Ronald Brownstein, "Bush's Immigration Failure Offers Obama a Lesson," *National Journal*, February 4, 2013; Michael Tarm, "Dennis Hastert Sentenced to 15 Months in Prison," Associated Press, April 27, 2016; Tamar Jacoby, "A Wedge Too Far," *Washington Examiner*, November 20, 2016.

7. Jason Noble, "Donald Trump Raises Sarah Root Case in Convention Speech,"

Des Moines Register, July 21, 2019; Todd Cooper and Bob Glissmann, "Systemic Failures Allowed Man Accused in Motor Vehicle Homicide to Vanish," *Omaha World-Herald,* February 22, 2016.

8. Michael Grabell, "What Happened When Health Officials Wanted to Close a Meatpacking Plant, but the Governor Said No," *ProPublica,* May 7, 2020, https://www .propublica.org/article/what-happened-when-health-officials-wanted-to-close-a -meatpacking-plant-but-the-governor-said-no; Christina Stella, "While Meatpacking Workers Fear Speaking Out on COVID-19, Their Children Organize for Them," NET Nebraska, June 3, 2020, http://netnebraska.org/article/news/1221888/while-meat packing-workers-fear-speaking-out-covid-19-their-children-organize; "Virus Cases Lead 2 Nebraska Meat Processing Plants to Close," Associated Press, May 5, 2020; Grant Schulte, "Fearing Virus, Nebraska Meatpacking Workers Briefly Walk Out," Associated Press, April 28, 2020; Alex Loroff, "Northeast Nebraska Feedlot Dealing with COVID-19 Impacts," News Channel Nebraska, May 21, 2020, https://www .newschannelnebraska.com/story/42161308/northeast-nebraska-feedlot-dealing -with-covid19-impacts; "Hy-Vee to Limit Meat Purchases," KETV 7 Omaha ABC, May 5, 2020.

9. Steve Liewer, "Immigrant Labor Has Fueled Meatpacking Industry since Its Earliest Days in Nebraska," *Omaha World-Herald,* June 28, 2020.

10. "Gov. Ricketts Opposes Bringing Syrian Refugees to Nebraska," KETV 7 Omaha ABC, November 16, 2015; Don Walton, "Ricketts Targeting Young Immigrant Bill," *Lincoln Journal Star,* March 30, 2016; Don Walton, "Governor Candidates Argue Illegal Immigrant Benefits," *Lincoln Journal Star,* February 26, 2014; Chris Dunker, "Nebraska Among 7 States Suing Federal Government to End DACA," *Lincoln Journal Star,* May 1, 2018; Fred Knapp, "Senators Override Ricketts On Professional Licenses For DACA Recipients," NET Nebraska, April 20, 2016.

11. Chatelain, *24th and Glory,* 30–31; Tekla Agbala Ali Johnson, *Free Radical: Ernest Chambers, Black Power, and the Politics of Race* (Lubbock: Texas Tech University Press, 2012), chap. 3, Kindle; Adam Fletcher Sasse, "A History of Redlining in Omaha," *North Omaha History,* August 2, 2015, https://northomahahistory.com/2015/08/02 /a-history-of-red-lining-in-north-omaha/.

12. Mike Tobias, "Nebraska's Hispanic/Latino Population Could Triple by 2050," NET News, August 20, 2013, http://netnebraska.org/article/news/nebraskas -hispaniclatino-population-could-triple-2050.

13. Alayna Treene, "Trump Isn't Matching Obama Deportation Numbers," Axios, June 21, 2019; Alicia Caldwell and Louise Radnofsky, "Why Trump Has Deported Fewer Immigrants Than Obama," *Wall Street Journal,* August 3, 2019.

14. "In the Vanguard," *Economist,* October 14, 1999; Sara Grell, "Nelson Critical of Operation Vanguard, Calls It Detrimental," *Grand Island Independent,* June 3, 1999; Michael Ventura, "Letters at 3 AM: Immigration Wildfires," *Austin Chronicle,* July 7, 2006.

15. Spencer Hsu and Kari Lydersen, "Illegal Hiring Is Rarely Penalized," *Washington Post*, June 19, 2006.

16. Henry Cordes, "'We Have a Workforce Crisis': Nebraska Leaders Sounding Alarm about Unfilled Jobs," *Omaha World-Herald*, March 31, 2019.

17. Tobias, "Nebraska's Hispanic/Latino Population Could Triple by 2050."

18. John Wenz, "Six Degrees North of Arizona: Nebraska's War on Immigration," *The Awl*, April 11, 2011, https://medium.com/the-awl/six-degrees-north-of-arizona -nebraskas-war-on-immigration-e96c94586e80.

19. Wenz, "Six Degrees North of Arizona."

20. Josh Swartzlander, "Osborne Flew Under the Radar in D.C.," *Lincoln Journal Star*, October 14, 2006; Don Walton, "Osborne Defends Immigration Record," *Lincoln Journal Star*, May 4, 2006; Don Walton, "Gov. Turns Back Osborne," *Lincoln Journal Star*, May 9, 2006; Don Walton, "High Noon Near," *Lincoln Journal Star*, May 7, 2006.

21. A. G. Sulzberger, "Immigration Law Moves to Center Stage," *New York Times*, October 2, 2010; Walton, "Osborne Defends Immigration Record"; Walton, "High Noon Near."

22. Kent Warneke, "Senators Override Prenatal Care Veto," *Norfolk Daily News*, April 19, 2012; Sulzberger, "Immigration Law Moves to Center Stage."

23. Aaron Blake, "Our Top 10 Most Popular Governors, Ranked," *Washington Post*, April 12, 2012.

24. Joanne Young, "Bills Would Downgrade Public Assistance," *Lincoln Journal Star*, February 3, 2011; Andrew Norman, "Sending a Message: Arizona-Style Law Would Task Nebraska Police with Immigration Enforcement," the Reader, February 24, 2011, https://thereader.com/news/sending-a-message-arizona-style-law-would -task-nebraska-police-with-immigra.

25. Don Walton, "Nelson Challenges Ricketts on Immigration," *Lincoln Journal Star*, May 29, 2006; David Welna, "Nebraska Senator Takes Tough Stand on Immigration," NPR, April 24, 2006; Ted Genoways, *The Chain: Farm, Factory and the Fate of Our Food* (New York: Harper, 2014), 56–57; Tom Curry, "The Money Strategy in Nebraska's Senate Race," NBC News, May 24, 2006.

26. Robynn Tysver, "Illegal Immigration Is the Latest Hot Topic in Nebraska Governor's Race," *Omaha World-Herald*, May 1, 2014. Joe Duggan, "As Nebraska Lawmakers Debate Immigrant Driver's Licenses, 'Dreamers' Get Day in Court," *Omaha World-Herald*, April 27, 2015.

27. "John C. Fremont, Pathfinder," Nebraskastudies.org, accessed January 20, 2020; Don Schaufelberger and Bill Beck, *The Only State: A History of Public Power in Nebraska* (Virginia Beach: Donning, 2009), 12; "Republican Party Founded," History .com, https://www.history.com/this-day-in-history/republican-party-founded, accessed January 20, 2020; Ryan Bell, "A Nebraskan and a New Yorker Cross Swords

over 'Coastal Bias' in Reporting," *Columbia Journalism Review*, February 7, 2018; Genoways, *The Chain*, 57–59.

28. Joanne Young, "Nebraska Leaders Respond to Trump's DACA Action; Issue Now in Hands of Congress," *Lincoln Journal Star*, September 6, 2017; Dunker, "Nebraska Among 7 States Suing Federal Government to End DACA."

29. Gustavo Lopez, Kristen Bialik, and Jynnah Radford, "Key Findings about U.S. Immigrants," Pew Research Center, November 30, 2018; Jeffrey Passel and D'Vera Cohn, "As Mexican Share Declined, U.S. Unauthorized Immigrant Population Fell in 2015 below Recession Level," Pew Research Center, April 25, 2017, https://www.pewre search.org/fact-tank/2017/04/25/as-mexican-share-declined-u-s-unauthorized-immi grant-population-fell-in-2015-below-recession-level/; Jeffrey Passel and D'Vera Cohn, "Mexicans Decline to Less than Half the U.S. Unauthorized Immigrant Population for the First Time," Pew Research Center, June 12, 2019, https://www.pewresearch.org /fact-tank/2019/06/12/us-unauthorized-immigrant-population-2017/.

30. Jack Crowe, "Sasse Warns Trump That National Emergency Could Set Dangerous Precedent," *National Review*, February 15, 2019; Jack Crowe, "Sasse Backs Trump's Emergency Declaration Despite Executive-Overreach Concern," *National Review*, March 14, 2019.

31. Ben Sasse, *Them: Why We Hate Each Other and How to Heal* (New York: St. Martin's Press, 2018), 121; Ian Schwartz, "Sen. Sasse: I Think About Leaving Republican Party Every Day," *RealClear Politics*, September 9, 2018, https://www.realclearpolitics .com/video/2018/09/09/sen_sasse_i_think_about_leaving_republican_party_every _day_trump_white_house_a_reality_tv_circus.html; "Tracking Congress in the Age of Trump," FiveThirtyEight, https://projects.fivethirtyeight.com/congress-trump-score/, accessed September 15, 2019; "Benjamin Eric Sasse," Voteview, https://voteview.com /person/41503/benjamin-eric-sasse, accessed September 15, 2019; Tim Alberta, *American Carnage: On the Front Lines of the Republican Civil War and the Rise of President Trump* (New York: Harper, 2019), 492.

32. Roseann Moring, "Saying Trump Needs Support, Businessman Matt Innis to Run for Sen. Ben Sasse's Seat," *Omaha World-Herald*, August 2, 2019; Voteview, https://voteview.com/congress/senate, accessed September 15, 2019; Sheryl Gay Stolberg, "Senator Ben Sasse, Vocal Trump Critic, Goes Mum after President's Endorsement," *New York Times*, September 12, 2019; Stephanie Akin, "Ben Sasse, One of the Senate's Last Remaining Republican Trump Critics, to Seek Reelection," Roll Call, August 5, 2019.

33. David French, "Ben Sasse Conducts a Two-Minute Master Class in American Civics," *National Review*, September 4, 2018; Ben Sasse, "Blame Congress for Politicizing the Court," *Wall Street Journal*, September 5, 2018; "Conservatism and Young People," C-SPAN, February 26, 2015; "Full Text: Senator Sasse Discusses Executive Unilateralism on the Senate Floor," U.S. Senator for Nebraska Ben Sasse website, December 17, 2015, https://www.sasse.senate.gov/public/index.cfm/2015/12/full-text.

34. Steve Jordon, "'We Need to Come Together': Political Leaders React to Nebraska Immigration Arrests," *Omaha World-Herald*, August 10, 2018.

35. "Taking Sides on Facebook: How Congressional Outreach Changed under President Trump," Pew Research Center, July 18, 2018, https://www.people-press.org/wp-content/uploads/sites/4/2018/07/TakingSides_FullReport.pdf.

36. Stefan Wojcik and Adam Hughes, "Sizing Up Twitter Users," Pew Research Center, April 24, 2019, https://www.pewresearch.org/internet/2019/04/24/sizing-up-twitter-users/; Mathew Ingram, "Do Journalists Pay Too Much Attention to Twitter?," *Columbia Journalism Review*, October 10, 2018; Nate Cohn and Kevin Quealy, "The Democratic Electorate on Twitter Is Not the Actual Democratic Electorate," *New York Times*, April 9, 2019.

37. Paul Waldman, "How Democrats Are Increasingly Becoming the Pro-Immigrant Party," *Washington Post*, January 29, 2018; Zac Auter and Justin Lall, "Republicans' Dissatisfaction with Immigration Down, Democrats' Up," Gallup, January 23, 2018, https://news.gallup.com/poll/226175/republicans-dissatisfaction-immigration-down-democrats.aspx; "More Say Immigrants Strengthen U.S. as the Partisan Divide Grows," Pew Research Center, October 4, 2017, https://www.people-press.org/2017/10/05/4-race-immigration-and-discrimination/4_9-3/.

38. Mary Pipher, *The Middle of Everywhere: The World's Refugees Come to Our Town* (New York: Harcourt, 2002), 6; Margaret Reist, "Refugee Resettlement Numbers Drop; Mayors, Governor Could Reject Additional Refugees," *Lincoln Journal Star*, December 2, 2019; Jynnah Radford and Phillip Connor, "Just 10 States Resettled More Than Half of Recent Refugees to U.S.," Pew Research Center, December 6, 2016, https://www.pewresearch.org/fact-tank/2016/12/06/just-10-states-resettled-more-than-half-of-recent-refugees-to-u-s/.

39. Nicholas Kristof, "Trump Voters Are Not the Enemy," *New York Times*, February 23, 2017.

40. Nate Cohn, "The Obama-Trump Voters Are Real. Here's What They Think," *New York Times*, August 15, 2017.

41. Michael Massing, "Journalism in the Age of Trump: What's Missing and What Matters," *Nation*, July 19, 2018.

42. Emily Nohr, "'A Welcoming State': Nebraska Led the Nation in Resettling Most Refugees Per Capita in the Last Year," *Omaha World-Herald*, December 9, 2019.

43. Rebekkah Rubin, "The Ugly History of American Immigration," the Week, September 21, 2017, https://theweek.com/articles/722998/ugly-history-american-immigration; Peter Duignan, "Making and Remaking America: Immigration into the United States," Hoover Institution, September 15, 2003; D'vera Cohn, "How U.S. Immigration Laws and Rules Have Changed through History," Pew Research Center, September 30, 2015, https://www.pewresearch.org/fact-tank/2015/09/30/how-u-s-immigration-laws-and-rules-have-changed-through-history/.

44. Gwen Aviles, "New York City Bans Use of 'Illegals' and 'Illegal Alien,'" NBC

News, October 3, 2019; Hans A. von Spakovsky and Patrick Featherston, "New York City Will Fine You for Saying 'Illegal Alien.' That's an Assault on the Constitution," Heritage Foundation, October 4, 2019, https://www.heritage.org/immigration /commentary/new-york-city-will-fine-you-saying-illegal-alien-thats-assault-the; "Legal Immigration," *Last Week Tonight with John Oliver*, September 15, 2019; Ronald Brownstein, "Immigration Backlash Is Coming from Places Least Touched by Immigration," CNN, January 30, 2018; Trip Gabriel, "Border Wall Is Out of Sync with the Southwest's Changing Politics," *New York Times*, January 25, 2019; Charles Garcia, "Why 'Illegal Immigrant' Is a Slur," CNN, July 6, 2012; Jack Dura, "North Dakota Senate Passes Resolution Supporting Southern U.S. Border Wall," *Bismarck Tribune*, March 28, 2019.

45. Frederick Luebke, *Nebraska: An Illustrated History* (Lincoln: University of Nebraska Press, 1995), 239.

46. Donald Hickey, *Nebraska Moments: Glimpses of Nebraska's Past* (Lincoln: University of Nebraska Press, 1992), 194–195; William Ross, *Forging New Freedoms: Nativism, Education and the Constitution 1917–1927* (Lincoln: University of Nebraska Press, 1994); William Ross, "Meyer v. Nebraska," in *The History of Nebraska Law,* edited by Alan Gless (Athens: Ohio University Press, 2008); Jack Rodgers, "The Foreign Language Issue in Nebraska, 1918–1923," *Nebraska History* 39 (1958): 1–22; Willa Cather, *Willa Cather in Person: Interviews, Speeches, and Letters* (Lincoln: University of Nebraska Press, 1990), 147.

47. Ross, "Meyer v. Nebraska," 272–273.

48. Ross, 276–277.

49. Ross, 276–277.

50. Ross, 278–284.

51. Ross, 284.

52. The Nebraska Republican Party 2016 Platform, adopted May 14, 2016; James Cunningham, "Meyer v. Nebraska Created an Interesting Story," *Southern Nebraska Register*, January 23, 2015; Nebraska State Constitution, Article I, Section 27.

53. Ephrat Livni, "Another Child Just Died in US Customs and Border Protection Custody," *Quartz*, December 25, 2018; David Smith, "Families Torn Apart: The Anatomy of Trump's Immigration U-Turn," *Guardian*, June 23, 2018; Nomaan Merchant, "Immigrant Kids Seen Held in Fenced Cages at Border Facility," Associated Press, June 18, 2018.

54. Rev. Bernard Starman, homily, August 12, 2018.

55. The Editors, "Cross the Bridge," *Commonweal*, August 7, 2019.

56. Luebke, *Nebraska: An Illustrated History*, 179; Míla Šašková-Pierce, "Czech-Language Maintenance in Nebraska," *Nebraska History* 74 (1993): 209–217; Clarence John Kubicek, "The Czechs of Butler County, 1870–1940" (master's thesis, University of Nebraska-Lincoln, 1958).

Chapter 3. The Cornhusker Kickback

1. "Frost Ready to Return Nebraska to Former Glory," ESPN, https://www.espn.com/video/clip?id=24494231, accessed April 10, 2019.

2. Jonathan Rodden, *Why Cities Lose: The Deep Roots of the Urban-Rural Political Divide* (New York, Basic, 2019); Jonathan Martin, "Across South, Democrats Who Speak Boldly Risk Alienating Rural White Voters," *New York Times*, November 24, 2018.

3. Micah Mertes, "New ABC Sitcom Is Set in Nebraska. It's About a Couple of City Slickers Who Decide to Live the Good Life," *Omaha World-Herald*, February 7, 2019.

4. Dennis Boyles, *Superior, Nebraska: The Common-Sense Values of America's Heartland* (New York: Doubleday, 2007), 39.

5. Robert Wuthnow, *The Left Behind: Decline and Rage in Small-Town America* (Princeton, NJ: Princeton University Press, 2018), 128.

6. Samer Kalaf, "No One Is Pissing Off Local Wrestling Crowds Like the 'Progressive Liberal,'" Deadspin, June 27, 2017, https://deadspin.com/no-one-is-pissing-off-local-wrestling-crowds-like-the-1796437497.

7. Katherine Cramer, *The Politics of Resentment: Rural Consciousness in Wisconsin and the Rise of Scott Walker* (Chicago: University of Chicago Press, 2016), chap. 3, Kindle; Sarah Smarsh, *Heartland: A Memoir of Working Hard and Being Broke in the Richest Country on Earth* (New York: Scribner, 2018), 272.

8. Vahe Gregorian, "Texas Coach Brown Praises Nebraska Fans," *St. Louis Post-Dispatch*, July 29, 2010.

9. J. D. Vance, *Hillbilly Elegy: A Memoir of a Family and Culture in Crisis* (New York: HarperCollins, 2016).

10. Daniel Funke, "Here's How the Deficit Performed Under Republican and Democratic Presidents, from Reagan to Trump," PolitiFact, August 2, 2019, https://www.politifact.com/factchecks/2019/jul/29/tweets/republican-presidents-democrats-contribute-deficit/; Ed Burmila, "State under Siege," *New Republic*, October 28, 2019; Nathan Arnosti and Amy Liu, "Why Rural America Needs Cities," *Brookings*, November 30, 2018, https://www.brookings.edu/research/why-rural-america-needs-cities/; Scott Olson, "Study: Urban Tax Money Subsidizes Rural Counties," *Indianapolis Business Journal*, January 12, 2010; Bruce Murphy, "Milwaukee Subsidizes the State," *Urban Milwaukee*, February 14, 2017; Brian Mann, *Welcome to the Homeland: A Journey to the Rural Heart of America's Conservative Revolution* (Hanover, NH: Steerforth, 2006), 185; Dan Clark, "The State Spends More on Western New York Than It Receives in Taxes from Region," PolitiFact, October 14, 2016, https://www.politifact.com/factchecks/2016/oct/14/chris-jacobs/state-spends-more-western-new-york-it-receives-tax/; Chris Grygiel, "King Co. Pays for the Rest of the State—Is that Fair?," *Seattle PI*, January 20, 2011, https://www.seattlepi.com/local/article/King-Co-pays-for-the-rest-of-the-state-is-that-969099.php.

11. Paul Krugman, "Why We Regulate," *New York Times*, May 13, 2013.

12. Henry Cordes, "Rural-Urban Divide Shows in Nebraska Vote to Approve Medicaid Expansion," *Omaha World-Herald*, November 7, 2018.

13. Penny Young Nance, "There Is No War on Women," Politico, October 4, 2013, https://www.politico.com/story/2013/10/there-is-no-war-on-women-097847; David French, "The Little Sisters of the Poor Just Beat the Obama Administration at the Supreme Court," *National Review*, May 16, 2016.

14. Tim Alberta, *American Carnage: On the Front Lines of the Republican Civil War and the Rise of President Trump* (New York: Harper, 2019), 62; James Taranto, "ObamaCare's Heritage," *Wall Street Journal*, October 19, 2011.

15. Amy Goldstein, "Nebraska Senator's Sweetener Now a Stumbling Block for Health-Care Bill," *Washington Post*, January 15, 2010; Steve Jordon, "Ex-Nebraska Sen. Ben Nelson, Whose Obamacare Vote Caused Controversy, Says Odds Are Against GOP on Health Care," *Omaha World-Herald*, July 21, 2017; Kevin O'Hanlon, "'Cornhusker Kickback' Part of Nelson's Senate Legacy," *Lincoln Journal Star*, December 27, 2011; "Excerpts from the Times's Interview with Trump," *New York Times*, July 19, 2017; Barack Obama, "A President Looks Back on His Toughest Fight," *New Yorker*, October 26, 2020.

16. Steve Jordon, "What Was the 'Cornhusker Kickback,' the Deal that Led to Nelson's Crucial ACA Vote?," *Omaha World-Herald*, July 20, 2017.

17. Jordon, "What was the Cornhusker Kickback"; Goldstein, "Nebraska Senator's Sweetener"; "Sen. Ben Nelson: His Side of the 'Cornhusker Kickback,'" Fox News, April 13, 2010.

18. Casey Mattox, "Three Ways Obamacare Forces Americans to Fund Big Abortion," *Federalist*, September 23, 2014.

19. Steven Ertlet, "Right to Life Will Oppose 'Pro-Life' Democrat Ben Nelson," Life News, December 14, 2011, https://www.lifenews.com/2011/12/14/right-to-life-will-oppose-pro-life-democrat-ben-nelson/; Crossroads GPS: "'Stakes' Nebraska," December 7, 2011, accessed via YouTube; Don Walton, "Nelson May Lose Pro-Life Supporter," *Lincoln Journal Star*, December 19, 2009; "National Right to Life PAC and Nebraska Right to Life PAC Will Oppose Sen. Ben Nelson for Re-Election," National Right to Life website, December 14, 2011; National Right to Life letter to Congress, Marcy 19, 2010; Manu Raju, "Nelson Tries to Repair Damage at Home," Politico, January 14, 2010, https://www.politico.com/story/2010/01/nelson-tries-to-repair-damage-at-home-031488.

20. David Herszenhorn and Carl Hulse, "Democrats Clinch Deal for Deciding Vote on Health Bill," *New York Times*, December 19, 2009; "President Bush Signs Unborn Victims of Violence Act into Law, after Dramatic One-Vote Win in Senate," National Right to Life website, April 6, 2004; Huma Khan, "Does Sen. Ben Nelson Stand in the Way of Health Care Victory for Democrats?," ABC News, December 18, 2009; Josh Gerstein, "Ben Nelson Is First Dem 'No' on Kagan," Politico, July 31, 2010, https://www.politico.com/blogs/under-the-radar/2010/07/ben-nelson-is-first-dem-no-on-kagan-028327; Michael New, "No, Trump-Administration Policies Won't Increase the

Abortion Rate," *National Review*, November 14, 2017; Stephanie Condon, "Ben Nelson to Offer Stupak Amendment for Senate Health Bill," CBS News, December 1, 2009.

21. Alberta, *American Carnage*, 68; Julian Pecquet, "Few Democrats Survive Health-care Vote," the Hill, November 2, 2010, https://thehill.com/policy/healthcare/127261 -few-democrats-survive-vote-in-favor-of-health-reform; Philip Klein, "Half of the Senators Who Voted for Obamacare Won't Be Part of New Senate," *Washington Examiner*, December 6, 2014; Catherine Dodge and Lisa Lerer, "Democrats Face Biggest House Midterm Defeat in Years," *Bloomberg*, November 2, 2010, https://www.bloomberg.com/news/articles/2010-11-02/republicans-approach-biggest-house-midterm-win-in-seven-decades; Daniel Hopkins, *The Increasingly United States: How and Why American Political Behavior Nationalized* (Chicago: University of Chicago Press, 2018), 239.

22. Rachel Leven, "Sen. Nelson Could Get $1M from K Street," the Hill, December 29, 2011, https://thehill.com/business-a-lobbying/201585-retiring-sen-ben-nelson -would-fetch-top-dollar-on-k-street; Jonathan Rodden, *Why Cities Lose: The Deep Roots of the Urban-Rural Divide* (New York: Basic , 2019), 8.

23. Hopkins, *The Increasingly United States*, 239.

24. Alex Pareene, "Senator Ben Nelson Will Vote against Kagan," *Salon*, July 31, 2010, https://www.salon.com/2010/07/30/ben_nelson_no_kagan/; Jeff Zeleny and Carl Hulse, "Senate Supports a Pullout Date in Iraq War Bill," *New York Times*, March 28, 2007; Jen Dimascio, "Nelson to Back 'Don't Ask' Repeal," Politico, May 26, 2010, https://www.politico.com/story/2010/05/nelson-to-back-dont-ask-repeal-037801.

25. Eric Palmer, "Shire's $800M Lialda Confronted by Generic Competition but Zydus Copy Will Fly Solo for Now," *Fierce Pharma*, June 9, 2017, https://www.fiercepharma.com/pharma/shire-s-800m-lialda-confronted-by-generic-but-zydus -copy-will-fly-solo-for-now.

26. Pedro Nicolaci da Costa, "An Alarming Number of Americans Are Worse Off Than Their Parents and We're Not Talking About It Enough," *Business Insider*, July 17, 2017.

27. Dan Mangan, "The Rate of Uninsured Americans Hits a Record Low as Obamacare's Future Remains a Question Mark," CNBC, February 14, 2017; Allen St. John, "How the Affordable Health Care Act Drove Down Personal Bankruptcy," *Consumer Reports*, May 2, 2017.

Chapter 4. An Undivided House Falls
1. Chris Dunker, "Ebke Implores Lawmakers to Cast Aside Political Obligations," *Lincoln Journal Star*, January 5, 2018.

2. Martha Stoddard and Emily Nohr, "8 of 14 Legislative Candidates Supported by Ricketts Win, Giving the Unicameral a More Conservative Bent," *Omaha World-Herald*, November 9, 2016; "Nebraska Campaign Finance," *Omaha World-Herald*, https://www.dataomaha.com/campaign-finance.

3. John Miller, "A Federalist Faces Down Lincoln's Powerful Legislature," *Wall Street Journal*, December 8, 2017.

4. Brian Doherty, "GOP to Libertarian Legislator: Your It's a Wonderful Life Screening Is against the Law," *Reason*, December 5, 2017, https://reason.com/2017/12/05/libertarian-state-sen-laura-ebke-breakin/; Email, Nebraska Accountability and Disclosure Commission, May 29, 2020.

5. George Norris, *Fighting Liberal: The Autobiography of George Norris*, (New York: Macmillan, 1945), 240–250; Richard Lowitt, *George W. Norris: The Triumph of a Progressive 1933–1944* (Chicago: University of Illinois Press, 1978), 65–67; Seth Masket and Boris Shor, "Polarization without Parties: Term Limits and Legislative Partisanship in Nebraska's Unicameral Legislature," *State Politics and Policy Quarterly* 15, no. 1 (2014): 67–90; James Olson and Ronald Naugle, *History of Nebraska*, 3rd ed. (Lincoln: University of Nebraska Press, 1997), 330.

6. Lowitt, *Norris: Triumph of a Progressive*, 66.

7. Donald Hickey, *Nebraska Moments: Glimpses of Nebraska's Past* (Lincoln: University of Nebraska Press, 1992), 222; University of Nebraska School of Journalism, *Behind These Doors Is the Story of Nebraska's Unicameral Legislature*, August 15, 1961, University of Nebraska–Lincoln library archives; Charlyne Berens, *One House: The Unicameral's Progressive Vision for Nebraska* (Lincoln: University of Nebraska Press, 2005), 206; "On Unicameralism," *Nebraska Legislature*, https://nebraskalegislature.gov/about/ou_experience.php, accessed May 22, 2020.

8. James Hewitt, "Nebraska's Unicameral Legislature," in *The History of Nebraska Law*, edited by Alan Gless (Athens: Ohio University Press, 2008), 145.

9. Martha Stoddard, "Gov. Ricketts, TD Ameritrade, Cubs Reject Racist, Anti-Muslim Emails by Joe Ricketts," *Omaha World-Herald*, February 5, 2019; David Earl, "Joe Ricketts Calls Concern over TD Ameritrade Job Losses 'Foolishness,'" KETV Omaha 7, January 14, 2020; Lynn Sweet, "Cubs Co-owner Todd Ricketts Expands Trump Fundraising Role," *Chicago Sun Times*, February 1, 2019; "Governors' Races Have Become Contests between Bajillionaires," *Economist*, October 19, 2017.

10. Amber Phillips, "Meet the Multi-Millionaire GOP Governor Using His Fortune to Push His Agenda—and Punish His Foes," *Washington Post*, November 6, 2016; Don Walton, "Ricketts Counts on Turnout," *Lincoln Journal Star*, October 25, 2006; Eric Ostermeier, "Ricketts Wins Nebraska GOP Gubernatorial Nod with Lowest Support in State History," *Smart Politics*, May 14, 2014, https://editions.lib.umn.edu/smartpolitics/2014/05/14/ricketts-wins-nebraska-gop-gub/.

11. Paul Hammel, "'Dark Money Group Tied to Ricketts Family Buys Ads Targeting State Legislature Candidates," *Omaha World-Herald*, May 11, 2018; Paul Hammel, "Ricketts' Campaign Manager Sells Her Business, But Still Will Work to Re-Elect Governor," *Omaha World-Herald*, July 5, 2018; "Axiom Strategies Announces the Formation of Media Buying Company," *Missouri Times*, November 29,

2017, https://themissouritimes.com/axiom-strategies-announces-the-formation-of
-media-buying-company/.

12. Hammel, "Dark Money Group"; Andrew Ozaki, "Candidates Targeted by
'Dark Money' Ads Speak Out," KETV Omaha, May 11, 2018.

13. Emily Nohr, "Ricketts and Political Group Deny Having Ties, but Have Same
Targets in Nebraska," *Omaha World-Herald*, November 1, 2016; Joanne Young,
"Americans for Prosperity's Former Nebraska Director Is New HHS Communications Administrator," *Lincoln Journal Star*, January 8, 2018; Kenneth Vogel, "How
the Kochs Launched Joni Ernst," Politico, November 12, 2015, https://www.politico
.com/story/2015/11/the-kochs-vs-the-gop-215672; Paul Blumenthal, "The Kochs' Dark
Money Reaches All the Way to NRA, Religious Groups," HuffPost, November 17,
2015, https://www.huffpost.com/entry/koch-brothers-2014-election_n_564b7680e4b
06037734b3987; John Nichols, "How the Koch Brothers Are Molding the Next Scott
Walkers," *Nation*, October 2, 2014, https://www.thenation.com/article/archive/exclu
sive-audio-how-koch-brothers-are-molding-next-scott-walkers/; Robynn Tysver, "In
Race for Governor, Pete Ricketts in Fundraising Lead, Followed by Beau McCoy and
Jon Bruning," *Omaha World-Herald*, April 15, 2014.

14. Margaret Reist, "NSEA Calls Governor's Denial of Proclamation Honoring Ed-
ucator Union 'Slap in the Face,'" *Lincoln Journal Star*, April 26, 2017; Aaron Hegarty,
"'One Nebraska' Book on Farm Family Is Divisive, Won't Get Proclamation, Ricketts
Says; Author Calls Move 'Shocking,'" *Omaha World-Herald*, January 8, 2019; Matthew
Hansen, "Ricketts Grants, Then Revokes Nebraska Navy Honors for UNL Lecturer,
Professor," *Omaha World-Herald*, February 10, 2018; Joe Duggan, Paul Hammel, Emily
Nitcher, and Martha Stoddard, "'A Monumental Day': Nebraska Executes Carey Dean
Moore in State's First Lethal Injection," *Omaha World-Herald*, August 15, 2018; Joe
Duggan, "Death Penalty Foe Ernie Chambers 'Outraged' that Requested Execution
Date Is His Birthday," *Omaha World-Herald*, June 1, 2018.

15. Paul Hammel, "Nebraska GOP Attacks Republican Candidate Challenging Sen.
Slama; Heineman Calls It 'Despicable,'" *Omaha World-Herald*, April 21, 2020; Don
Walton, tweet, April 20, 2020; Don Walton, "Kerrey, Heineman Urge Slama to Apol-
ogize for 'Racist Campaigning,'" *Lincoln Journal Star,* June 13, 2020; Bob Kerrey and
Dave Heineman, letter to Senator Julie Slama, June, 12, 2020.

16. Jerry Johnson, "Yes, I Voted to Repeal the Death Penalty," *Fremont Tribune*,
May 27, 2015; Grand Schulte, "Nebraska Set for Execution after About-Face on Death
Penalty," Associated Press, August 13, 2018.

17. American Conservative Union, "2015 Ratings of Nebraska," http://acuratings
.conservative.org/wp-content/uploads/sites/5/2016/04/Nebraska_2015_web2.pdf; and
"2018 Ratings of Nebraska," http://acuratings.conservative.org/wp-content/uploads
/sites/5/2018/10/Nebraska_2018_web-1.pdf.

18. Tekla Agbala Ali Johnson, *Free Radical: Ernest Chambers, Black Power, and the*

Politics of Race (Lubbock: Texas Tech University Press, 2012), chap. 7, Kindle; Jonathan Stein, "Ernie Chambers, Nebraska's Leading Hellraiser, Sues God," *Mother Jones*, September 18, 2007, https://www.motherjones.com/politics/2007/09/ernie-chambers -nebraskas-leading-hellraiser-sues-god/; Katherine Timpf, "Nebraska State Senator: ISIS Has Never 'Terrorized Us' Like the Police Do," *National Review*, March 25, 2015, https://www.nationalreview.com/2015/03/nebraska-senator-isis-has-never-terrorized -us-police-do-katherine-timpf/.

19. Gerald Wright and Brian Schaffer, "The Influence of Party: Evidence from the State Legislatures," *American Political Science Review* 96, no. 2 (2002): 367–379.

20. Paul Hammel, "Heineman Stands Out for Efforts to Elect GOP Lawmakers," *Omaha World-Herald Bureau*, October 15, 2012, available at https://www.kearneyhub. com/news/local/heineman-stands-out-for-efforts-to-elect-gop-lawmakers/article _a9e6894e-16c5-11e2-842d-001a4bcf887a.html; Bob Krist, "Heineman Threw Legislature under the Bus," *Grand Island Independent*, October 27, 2012; Seth Masket and Boris Shor, "Polarization without Parties: Term Limits and Legislative Partisanship in Nebraska's Unicameral Legislature," *State Politics and Policy Quarterly* 15, no. 1 (2014): 67–90.

21. Seth Masket, *The Inevitable Party: Why Attempts to Kill the Party System Fail and How They Weaken Democracy* (New York: Oxford University Press, 2016), 59–84; Jack Rodgers, Robert Sittig, and Susan Welch, "The Legislature," in *Nebraska Government and Politics*, edited by Robert Miewald (Lincoln: University of Nebraska Press, 1984), 79.

22. Berens, *One House*, 143–145.

23. Masket and Shor, "Polarization without Parties."

24. Josh Gerstein, "Gorsuch Takes Victory Lap at Federalist Dinner," Politico, November 16, 2017, https://www.politico.com/story/2017/11/16/neil-gorsuch-federalist -society-speech-scotus-246538; "Gov. Ricketts Appoints La Grone in LD49,"Nebraska .gov, December 17, 2018, https://governor.nebraska.gov/press/gov-ricketts-appoints-la -grone-ld49; Martha Stoddard, "Ricketts Names Campaign Press Secretary Julie Slama as State Lawmaker," *Omaha World-Herald*, December 27, 2018; Miller, "A Federalist Faces Down Lincoln's Powerful Legislature"; Nebraska Republican Party 2016 Platform, adopted May 14, 2016.

25. Nebraska Legislature, Adopt the Redistricting Act, LB 580, introduced January 21, 2015; Don Walton, "Murante Won't Contest Redistricting Reform Veto," *Lincoln Journal Star*, April 19, 2016; J. L. Schmidt, "12 New Faces as the 106th Legislature Convenes Jan. 9," *Columbus Telegram*, January 2, 2019; Aaron Sanderford, "Support of Prominent Republicans Carries John Murante to Victory over Taylor Royal in State Treasurer's Race," *Omaha World-Herald*, May 16, 2019; Paul Hammel and Martha Stoddard, "Gov. Pete Ricketts: State Treasurer Should Have Been More Mindful with Outreach Office, Advertising," *Omaha World-Herald*, December 23, 2019; Paul Hammel, "State Treasurer Opened New Omaha Office in September but Hasn't Alerted the Public," *Omaha World-Herald*, December 21, 2019.

26. Nebraska Legislature, Provide for Restoration of Voting Rights upon Completion of a Felony Sentence or Probation for a Felony, LB 75, introduced January 5, 2017.

27. Charles Pallesen and Samuel Van Pelt, *Big Jim Exon: A Political Biography* (Lincoln: Infusionmedia, 2012), 146.

28. University of Nebraska School of Journalism, *Behind These Doors Is the Story of Nebraska's Unicameral Legislature.*

29. University of Nebraska School of Journalism, *Behind These Doors Is the Story of Nebraska's Unicameral Legislature.*

30. Kimberly Reed, "Dark Money," PBS documentary, 2018.

31. Reed, "Dark Money"; Jane Mayer, *Dark Money: The Hidden History of the Billionaires behind the Rise of the Radical Right* (New York: Doubleday, 2016), 229–231.

32. Kevin O'Hanlon, "Supreme Court Overturns Campaign Finance Law," *Lincoln Journal Star*, August 3, 2012; Chris Cillizza, "Winners and Losers from the McCutcheon v. SEC Ruling," *Washington Post*, April 2, 2014.

33. "Donor Demographics," Center for Responsive Politics website, accessed October 30, 2019; Lee Drutman, "The Political 1% of the 1% in 2012," Sunlight Foundation website, June 24, 2013; Paul Hammel, "Ricketts Family Spends Nearly $1 Million This Election Cycle," *Omaha World-Herald*, November 1, 2020.

34. Mayer, *Dark Money*, 239, 332.

35. Bradley Jones, "Most Americans Want to Limit Campaign Spending, Say Big Donors Have Greater Political Influence," Pew Research Center, May 8, 2018, https://www.pewresearch.org/fact-tank/2018/05/08/most-americans-want-to-limit-campaign-spending-say-big-donors-have-greater-political-influence/.

36. National Conference of State Legislatures, "State Limits on Contributions to Candidates 2017–2018 Election Cycle," updated June 27, 2017; "The 2016 State of Nebraska Summary of Campaign Financing," Nebraska Accountability and Disclosure Commission, https://nadc.nebraska.gov/cf/publications.html, accessed January 10, 2020; "The 2000 State of Nebraska Summary of Campaign Financing," Nebraska Accountability and Disclosure Commission, https://nadc.nebraska.gov/cf/publications.html, accessed January 10, 2020; email with Nebraska Accountability and Disclosure Commission, May 29, 2020.

37. Joe Duggan, "Bill to Make Nebraska's Electoral College Votes Winner-Take-All Is Headed to Legislature Floor," *Omaha World-Herald*, April 20, 2017; Joe Duggan, "Bill to Make Nebraska's Electoral Votes Winner-Take-All Moves Ahead but Still Too Close to Call," *Omaha World-Herald*, March 3, 2015.

Chapter 5. Dear Old Nebraska U

1. "Full Call between Reyn Archer and Ari Kohen," *Seeing Red Nebraska*, November 1, 2018, accessed via YouTube.

2. Chris Dunker, "Fortenberry Complains about Facebook Reaction to Vandalized Sign; UNL Professor Says He's Bullying," *Lincoln Journal Star*, November 1, 2018.

3. Robert Knoll, *Prairie University: A History of the University of Nebraska* (Lincoln: University of Nebraska Press, 1995), 43; James Olson and Ronald Naugle, *History of Nebraska*, 3rd ed. (Lincoln: University of Nebraska Press, 1997), 258.

4. Donald Hickey, *Nebraska Moments: Glimpses of Nebraska's Past* (Lincoln: University of Nebraska Press, 1992), 194–195; "Faculty on Campus," Nebraska U: A Collaborative History from the Archives of the University of Nebraska–Lincoln, http://unlhistory.unl.edu/exhibits/show/1910-1919/faculty, accessed June 10, 2020.

5. Knoll, *Prairie University*, 88–89; Hickey, *Nebraska Moments*, 224–225.

6. Knoll, *Prairie University*, 114, 133; "Nebraska's Loyalty Oath," Nebraskastudies.org, http://www.nebraskastudies.org/1950-1974/the-red-menace/nebraskas-loyalty-oath/, accessed June 11, 2020.

7. Stephen Witte, "UNL Reaction to the Cambodian Incursion and the Kent State Shootings, May 1970," *Nebraska History* 75 (1994): 261–271; Olson and Naugle, *History of Nebraska*, 363–368.

8. "Proseminar in Homophile Studies," Nebraska U: A Collaborative History from the Archives of the University of Nebraska–Lincoln, http://unlhistory.unl.edu/exhibits/show/proseminar-homophile/proseminar-homophile, accessed January 3, 2020; Knoll, *Prairie University*, 149, 158.

9. Turning Point USA, https://www.tpusa.com/, accessed December 10, 2019; Charlie Kirk, *The Campus Battlefield: How Conservatives Can Win the Battle on Campus and Why It Matters* (New York: Post Hill, 2018), xii–16, 128; Alex Kotch, "Who Funds Conservative Campus Group Turning Point USA? Donors Revealed," *International Business Times*, November 28, 2017; Joseph Guinto, "Trump's Man on Campus," Politico, April 6, 2018, https://www.politico.com/magazine/story/2018/04/06/trump-young-conservatives-college-charlie-kirk-turning-point-usa-217829; "A Profile of Charlie Kirk," *Dartmouth Review*, November 1, 2019; Internal Revenue Service, Form 990, Ending Spending Inc., 2016, https://pdf.guidestar.org/PDF_Images/2016/272/189/2016-272189012-0e93d7a2-9O.pdf.

10. "My Effing First Amendment," *This American Life*, NPR, May 4, 2018.

11. Allison Stanger, "Understanding the Angry Mob at Middlebury That Gave Me a Concussion," *New York Times*, March 13, 2017; Thomas Fuller and Christopher Mele, "Berkeley Cancels Milo Yiannopoulos Speech, and Donald Trump Tweets Outrage," *New York Times*, February 1, 2017.

12. Rick Ruggles, "Amid Free Speech Firestorm, NU Grapples with Keeping Debate Robust but Respectful," *Omaha World-Herald*, September 3, 2017; Steve Erdman, "UNL Professor, Teaching Assistant Need to Be Terminated," *Scottsbluff Star-Herald*, September 7, 2017.

13. Steve Halloran, Steve Erdman, and Tom Brewer, "5 Questions for UNL," *Hastings Tribune*, October 30, 2017; Steve Kolowich, "State of Conflict: How a Tiny Protest at the U. of Nebraska Turned into a Proxy War for the Future of Campus Politics," *Chronicle of Higher Education*, April 27, 2018; Senator Steve Halloran, Facebook post, September 8, 2017.

14. Shirley Koeing, "Liberal Bias at UNL," *Hastings Tribune*, November 7, 2017; John Grinvalds, "Nebraska Senators' Letter to UNL Questioned by English Department," *Daily Nebraskan*, November 3, 2017; emails to the University of Nebraska Office of the President, August 2017.

15. Kolowich, "State of Conflict"; emails to the University of Nebraska Office of the President, August 2017.

16. "Academic Freedom and Tenure: University of Nebraska–Lincoln," AAUP, May 2018; Chris Pandolfo, "UNL Campus Not 'Safe' for Conservatives, Public Records Reveal," Conservative Review, November 21, 2017, https://www.conservativereview.com/news/unl-campus-not-safe-for-conservatives-public-records-reveal/; Kolowich, "State of Conflict"; emails to University of Nebraska communication staff, August 2017 to November 2017.

17. Emails to University of Nebraska communication staff, August 2017 to November 2017.

18. Chris Dunker, "'This Is a Witch-Hunt': Conservative Faculty, Students at UNL Weigh in on Senators' Call for Changes amid Political Debate," *Lincoln Journal Star*, November 5, 2017; Rick Ruggles, "Ricketts Campaign Survey Asks Donors to Weigh in on 'Bullying' of Conservative NU Students," *Omaha World-Herald*, December 30, 2017; Rick Ruggles, "2 PR Leaders at UNL Resign after Campus Controversy," *Omaha World-Herald*, November 19, 2017.

19. Chris Dunker, "Nebraska Attorney General: Records from Lawmakers to NU Should Be Made Public," *Lincoln Journal Star*, January 24, 2018; Chris Dunker, "NU Releases Senators' Emails Triggered by Politically Charged Confrontation on Campus," *Lincoln Journal Star*, February 2, 2018.

20. Rick Ruggles, "Former NU Lobbyist: UNL Professors Are in Danger of Alienating State Leaders," *Omaha World-Herald*, December 5, 2017; "An Open Letter from University of Nebraska Faculty on Recent Attacks on Our Institution," November 27, 2017, https://aaup-ne.org/2017/11/27/an-open-letter-from-university-of-nebraska-faculty-on-recent-attacks-on-our-institution/; emails between Nebraska state senators, University of Nebraska regents and Office of the President, September 2017 to November 2017; Rick Ruggles, "UNL Professors Defend Academic Freedom after Dustup Involving Lecturer, Student Recruiting for Conservative Group," *Omaha World-Herald*, September 20, 2017.

21. Steve Kolowich, "U. of Nebraska Wondered Whether Conservative Students Were Being Silenced. Here's What It Found Out," *Chronicle of Higher Education*, September 13, 2018; "The University of Nebraska System Climate Study: Understanding Perceptions of Students, Faculty, Staff and Alumni," Gallup, September 2018, https://nebraska.edu/~/media/UNCA/docs/news/NU_2018_Climate_Study_Full_Report.pdf.

22. John Gage, "College Student Taunted as 'Neo-Fascist Becky' Joins Trump for Signing of Free Speech Order," *Washington Examiner*, March 22, 2019; "My Effing First

Amendment," *This American Life*; Kolowich, "U. of Nebraska Wondered Whether Conservative Students Were Being Silenced."

23. "An Open Letter from University of Nebraska Faculty on Recent Attacks on Our Institution," November 27, 2017; "Public Remarks by Delegates on Censure of University of Nebraska," AAUP, June 19, 2018, https://www.aaup.org/news /public-remarks-delegates-censure-university-nebraska.

24. Colleen Flaherty, "AAUP Censure for Nebraska," *Inside Higher Ed*, June 18, 2018, https://www.insidehighered.com/news/2018/06/18/aaup-votes-censure-u-nebraska -alleged-violations-academic-freedom-courtney-lawton.

25. Kolowich, "State of Conflict"; FIRE Letter to the University of Nebraska, Lincoln, December 8, 2017, https://www.thefire.org/fire-letter-to-the-university-of-ne braska-lincoln-december-8-2017/; Cecilia Capuzzi Simon, "Fighting for Free Speech on America's Campuses," *New York Times*, August 1, 2016; Rick Ruggles, "UNL Under Fire from National Groups for Punishing Lecturer after Clash with Conservative Student," *Omaha World-Herald*, December 18, 2017.

26. Rick Ruggles, "UNL Faculty Senate Leader's Rocky Tenure Ends with His Ouster," *Omaha World-Herald*, October 3, 2018; "Leader Resigns from Professor Group over UNL Campus Incident," Associated Press, February 5, 2018; Mary Zoeller, "University of Nebraska Board of Regents Approves 'Commitment to Free Expression' Statement," FIRE, January 30, 2018, https://www.thefire.org/university-of-ne braska-board-of-regents-approves-commitment-to-free-expression-statement/; Chris Dunker, "UNL Faculty Say Free Speech Bill an Attempt to Squash Dissenting Opinions," *Lincoln Journal Star*, January 30, 2018; transcript prepared by the clerk of the Legislature Transcriber's Office, Education Committee, January 30, 2018, 78–137; Margaret Reist, "Proposed Resolution to Abolish Nebraska Board of Education Gets Little Support," *Lincoln Journal Star*, February 20, 2018; Nebraska Legislature, Constitutional Amendment to Eliminate the State Board of Education, LR 285CA, introduced January 16, 2018.

27. Steve Erdman, "Straight Talk from Steve," Nebraska Legislature, July 20, 2018, http://news.legislature.ne.gov/dist47/2018/07/20/straight-talk-from-steve-63/; Matthew Hansen, "Sen. Erdman's View of UNL as Hostile to Conservative White Men Is Bewildering," *Omaha World-Herald*, August 30, 2018; Rick Ruggles, "State Senator: UNL Plan for Diversity Director Puts 'White Christian Conservative Males' at Risk," *Omaha World-Herald*, August 23, 2018; Kolowich, "State of Conflict."

28. Steve Erdman, "Straight Talk from Steve," Nebraska Legislature, October 22, 2018, http://news.legislature.ne.gov/dist47/2018/10/22/straight-talk-from-steve-74/.

29. Erdman, "Straight Talk from Steve," October 22, 2018.

30. Grace Gorenflo, "UNL Professor Suing State Senator Over Alleged Defamatory Statements," *Daily Nebraskan*, April 9, 2019.

31. "Who Is Gerard Harbison," *The Gerard Harbison Files* (blog), October 10, 2008.

32. Gerard Harbison v. Steve Erdman, County Court of Lancaster County, Nebraska, March 27, 2019.

33. Kolowich, "State of Conflict."

34. Ruggles, "Ricketts Campaign Survey Asks Donors to Weigh in on 'Bullying.'"

35. "Bennett Bressman: Nebraska Governor's Field Director," Anti-Fascist Action Nebraska, March 11, 2019, https://antifaneb.noblogs.org/post/2019/03/11/bennett-bressman-governors-state-field-director/; Emma Pettit, "How 'the Jewish Professor' on Campus Responded to a Former Student's Anti-Semitism," *Chronicle of Higher Education*, March 12, 2019.

36. Tyler Tynes and Richard Johnson, "Emails Show a Nebraska Regent Was 'Embarrassed' by Cornhusker Football Players' Protest," *SB Nation*, October 25, 2016, https://www.sbnation.com/college-football/2016/10/25/13337820/nebraska-cornhusker-football-players-protest-kneel-national-anthem; emails sent to University of Nebraska administrators, September 2016; "Michael Rose-Ivey's Statement on Kneeling during the National Anthem," KETV NewsWatch 7, September 26, 2016, accessed via YouTube.

37. "Michael Rose-Ivey Press Conference Quotes," Huskers.com, September 26, 2016, https://huskers.com/news/2016/9/26/211191531.aspx.

38. Chris Heady, "One Year Later, Former Husker Michael Rose-Ivey Stands by His Decision to Kneel during National Anthem," *Omaha World-Herald*, September 27, 2017.

39. Sam McKewon, "Nebraska's Mike Riley on Criticism from Gov. Pete Ricketts and Hal Daub: 'I'm Certain of How We're Handling It,'" *Omaha World-Herald*, September 26, 2016; Sam McKewon, "McKewon: Daub, Ricketts Comments Create Another Obstacle in Nebraska's Uphill Recruiting Battle," *Omaha World-Herald*, September 28, 2016; Chris Dunker, "Emails Shed Light on Regent's Comments Critical of Husker Players," *Lincoln Journal Star*, October 26, 2016.

40. Matt Lamb, "No Republican Professors Found Teaching Theology at Catholic University," College Fix, December 31, 2015, https://www.thecollegefix.com/no-republican-professors-found-teaching-theology-catholic-university/; Matt Lamb, "ROTC Student Banned from Starting Conservative Club, University Refuses to Say Why," College Fix, February 26, 2016, https://www.thecollegefix.com/rotc-student-banned-starting-conservative-club-university-refuses-say/; Anthony Gockowski, "Turning Point USA on Watch at America's Colleges," Campus Reform, April 28, 2016, https://www.campusreform.org/?ID=7536; Jacob Tilstra, "Affirmative Action Is Not Racist Cookies," Creightonian, November 1, 2017, https://www.creightonian.com/opinion/article_12afc060-bf1f-11e7-b2f7-2ffd28974713.html; Owen Amos, "Turning Point USA: Are Conservatives Fighting Back on Campus?," BBC News, March 19, 2018; "Creighton University Professor: Criticize Donald Trump for Bonus Points," Fox News, May 3, 2016; Rebecca Downs, "Professor's Secret Letter Targets Conservative Students,

Calls Trump 'the Anti-Christ,'" *Washington Examiner*, May 1, 2016; "Nebraska GOP Critical of College Speaker's Abortion Stance," Associated Press, April 12, 2019.

41. "UNL Cancels Outdoor Graduation Ceremonies," KETV Omaha ABC Channel 7, May 4, 2013.

42. Tom Brewer, "Taxes, Gun Rights Top Agenda," *North Platte Telegraph*, August 18, 2019.

43. Olson and Naugle, *History of Nebraska*, 138, 330; Don Walton, "Kay Orr Looks Back at the Drama," *Lincoln Journal Star*, February 11, 2013; Frederick Luebke, "Tiemann, Taxes, and the Centennial Legislature of 1967: Beginning Nebraska's Second Century," *Nebraska History* 71 (1990): 106–120.

44. Olson and Naugle, *History of Nebraska*, 138, 330; Michael Wasylenko and John Yinger, "Nebraska Comprehensive Tax Study," Maxwell School of Syracuse University, July 1988, https://nebraskalegislature.gov/pdf/reports/committee/select_special/taxmod/lr155_syracuse.pdf.

45. "Ricketts Signs First Bill to Cut Nebraska State Budget," Associated Press, February 15, 2017.

46. Brewer, "Taxes, Gun Rights Top Agenda"; "Introduction of Bills Begins," *Unicameral Update*, January 8, 2020.

47. "Nebraska Lobbying Report 2020," Common Cause, https://www.commoncause.org/nebraska/wp-content/uploads/sites/18/2020/05/NebraskaLobbyingReport2020_WEB.pdf, accessed June 14, 2020; Brad Davis, "Senator Resigns to Become NU Lobbyist," *Daily Nebraskan*, June 16, 2006; Rick Ruggles, "Former Mayoral Candidate Heath Mello Will Serve as Chief Lobbyist for University of Nebraska," *Omaha World-Herald*, December 6, 2017.

48. Martha Stoddard, "Governor Candidate Bob Krist Criticizes Gov. Ricketts for Cutting NU Funding," *Omaha World-Herald*, August 22, 2018; Knoll, *Prairie University*, 35–36, 88–89; Cassie Wade, "University of Nebraska Braces Itself for Additional Budget Cuts," *UNO Gateway*, January 22, 2018, http://unothegateway.com/university-nebraska-braces-additional-budget-cuts/; "Senators Reject Deeper Cuts to University of Nebraska," NET Nebraska, March 21, 2018, http://netnebraska.org/article/news/1121825/senators-reject-deeper-cuts-university-nebraska.

49. Chris Dunker, "Decades-Old State Supreme Court Decision on Legislature's Power in Governing NU System a Renewed Topic at Capitol," *Lincoln Journal Star*, February 4, 2018; Knoll, *Prairie University*, 157, 171, 180; Charles Pallesen and Samuel Van Pelt, *Big Jim Exon: A Political Biography* (Lincoln: Infusionmedia, 2012), 155; Ivy Harper, *Waltzing Matilda: The Life and Times of Nebraska Senator Robert Kerrey* (New York: St. Martin's Press, 1992), 93, 167.

50. Walton, "Kay Orr Looks Back at the Drama"; Don Walton, "Norbert Tiemann Remembered as Dynamic State Leader," *Lincoln Journal Star*, June 20, 2012; Kim Parker, "The Growing Partisan Divide in Views of Higher Education," Pew Research Center, August 19, 2019, https://www.pewsocialtrends.org/essay/the

-growing-partisan-divide-in-views-of-higher-education/; Charlyne Berens, "Senator Jerome Wagner: Leaving His Mark," University of Nebraska-Lincoln College of Journalism and Mass Communications Archive, accessed January 10, 2020.

51. Transcript prepared by the clerk of the Legislature's Transcriber's Office, Floor Debate, May 8, 2019, 71–73; "Senators Reject Deeper Cuts to University of Nebraska," NET Nebraska; Brent Martin, "Gov. Ricketts Says NU Must Deal with Budget Cuts Just Like the Rest of the State," Associated Press, June 30, 2018.

52. Analysis of University of Nebraska General Operating Budgets 2010–2020; "NU Funding Sources," accessed June 10, 2020, https://sdn.unl.edu/funding_sources.

53. "Public Research Universities: Changes in State Funding," *American Academy of Arts & Sciences*, 2015, 13, https://www.amacad.org/sites/default/files/academy /multimedia/pdfs/publications/researchpapersmonographs/PublicResearchUniv _ChangesInStateFunding.pdf; "Two Decades of Change in Federal and State Higher Education Funding," *Pew Charitable Trusts*, October 15, 2019, https://www.pewtrusts .org/en/research-and-analysis/issue-briefs/2019/10/two-decades-of-change-in-federal -and-state-higher-education-funding.

54. Daniel Showalter et al., "Why Rural Matters 2018–2019: The Time Is Now," *Rural School and Community Trust*, November 2019; "Fall Symposium Presentation," OpenSky Policy Institute, accessed April 24, 2020; "Public Education Finances: 2015," United States Census Bureau, June 2017, https://www.census.gov/content/dam/Cen sus/library/publications/2017/econ/g15-aspef.pdf.

55. Grant Schulte, "Nebraska Senators Struggle to Fund Schools and Cut Taxes," Associated Press, September 16, 2018.

56. "Report to the Legislature: LR155," Nebraska's Tax Modernization Committee, 2013, https://nebraskalegislature.gov/pdf/reports/committee/select_special/taxmod/lr 155_taxmod2013.pdf; "Nebraska Agriculture Fact Card," Nebraska Department of Agriculture, February 2020, https://nda.nebraska.gov/facts.pdf; Salman Ahmed et al., "US Foreign Policy for the Middle Class: Perspectives from Nebraska," University of Nebraska Public Policy Center, 2020, https://carnegieendowment.org/files/USFP_Ne braska_full_final.pdf; Jim Jansen, Jeff Stokes, and Glennis McClure, "Nebraska Farm Real Estate and Financial Considerations in 2020," *University of Nebraska Institute of Agriculture and Natural Resources Cropwatch*, December 13, 2019, https://cropwatch .unl.edu/2019/nebraska-farm-real-estate-and-financial-considerations-2020; Jim Jansen and Jeff Stokes, "Nebraska Farm Real Estate Market Highlights 2018–2019," University of Nebraska–Lincoln Department of Agricultural Economics; Blake Hurst, "Is a Farmland Price Crash on the Horizon?" *Agri-Pulse*, January 28, 2019, https://www .agri-pulse.com/articles/11841-opinion-is-a-farmland-price-crash-on-the-horizon; Martha Stoddard, "Ag Land Leads Valuation Increases in Nebraska—Again," *Omaha World-Herald*, April 17, 2015.

57. Tekla Agbala Ali Johnson, *Free Radical: Ernest Chambers, Black Power, and the Politics of Race* (Lubbock: Texas Tech University Press, 2012), chap. 5, Kindle;

"Nebraska Panel Advances Tax Break for Emergency Responders," 10/11 KOLN/KGIN, March 2, 2016; J. David Aiken, "2007 Legislature Repeals Estate Tax and Reduces Inheritance Tax," *Cornhusker Economics,* July 11, 2007, https://digitalcommons.unl .edu/cgi/viewcontent.cgi?article=1324&context=agecon_cornhusker; Paul Hammel, "Tax-Increment Financing Blight Fix or Scheme Run Amok?," *Omaha World-Herald,* February 25, 2015; Martha Stoddard, "Sale of TD Ameritrade Stirs Debate about Nebraska's Business Tax Incentives," *Omaha World-Herald,* November 29, 2019.

58. Paul Hammel, "Teachers Union Criticizes Ricketts for Calling Nebraska's Public Schools 'Government Schools,'" *Omaha World-Herald,* February 12, 2020; Don Walton, "Ricketts Would Further Limit Spending Growth in 'Government Schools,'" *Lincoln Journal Star,* February 11, 2020; Governor Pete Rickets, "Delivering Property Tax Relief for Nebraskans," Official Nebraska Government website, February 11, 2020, https://governor.nebraska.gov/press/delivering-property-tax-relief-nebraskans.

59. Sharon Lerner, "Segregation Nation," American Prospect, June 9, 2011, https:// prospect.org/civil-rights/segregation-nation/; Adam Fletcher Sasse, "A History of Segregated Schools in Omaha, Nebraska," North Omaha History, February 6, 2018, https://northomahahistory.com/2018/02/06/a-history-of-segregated-schools-in-oma ha-nebraska/; "Nebraska Segregation Law Draws National Attention," Daily Kos, April 15, 2006, https://www.dailykos.com/stories/2006/4/15/202422/-; "Omaha Public Schools Issues and Implications of Nebraska Legislative Bill 1024," U.S. Commission on Civil Rights, https://www.usccr.gov/pubs/docs/OmahaFinal.pdf, accessed March 25, 2020; Dirk Chatelain, "Some Folks in West Omaha Didn't Want to Live Next to a Black Family—Even Bob Gibson's," *Omaha World-Herald,* July 6, 2019; transcript prepared by the clerk of the Legislature's Transcriber's Office, Education Committee, February 6, 2007, 21–45; Jennifer Jellison Holme, Sarah Diem, and Katherine Cumings Mansfield, "Using Regional Coalitions to Address Socioeconomic Isolation: A Case Study of the Omaha Metropolitan Agreement," Charles Hamilton Houston Institute for Race and Justice, Harvard Law School, May 2009, http://charleshamiltonhouston. org/wp-content/uploads/2013/06/OmahaMetroAgreement_Smaller.pdf.

60. "Public Education Finances," United States Census Bureau; "State and Local Financing of Public Schools," Congressional Research Service, August 26, 2019, https://fas.org/sgp/crs/misc/R45827.pdf; Dave Aiken, "2019 Nebraska Property Tax–School Funding Issues," *Cornhusker Economics,* February 27, 2019, https://agecon.unl .edu/cornhusker-economics/2019/nebraska-property-tax-school-funding-issues.

61. Rebecca Vogt et al., "Nebraska Rural Poll: Media, Institutions and Voting," University of Nebraska–Lincoln, September 2017, https://ruralpoll.unl.edu/pdf/17me diainstitutionsvoting.pdf.

62. Jonathan Haidt and Greg Lukianoff, *The Coddling of the American Mind: How Good Intentions and Bad Ideas Are Setting Up a Generation for Failure* (New York: Penguin, 2018), 15, 30, 48, 121–125, 148, 200; Erwin Chemerinsky and Howard Gillman, *Free*

Speech on Campus (New Haven, CT: Yale University Press, 2017); Sigal Ben-Porath, *Free Speech on Campus* (Philadelphia: University of Pennsylvania Press, 2017); Bruce Bawer, *The Victims' Revolution: The Rise of Identity Studies and the Closing of the Liberal Mind* (New York: Broadside, 2012).

63. Lukas Mikelionis, "Professor Found Guilty of Spraying Fake Blood at NRA Lobbyist's Home," Fox News, May 23, 2018.

64. Ruggles, "Former NU Lobbyist: UNL Professors are in Danger of Alienating State Leaders."

65. "My Effing First Amendment," *This American Life*; Hannah Scherlacher, "Video: Profs Bully TPUSA Prez While She Recruits on Campus," Campus Reform, August 25, 2017, https://www.campusreform.org/?ID=9649.

66. "My Effing First Amendment," *This American Life*; Bill Bishop and Robert Cushing, *The Big Sort: Why the Clustering of Like-Minded America Is Tearing Us Apart* (New York: Houghton Mifflin, 2008), 286–287; David French, "America's Most Educated, Engaged Citizens Are Making Politics Worse," *National Review*, June 24, 2019; "The Perception Gap," More in Common, https://perceptiongap.us/, accessed January 20, 2020; Peter Berkowitz, "The Most Politically Intolerant Americans," Real Clear Politics, March 21, 2019, https://www.realclearpolitics.com/articles/2019/03/21/the_most_politically_intolerant_americans_139810.html; Amanda Ripley, Rekha Tenjarla, and Angela He, "The Geography of Partisan Prejudice," *Atlantic*, March 4, 2019.

67. Andrew Kirell, "Serial Plagiarist Benny Johnson Joining Charlie Kirk's Turning Point USA," Daily Beast, February 6, 2019, https://www.thedailybeast.com/serial-plagiarist-benny-johnson-joining-charlie-kirks-turning-point-usa.

68. Christopher Ingraham, "The Dramatic Shift among College Professors That's Hurting Students' Education," *Washington Post*, January 11, 2016; Lukianoff and Haidt, *The Coddling of the American Mind*, 110–112; Mitchell Langbert, Anthony Quain, and Daniel Klein, "Faculty Voter Registration in Economics, History, Journalism, Law, and Psychology," *Econ Journal Watch* 13, no. 3 (2016): 422–451; Erik Wemple, "Dear Mainstream Media: Why so Liberal?," *Washington Post*, January 27, 2017.

69. Lydia Saad, "U.S. Still Leans Conservative, but Liberals Keep Recent Gains," Gallup, January 8, 2019, https://news.gallup.com/poll/245813/leans-conservative-liberals-keep-recent-gains.aspx; "Party Affiliation," Gallup, accessed December 10, 2019, https://news.gallup.com/poll/15370/party-affiliation.aspx; Scott Jaschik, "Professors and Politics: What the Research Says," *Inside Higher Ed*, February 27, 2017, https://www.insidehighered.com/news/2017/02/27/research-confirms-professors-lean-left-questions-assumptions-about-what-means.

70. Adam Goldstein, "Iowa Bill Seeking Partisan Balance in Higher Ed Faculty Likely Unconstitutional," FIRE, March 1, 2017, https://www.thefire.org/iowa-bill-seeking-partisan-balance-in-higher-ed-faculty-likely-unconstitutional/; William Petroski and Brianne Pfannenstiel, "Political Diversity among Faculty Won't Be Required.

Here Are Some Bills That Died in the 2017 Iowa Legislature," *Des Moines Register*, April 22, 2017; Corky Siemaszko, "Iowa Pol's Bio Changed after 'Sizzler U' Discrepancy Emerges," NBC News, March 1, 2017; Corky Siemaszko, "Iowa Pol Pushing Bill to Get More GOP Profs on College Campuses," NBC News, February 24, 2017; Madeline Will, "Iowa Legislator Wants to Give Students the Chance to Fire Underwhelming Faculty," *Chronicle of Higher Education*, April 23, 2015; O. Kay Henderson, "Senators Squabble over Preschool," Radio Iowa, February 14, 2011, https://www.radioiowa .com/2011/02/14/senators-squabble-over-preschool-pre-preschool/.

71. Rebecca Vogt et al., "Nebraska Rural Poll: Higher Education Opinions and Participation among Nonmetropolitan Nebraskans," University of Nebraska–Lincoln, November 2015, https://ruralpoll.unl.edu/pdf/15education.pdf; Rebecca Vogt et al., "Nebraska Rural Poll: Perceptions of Higher Education in Nonmetropolitan Nebraska," University of Nebraska–Lincoln, October 2019, https://ruralpoll.unl.edu/pdf/19educa tion.pdf; Jackie Ourada, "New Poll Shows Rural Nebraskans Have Mixed Feelings on Higher Education," KETV Omaha ABC Channel 7, November 1, 2019; Parker, "The Growing Partisan Divide in Views of Higher Education"; Jeffrey Jones, "Confidence in Higher Education Down Since 2015," Gallup, October 9, 2015, https://news.gallup.com /opinion/gallup/242441/confidence-higher-education-down-2015.aspx.

72. Marc Tracy, "Harvard Crimson Under Fire from Student Activists," *New York Times*, October 23, 2019; Jacey Fortin, "The Daily Northwestern Apologizes to Student Protestors for Reporting," *New York Times*, November 12, 2019; Howard Gillman and Erin Chemerinsky, "Professors Are Losing Their Freedom of Expression," *Washington Post*, November 15, 2017.

73. José Duarte et al., "Political Diversity Will Improve Social Psychological Science," *Behavioral and Brain Sciences* 38 (2015): 1–58.

74. John Villasenor, "Views Among College Students Regarding the First Amendment: Results from a New Survey," Brookings, September 18, 2017, https://www.brook ings.edu/blog/fixgov/2017/09/18/views-among-college-students-regarding-the-first -amendment-results-from-a-new-survey/; Jacob Poushter, "40% of Millennials OK with Limiting Speech Offensive to Minorities," Pew Research Center, November 20, 2015, https://www.pewresearch.org/fact-tank/2015/11/20/40-of-millennials-ok-with-lim iting-speech-offensive-to-minorities/; "The First Amendment on Campus 2020 Report: College Students' Views of Free Expression," *Knight Foundation* and Gallup, accessed June 22, 2020, https://knightfoundation.org/wp-content/uploads/2020/05 /First-Amendment-on-Campus-2020.pdf; "Free Expression on College Campuses," *Knight Foundation* and *College Pulse*, May 2019, https://kf-site-production.s3.ama zonaws.com/media_elements/files/000/000/351/original/Knight-CP-Report-FINAL .pdf; Lukianoff and Haidt, *Coddling of the American Mind*, 30–48.

75. "Daniel Kleve, UNL Student, Vanguard America Member," Anti-Fascist Action Nebraska, September 6, 2017, https://antifaneb.noblogs.org/post/2017/09/06/daniel -kleve-unl-student-vanguard-america-member/; John Grinvalds, "UNLPD Reviews

Student Video Discussing Violence, White Nationalism," *Daily Nebraskan*, February 6, 2018; Rick Ruggles, "About 300, including Coach Tim Miles, Attend UNL Rally against White Nationalist Student," *Omaha World-Herald*, February 8, 2018; "University of Nebraska-Lincoln's Violent Student Problem," Anti-Fascist Action Nebraska, via YouTube, February 5, 2018.

76. "Dan Kleve Update (ATTN Florida)," Anti-Fascist Action Nebraska, February 10, 2019, https://antifaneb.noblogs.org/post/2019/02/10/dan-kleve-update-attn-florida/; Nebraska Left Coalition, Facebook post, October 21, 2017; Michael Edison Hayden, "Nebraska White Supremacist Who Praises Violence Poses Unique Challenges to Campus Free Speech," *Newsweek*, February 13, 2018.

77. Troy Fedderson, "'Hate Will Never Win' Rally Draws 1500+," University of Nebraska Newsroom, February 14, 2018, https://news.unl.edu/newsrooms/today/article/hate-will-never-win-rally-draws-1500/; "Free 'Hate Will Never Win' Shirts Available," University of Nebraska Newsroom, https://newsroom.unl.edu/announce/engineering/7728/43747, accessed December 10, 2019; Ruggles, "About 300, including Coach Tim Miles, Attend UNL Rally."

78. Journal Star Editorial Board, "'Hate Will Never Win' Is Needed Response to UNL's White Nationalist," *Lincoln Journal Star*, February 13, 2018.

Chapter 6. Democratic Disarray and Hidden Progressivism

1. Bob Kerrey, *When I Was a Young Man: A Memoir by Bob Kerrey* (New York: Harcourt, 2002), 35.

2. Mark Shields, "Nebraska's 'First Lady Friend,'" *Washington Post*, October 11, 1985.

3. Jeff Goodell, "Bob Kerrey: Un-Candidate," *Rolling Stone*, February 6, 1992; Ivy Harper, *Waltzing Matilda: The Life and Times of Nebraska Senator Robert Kerrey* (New York: St. Martin's Press, 1992), xi, 156; Mary Vespa, "A Tornado Named Debra Winger Has a Whirl with Nebraska's Governor—Rockin' Bob Kerrey," *People*, June 6, 1983; "A Loss for the Senate and the Nation," *Buffalo News*, January 24, 2000.

4. James Olson and Ronald Naugle, *History of Nebraska*, 3rd ed. (Lincoln: University of Nebraska Press, 1997), 388–393; Sarah Muller, "Speaking Out: Who Opposed DOMA during 1996 Debate?," MSNBC, March 29, 2013.

5. Stephen Chapman, "Bill Clinton and the Boy Who Cried Wolf," *Chicago Tribune*, January 25, 1998.

6. "Kerrey Surges Despite Dwindling Democratic Electoral Muscle," NewsNetNebraska, November 1, 2012, https://web.archive.org/web/20200327200602/http://www.newsnetnebraska.org/2012/11/01/kerrey-surges-despite-dwindling-democratic-electoral-muscle/.

7. Manu Raju, "For Bob Kerrey, Buffett Rules," Politico, June 25, 2012, https://www.politico.com/story/2012/06/for-bob-kerrey-buffet-rules-077819; Janet Hook, "Hagel to Endorse Kerrey in Nebraska," *Wall Street Journal*, October 31, 2012; Dan Amira,

"Steve Martin Gives Nontraditional Endorsement to Bob Kerrey," *New York* magazine, October 5, 2012.

8. Christopher Heine, "In the Middle of the Fight: Cosmic Bob Lands on the 9–11 Commission," *Omaha Weekly Reader*, 2002, http://web.archive.org/web/20040606 033401/www.thereader.com/createpage.asp?contentID=2366; Colin Moynihan and Trymaine Lee, "Protest at The New School Turns Unruly," *New York Times*, December 18, 2008; Ariel Kaminer, "Kerrey, in Reversal, Decides to Quit Job at New School," *New York Times*, February 1, 2013; Marc Santora and Lisa Foderaro, "New School Faculty Votes No Confidence in Kerrey," *New York Times*, December 10, 2008; Meryl Gordon, "Bob Kerrey's New War," *New York* magazine, April 18, 2003; Ted Genoways, "Bob Kerrey Will Call Your Bullshit," *Mother Jones*, October 2012; "Memories of a Massacre: Varying Accounts of a Night in 1969," *60 Minutes*, May 1, 2001.

9. Scott Voorhees, "Democratic Party Tells Janicek ENOUGH," KFAB, June 16, 2020, https://kfab.iheart.com/featured/voorhees/content/2020-06-16-democratic-party -tells-janicek-enough/.

10. "Nebraska Democratic Party Demands that Chris Janicek Drop Out of Senate Race after Sexual Harassment Complaint," Nebraska Democratic Party, June 16, 2020, https://nebraskademocrats.org/press-releases/nebraska-democratic-party-demands -that-chris-janicek-drop-out-of-senate-race-after-sexual-harassment-complaint/; Maggie Astor, "Nebraska Democrat Urged to Quit Senate Race over Sexual Texts to Aide," *New York Times*, June 16, 2020; "Editorial 6/21: If You Want Football in 2020, Wear Your Mask," *Lincoln Journal Star*, June 20, 2020; "Chris Janicek Should Drop Out of Election," *Grand Island Independent*, June 19, 2020; "Janicek Must Exit Senate Race. Dems, GOP Need Strong Policy Debate," *Omaha World-Herald*, June 21, 2020.

11. Aaron Sanderford, "Democratic Nominee in Nebraska's 3rd District Wants to Switch Sides, Form New Marijuana Party," *Omaha World-Herald*, June 19, 2020.

12. Mark Elworth Jr., Facebook posts, June 16–22, 2020.

13. "Bob Krist Wins Nebraska Democratic Governor Nod," WOWT Channel 6 News, May 15, 2018; Don Walton, "Ricketts, Fischer Win Re-Election," *Lincoln Journal Star*, November 7, 2018; Roseann Moring, "Attorney General Candidate Steps Down amid Strangulation Charge; Democrats Plan a Replacement," *Omaha World-Herald*, June 25, 2018.

14. Brian Mann, *Welcome to the Homeland: A Journey to the Rural Heart of America's Conservative Revolution* (Hanover, NH: Steerforth, 2006), 97; Bob Moser, *Blue Dixie: Awakening the South's Democratic Majority* (New York: Times Books, 2008), 39; Jane Kleeb, *Harvest the Vote: How Democrats Can Win Again in Rural America* (New York: Ecco, 2020), 163; Chris Cillizza, "Barack Obama's Presidency Has Been a Very Good Thing for Republicans," *Washington Post*, February 3, 2016; Mara Liasson, "The Democratic Party Got Crushed during the Obama Presidency. Here's Why," NPR, March 4, 2016, https://www.npr.org/2016/03/04/469052020/the -democratic-party-got-crushed-during-the-obama-presidency-heres-why.

15. Sarah Jones, "How Can Democrats Win Back Rural America?," *New York* magazine, November 5, 2019.

16. Nebraska Secretary of State website, https://sos.nebraska.gov/, accessed October 25, 2019.

17. Emily Badger, "How the Rural-Urban Divide Became America's Political Fault Line," *New York Times*, Mary 21, 2019.

18. Niels Lesniewski, "Democrat Brad Ashford Falls in Nebraska's 2nd District," Roll Call, November 3, 2016.

19. Matt Olberding, "Census: Nebraska's Big Counties Growing, Rest of State Not," *Lincoln Journal Star*, March 22, 2018; David Drozd, "Percentage Change in Population for Nebraska Counties: 2010 to 2016," University of Nebraska-Omaha Center for Public Affairs Research, March 21, 2017, https://www.unomaha.edu/college-of-public-affairs-and-community-service/center-for-public-affairs-research/documents/population-changes-in-nebraska-counties-2016.pdf.

20. Patrick Carr and Maria Kefalas, *Hollowing Out the Middle: The Rural Brain Drain and What It Means for America* (Boston: Beacon, 2009), ix–x.

21. Henry Cordes, "'We Have a Workforce Crisis': Nebraska Leaders Sounding Alarm about Unfilled Jobs," *Omaha World-Herald*, March 31, 2019; "Census Shows 'Brain Drain' Continues in Nebraska," Associated Press, December 8, 2016.

22. Truman Capote, *In Cold Blood: A True Account of a Multiple Murder and Its Consequences* (London: Transaction, 1965), 40.

23. Bill Bishop and Robert Cushing, *The Big Sort: Why the Clustering of Like-Minded America Is Tearing Us Apart* (New York: Houghton Mifflin, 2008), 14, 39.

24. Kim Parker et. al, "Demographic and Economic Trends in Urban, Suburban and Rural Communities," Pew Research Center, May 22, 2018, https://www.pewsocialtrends.org/2018/05/22/demographic-and-economic-trends-in-urban-suburban-and-rural-communities/.

25. "Bitter Campaigns Seem Sure for Both Parties in Nebraska," *New York Times*, March 16, 1970; Dirk Chatelain, "Slumlords, Ghettos, Segregation: Housing Issues Split Nebraska Lawmakers—and Landed at an NBA Star's Doorstep," *Omaha World-Herald*, July 8, 2019; Don Walton, "Norbert Tiemann Remembered as Dynamic State Leader," *Lincoln Journal Star*, June 20, 2012; Don Walton, "50 Years Ago, Nebraskans 'Aroused to the Point of Fury' Over Taxes," *Lincoln Journal Star*, April 10, 2017; Don Walton, "Big Decisions Loom for 2019 Legislature," *Lincoln Journal Star*, July 29, 2018; Susan Welch, "The Governor and Other Elected Executives," in *Nebraska Government and Politics*, edited by Robert Miewald (Lincoln: University of Nebraska Press, 1984), 47; Frederick Luebke, "Tiemann, Taxes, and the Centennial Legislature of 1967: Beginning Nebraska's Second Century," *Nebraska History* 71 (1990): 106–120; Charles Pallesen and Samuel Van Pelt, *Big Jim Exon: A Political Biography* (Lincoln: Infusionmedia, 2012), 70–81, 403.

26. "Lee Raymond Terry," Voteview, https://voteview.com/person/29921/lee-ray

mond-terry, accessed June 10, 2020; Aaron Blake, "Rep. Lee Terry (R-Neb.) Survives Primary Scare," *Washington Post*, May 13, 2014; Robynn Tysver, "Rep. Lee Terry's Seat Is in an Increasingly Endangered Political Species: The Swing District," *Omaha World-Herald*, July 29, 2014.

27. Martha Stoddard, "Ricketts Names Campaign Press Secretary Julie Slama as State Lawmaker," *Omaha World-Herald*, December 27, 2018; Martha Stoddard, "Legislative Employee Will Replace His Boss, John Murante, in Nebraska Legislature," *Omaha World-Herald*, December 18, 2018.

28. Senator John McCollister, Facebook post, March 10, 2020.

29. "Nebraska Republicans Respond to McCollister's Statements," Associated Press, August 5, 2019.

30. Journal Star Editorial Board, "Nebraska GOP Offer to Boot McCollister Is Pure Pettiness," *Lincoln Journal Star*, August 8, 2019.

31. Joseph Morton, "Nebraska Lawmaker, a Republican, Says His Own Party Enables White Supremacy," *Omaha World-Herald*, August 6, 2019; "State Senator Says Risk Is Minimal for Calling Out 'Racist' Activity," MSNBC, August 7, 2019.

32. Michael Tomasky, "The Party Cannot Hold," *New York Review of Books*, March 26, 2020.

33. Roseann Moring, "At Meeting, Nebraska Democrats Debate Party Leaders' Role in Primaries," *Omaha World-Herald*, February 5, 2018; Roseann Moring and Aaron Sanderford, "How Did the Blue Wave Pass Over Nebraska's 2nd Congressional District?" *Omaha World-Herald*, November 11, 2018; Jessica Wade, "'I Won't Be Silent': Facebook Post Shows Tensions between Nebraska Democratic Party Leaders," *Omaha World-Herald*, November 3, 2019; Jane Fleming Kleeb, Facebook post, November 2, 2019; Aaron Sanderford, "Chair of Douglas County Democratic Party Won't Run Again Following Feud with State Party," *Omaha World-Herald*, April 30, 2020; Aaron Sanderford, "Top Democrats' Fight over Who Steers Strategy, Fundraising in Omaha Is Coming to a Head," *Omaha World-Herald*, March 1, 2020.

34. Joe Jordan, "Democrats' Family Feud Still Simmering, Love Ready to Place Peacemaker," *Sandhills Express*, November 27, 2018; Joe Jordan, "Democrats' Feud Escalates, Finds Crucial Votes in the Crosshairs," *Sandhills Express*, October 11, 2018; Joe Jordan, "Democrats' Family Feud Reaching Boiling Point amid Charges of Racism," *Sandhills Express*, October 12, 2018; Chelsey Gentry-Tipton, Facebook post, October 18, 2018.

35. Moring, "At Meeting, Nebraska Democrats Debate Party Leaders' Role in Primaries"; "Nebraska Democratic Party Passes Primary Fairness Resolution," Nebraska Democratic Party, February 5, 2018, https://nebraskademocrats.org/blog/nebraska -democratic-party-passes-primary-fairness-resolution/.

36. Don Walton, "Powers Withdraws in Face of Democratic Turmoil," *Lincoln Journal Star*, June 8, 2016; Robynn Tysver, "Nebraska Democratic Party Chairman Powers Says He Won't Run for Re-election; He Was Part of 'Unity Ticket,'" *Omaha*

World-Herald, June 9, 2016; Pallesen and Van Pelt, *Big Jim Exon,* 31; Paolo Coletta, "The Nebraska Democratic State Convention of April 13–14, 1892," *Nebraska History* 39 (1958): 317–333.

37. Oliver Laughland and Jon Swaine, "Virginia Shooting: Gunman Was Leftwing Activist with Record of Domestic Violence," *Guardian,* June 15, 2017.

38. Christopher Burbach, "Nebraska Democratic Party Chair Removes Official after Offensive Remarks About Congressman's Shooting," *Omaha World-Herald,* June 23, 2017; "Nebraska Democrat Phil Montag Glad Republican Senator Scalise Was Shot; Wish He Was Dead," accessed via YouTube, October 20, 2019.

39. Christopher Burbach, "Black Caucus Leaders Vote to Remove Nebraska Democratic Party Official after Remarks About Shooting of Congressman," *Omaha World-Herald,* July 19, 2017; Christopher Burbach, "Extended Recording Reveals Conversation Leading Up to Fired Democratic Official's Remark That He Was 'Glad' Congressman Was Shot," *Omaha World-Herald,* June 28, 2017.

40. Burbach, "Nebraska Democratic Party Chair Removes Official after Offensive Remarks About Congressman's Shooting."

41. Paul Hammel, "Eminent Domain Process for Keystone XL Pipeline Begins in Nebraska," *Omaha World-Herald,* September 28, 2019; Paul Hammel, "Opponents of Keystone XL Pipeline Seek Rehearing of Nebraska Supreme Court Ruling," *Omaha World-Herald,* August 30, 2019; "Nebraska Landowners Sue Keystone XL Developer," *Reuters,* January 17, 2015; Paul Hammel, "In Possible Roadblock for Keystone XL, Pipeline Opponents Gift Land to Ponca," *Omaha World-Herald,* June 15, 2018; Lori Pilger, "Attorneys Make Final Pitches to Nebraska Supreme Court in Keystone XL Appeal," *Lincoln Journal Star,* November 1, 2018; Sam Ross-Brown, "Nebraska Approves Keystone XL Pipeline, but Fight Continues," American Prospect, November 21, 2017, https://prospect.org/power/nebraska-approves-keystone-xl-pipeline-fight-contin ues/; "Nebraska Governor Asks Obama to Nix Keystone Pipeline," Reuters, August 31, 2011; Emily Sullivan, "In a Setback for Trump, Judge Blocks Keystone XL Pipeline Construction," NPR, November 9, 2018.

42. Saul Elbein, "Jane Kleeb vs. the Keystone Pipeline," *New York Times,* May 16, 2014; Joe Duggan, "Willie Nelson, Neil Young Lend Their Talents to Keystone XL Fight," *Omaha World-Herald,* September 29, 2014; Bill Schammert, "Planting a Symbolic Protest to the Keystone XL Pipeline," 10/11 Now, May 21, 2017, https:// www.1011now.com/content/news/Planting-a-symbolic-protest-to-the-Keystone-XL -pipeline-423528393.html; Joe Duggan, "Investor Tom Steyer Helps Dedicate 'Clean Energy' Barn in Pipeline's Path," *Omaha World-Herald,* September 22, 2013; Mitch Smith, "Pumpkin Carvers Protest Pipeline," *Lincoln Journal Star,* October 22, 2011; Kevin Abourezk, "Huskers Cut Off Deal with TransCanada," *Lincoln Journal Star,* September 14, 2011.

43. Merrill Fabry, "This Is Why Arbor Day Is a Thing," *Time,* April 28, 2017; Matt Olberding, "Report: Nebraska Led Nation in Wind Energy Growth," *Lincoln Journal*

Star, April 9, 2019; Jason Samenow, "Blowing Hard: The Windiest Time of Year and Other Fun Facts on Wind," *Washington Post*, March 31, 2016.

44. "Annual Average Electricity Price Comparison by State," Nebraska Energy Office, https://neo.ne.gov/programs/stats/inf/204.htm, accessed October 7, 2019; "Looking Deeper: The Choose Energy Rate Report," Choose Energy, https://www.chooseenergy.com/electricity-rates-by-state/, accessed October 7, 2019.

45. Frederick Luebke, *Nebraska: An Illustrated History* (Lincoln: University of Nebraska Press, 1995), 293; Don Schaufelberger and Bill Beck, *The Only State: A History of Public Power in Nebraska* (Virginia Beach, VA: Donning, 2009), 25–30.

46. Schaufelberger and Beck, *The Only State*, 252.

47. Ted Genoways, "Inside the Unlikely Coalition That Just Got the Death Penalty Banned in Nebraska," *Mother Jones*, May 28, 2015; Griselda Nevarez, "Nebraska Ends Ban on Driver's Licenses for Young Immigrants," NBC News, May 28, 2015; Grant Schulte, "Nebraska, Iowa Road Projects See Boost from Gas Tax Increase," Associated Press, November 28, 2017; Chris Dunker, "Nebraska Voter ID Proposal Dead after Short Debate," *Lincoln Journal Star*, April 5, 2018; Emily Nitcher, "Nebraska Legislature Panel Recommends Smaller Funding Cuts for NU, Colleges than Ricketts Wanted," *Omaha World-Herald*, February 24, 2018; David Bailey and Fiona Ortiz, "Nebraska Legislature Repeals Death Penalty, Overriding Governor's Veto," Reuters, May 27, 2015.

48. Olson and Naugle, *History of Nebraska*, 264; Josh Barro, "Four States Vote to Raise Minimum Wage," *New York Times*, November 3, 2014; Henry Cordes, "Nebraskans Approve Expanding Medicaid to Cover More of the State's Low-Income Residents," *Omaha World-Herald*, November 7, 2018; World-Herald Editorial, "Nebraska Continues Its Strong Tradition of Helping Refugees," *Omaha World-Herald*, January 24, 2018; Jens Manuel Krogstad, "Key Facts About Refugees to the U.S.," Pew Research Center, October 7, 2019, https://www.pewresearch.org/fact-tank/2019/10/07/key-facts-about-refugees-to-the-u-s/.

49. Bishop and Cushing, *The Big Sort*, 255.

50. Martha Stoddard, "Lincoln State Senator Wants to Give 16-Year-Olds the Vote in Nebraska," *Omaha World-Herald*, October 24, 2018; Grant Schulte, "Medical Marijuana Petition Drive Running Strong in Nebraska," Associated Press, July 21, 2019; "Nebraska Ballot Drive Seeks to Cap Payday Loan Rates," Associated Press, September 13, 2019; Don Walton, "Redistricting Ruling Could Prompt Nebraska Ballot Initiative," *Lincoln Journal Star*, July 2, 2019; "Nebraska Voters May Vote on Casino Gambling," Associated Press, June 30, 2019; Mason Dockter, "Ho-Chunk CEO: Expanded Gaming and Horse Races Would Boost Rural Nebraska," *Sioux City Journal*, September 15, 2019; Paul Hammel, "Nebraskans Vote Overwhelmingly to Restore Death Penalty, Nullify Historic 2015 Vote by State Legislature," *Omaha World-Herald*, November 9, 2016; "Timeline of Action on Nebraska's Gay Marriage Ban," *Omaha World-Herald*, March 3, 2015.

51. Tom Brewer for Legislature, accessed October 10, 2019; Tom Brewer, "Medicaid Expansion Is Unaffordable," *Scottsbluff Star-Herald*, October 14, 2018.

52. Caroline Tolbert and Daniel Smith, "The Educative Effects of Ballot Initiatives on Voter Turnout," *American Politics Research* 33, no. 2 (2005): 283–309.

Conclusion

1. "Americans in Rural Areas More Likely to Die by Suicide," CDC Newsroom, October 5, 2017, https://www.cdc.gov/media/releases/2017/p1005-rural-suicide-rates .html.

2. Kim Parker et al., "What Unites and Divides Urban, Suburban and Rural Communities," Pew Research Center, May 22, 2018, https://www.pewsocialtrends.org/2018 /05/22/what-unites-and-divides-urban-suburban-and-rural-communities/; Don Walton, "Impeachment, Medicaid, Lucy and the Football," *Lincoln Journal Star*, December 23, 2019; Paul Starr, "The Battle for the Suburbs," *New York Review of Books*, September 26, 2019; "Nebraska Voter Turnout 2014, 2016, 2018," University of Nebraska-Omaha Center for Public Affairs Research, https://www.unomaha.edu/college-of-public-af fairs-and-community-service/center-for-public-affairs-research/documents/nebras ka-voter-turnout-2014-2016-2018.pdf, accessed June 15, 2020.

3. Gabriel Sherman, *The Loudest Voice in the Room: How the Brilliant, Bombastic Roger Ailes Built Fox News and Divided a Country* (New York: Random House, 2014), 360.

4. Tony Herman, "Nebraska Lags Behind Neighbors in Campaign Finance Regulation," *Hastings Tribune*, September 27, 2019; Emily Nohr, "After Ricketts' Constitutional Objections, Murante Won't Seek Veto Override for Redistricting Bill," *Omaha World-Herald*, April 20, 2016.

5. Bill Bishop and Robert Cushing, *The Big Sort: Why the Clustering of Like-Minded America Is Tearing Us Apart* (New York: Houghton Mifflin, 2008), 291.

6. Bradley Jones, "Most Americans Want to Limit Campaign Spending, Say Big Donors Have Greater Political Influence," Pew Research Center, May 8, 2018, https:// www.pewresearch.org/fact-tank/2018/05/08/most-americans-want-to-limit-campaign -spending-say-big-donors-have-greater-political-influence/.

7. Jeff Barker, "U.S. Supreme Court Tackles Maryland Gerrymandering Case That's Split Democrats and Republicans," *Baltimore Sun*, March 26, 2019.

8. "Number of States Using Redistricting Commissions Growing," Associated Press, March 21, 2019; Eric Lindgren and Priscilla Southwell, "The Effect of Redistricting Commissions on Electoral Competitiveness in US House Elections, 2002–2010," *Journal of Politics and Law* 6 (2013): 13–18.

9. Jill Lepore, "Rock, Paper, Scissors: How We Used to Vote," *New Yorker*, October 6, 2008.

10. Tim Alberta, *American Carnage: On the Front Lines of the Republican Civil War and the Rise of President Trump* (New York: Harper, 2019), 82; "O'Donnell Winning

Tea Party, Losing Delaware," Fairleigh Dickson University's PublicMind Poll, October 28, 2010, http://publicmind.fdu.edu/winsome/final.pdf.

11. Eric McGhee et al., "A Primary Cause of Partisanship? Nomination Systems and Legislator Ideology," *American Journal of Political Science* 58, no. 2 (2014): 337–351.

12. Sarah John and Andrew Douglas, "Candidate Civility and Voter Engagement in Seven Cities with Ranked Choice Voting," *National Civic Review* 106, no. 1 (2017): 25–29; Lee Drutman, "Laboratories of Democracy: San Francisco Voters Rank Their Candidates. It's Made Politics a Little Less Nasty," Vox, July 31, 2019, https://www.vox .com/the-highlight/2019/7/24/20700007/maine-san-francisco-ranked-choice-voting; Craig Burnett and Vladimir Kogan, "Ballot (and Voter) 'Exhaustion' under Instant Runoff Voting: An Examination of Four Ranked-Choice Elections," *Electoral Studies* 37 (2015): 41–49; "The Frustrated Public: Views of the 2016 Campaign, the Parties, and the Electoral Process," Associated Press–NORC Center for Public Affairs Research, May 2016, http://www.apnorc.org/projects/Pages/the-frustrated-public-americans-views-of -the-election.aspx; Emily Swanson and Aamer Madhani, "AP-NORC Poll: Democrats Feel Mixed About Nomination Process," Associated Press, February 21, 2020, https:// apnews.com/e9d83a65fda49a3a1dec01f2fcc03ccf.

13. David Dayen, "How a Progressive Populist Plans to Win a Rural Republican District," American Prospect, August 7, 2019, https://prospect.org/power/progressive -populist-plans-win-rural-republican-district/; Rebecca Vogt et al., "Nebraska Rural Poll: Perceptions of Immigration Among Nonmetropolitan Nebraskans," University of Nebraska–Lincoln, August 2019, https://ruralpoll.unl.edu/pdf/19immigration.pdf.

14. Peter Salter, "'A Gift Sent from the Heavens'—Magic Beer Fridge Found in Flooded Field," *Lincoln Journal Star*, March 19, 2019; Chris Peters, "After the Flood, 2 Nebraska Buddies Find an Indestructible Beer Fridge Miles from Its Home," *Omaha World-Herald*, March 21, 2019; Nancy Gaarder, "Record Snowfall, 'Historic' Bomb Cyclone Are Forces behind Nebraska Floods, Blizzard," *Omaha World-Herald*, March 17, 2019; Margaret Resit, "North Bend School Becomes Town Center after Floods, but Lessons Still Plentiful for Students," *Lincoln Journal Star*, March 31, 2019; "Why Midwestern Farmers Are Not Thinking of Quitting after Historic Floods," Vice, April 5, 2019, https://video.vice.com/en_us/video/why-midwestern-farmers-are-not-think ing-of-quitting-after-historic-floods/5c9e9112be4077399458d648; Steve Liewer, "Columbus Man Who Died Trying to Rescue Motorist from Floodwaters Was 'Always the First to Go Help,'" *Omaha World-Herald*, March 16, 2019; Todd Cooper, "The Nebraska Flood of 2019 Isn't Just Historic. It's Almost Apocalyptic," *Omaha World-Herald*, March 19, 2019; Joseph Morton, "President Trump Approves Disaster Declaration for Nebraska after Severe Winter Weather, Flooding," *Omaha World-Herald*, March 21, 2019; Matt Lindberg, "Colfax County Unites during Stressful Flooding," *Schuyler Sun*, March 16, 2019; Sarah Baker Hansen, "How 2 Farmers and a Bunch of Volunteers Saved the World's Largest Herd of Rare Goats from Flooding," *Omaha World-Herald*, March 21, 2019; Steve Liewer, "Flood Recovery at Offutt

Could Cost $1 Billion and Take Five Years," *Omaha World-Herald*, September 16, 2019; Allison Mollenkamp, "Ricketts Honors Flood Heroes at Capitol Ceremony," NET News, December 17, 2019, http://netnebraska.org/article/news/1200524/ricketts-honors-flood-heroes-capitol-ceremony.

15. Jim Geraghty, "Chuck Schumer: Democrats Will Lose Blue-Collar Whites but Gain in the Suburbs," *National Review*, July 28, 2016; Holly Bailey, "Still Traumatized from 2016 Loss, Democrats Weigh How Much to Reach Out to Rural America," *Washington Post*, May 8, 2019.